MW01043080

The Targum Onqelos to Exodus

THE ARAMAIC BIBLE

• THE TARGUMS •

The Aramaic Bible

Volume 7

The Targum Onqelos to Exodus

Translated, with Apparatus, and Notes

BY

Bernard Grossfeld

A Michael Glazier Book

LITURGICAL PRESS
Collegeville, Minnesota

www.litpress.org

About the Translator

Bernard Grossfeld is Professor of Hebrew and Aramaic at the University of Wisconsin-Milwaukee, and founding member of the Association for Targumic Studies. He holds a B.A. in Hebrew Literature from UCLA, an M.A. in Semitic Literature from the University of California-Berkeley, and a Ph.D. in Near Eastern Studies from Johns Hopkins University. Professor Grossfeld has published extensively on the Targum. He is the author of *A Bibliography of Targum Literature* (1972, 1977), *The First Targum of Esther* (1983) and its companion volume *Concordance of the First Targum to the Book of Esther* (1984), as well as the co-author of *Targum Onqelos on Genesis 49* (1976) and *Targum Onkelos to the Book of Genesis* (1982).

Library of Congress Catalog Card Number: 88-45083

ISBN 0-8146-5486-X

Typography by Laura Burke.
Logo design by Florence Bern.

Table of Contents

EDITORS' FOREWORD

While any translation of the Scriptures may in Hebrew be called a Targum, the word is used especially for a translation of a book of the Hebrew Bible into Aramaic. Before the Christian era Aramaic had in good part replaced Hebrew in Palestine as the vernacular of the Jews. It continued as their vernacular for centuries later and remained in part as the language of the schools after Aramaic itself had been replaced as the vernacular.

Rabbinic Judaism has transmitted Targums of all books of the Hebrew Canon, with the exception of Daniel and Ezra-Nehemiah, which are themselves partly in Aramaic. We also have a translation of the Samaritan Pentateuch into the dialect of Samaritan Aramaic. From the Qumran Library we have sections of a Targum of Job and fragments of a Targum of Leviticus, chapter 16, facts which indicate that the Bible was being translated in Aramaic in pre-Christian times.

Translations of books of the Hebrew Bible into Aramaic for liturgical purposes must have begun before the Christian era, even though none of the Targums transmitted to us by Rabbinic Judaism can be shown to be that old and though some of them are demonstrably compositions from later centuries.

In recent decades there has been increasing interest among scholars and a larger public in these Targums. A noticeable lacuna, however, has been the absence of a modern English translation of this body of writing. It is in marked contrast with most other bodies of Jewish literature for which there are good modern English translations, for instance the Apocrypha and Pseudepigrapha of the Old Testament, Josephus, Philo, the Mishnah, the Babylonian Talmud and Midrashic literature, and more recently the Tosefta and Palestinian Talmud.

It is hoped that this present series will provide some remedy for this state of affairs.

The aim of the series is to translate all the traditionally-known Targums, that is those transmitted by Rabbinic Judaism, into modern English idiom, while at the same time respecting the particular and peculiar nature of what these Aramaic translations were originally intended to be. A translator's task is never an easy one. It is rendered doubly difficult when the text to be rendered is itself a translation which is at times governed by an entire set of principles.

All the translations in this series have been specially commissioned. The translators have made use of what they reckon as the best printed editions of the Aramaic Targum in question or have themselves directly consulted the manuscripts.

The translation aims at giving a faithful rendering of the Aramaic. The introduction to each Targum contains the necessary background information on the particular work. In general, each Targum translation is accompanied by an apparatus and notes. The former is concerned mainly with such items as the variant readings in the Aramaic texts, the relation of the English translation to the original, etc. The notes give what explanations the translator thinks necessary or useful for this series.

Not all the Targums here translated are of the same kind. Targums were translated at different times, and most probably for varying purposes, and have more than one interpretative approach to the Hebrew Bible. This diversity between the Targums themselves is reflected in the translation and in the manner in which the accompanying explanatory material is presented. However, a basic unity of presentation has been maintained. Targumic deviations from the Hebrew text, whether by interpretation or paraphrase, are indicated by italics.

A point that needs to be stressed with regard to this translation of the Targums is that by reason of the state of current targumic research, to a certain extent it must be regarded as a provisional one. Despite the progress made, especially in recent decades, much work still remains to be done in the field of targumic study. Not all the Targums are as yet available in critical editions. And with regard to those that have been critically edited from known manuscripts, in the case of the Targums of some books the variants between the manuscripts themselves are such as to give rise to the question whether they have all descended from a single common original.

Details regarding these points will be found in the various introductions and critical notes.

It is recognised that a series such as this will have a broad readership. The Targums constitute a valuable source of information for students of Jewish literature, particularly those concerned with the history of interpretation, and also for students of the New Testament, especially for those interested in its relationship to its Jewish origins. The Targums also concern members of the general public who have an interest in the Jewish interpretation of the Scriptures or in the Jewish background to the New Testament. For them the Targums should be both interesting and enlightening.

By their translations, introductions and critical notes the contributors to this series have rendered an immense service to the progress of targumic studies. It is hoped that the series, provisional though it may be, will bring significantly nearer the day when the definitive translation of the Targums can be made.

Kevin Cathcart Martin McNamara, M.S.C. Michael Maher, M.S.C.

PREFACE

The invitation by Father Martin MacNamara to be responsible in this series for Targum Onqelos to the Torah was especially welcomed as it provided me, first of all in the Genesis volume, the chance to revise, expand, and update my earlier works *Targum Onqelos on Genesis 49,* Society of Biblical Literature Aramaic Studies 1, Missoula-Montana (Scholars Press), 1976, and *Targum Onkelos to Genesis,* New York (Ktav Publishing House, Inc.), 1982, both of which were co-authored with Professor Moses Aberbach, to whom I am grateful for his permission to utilize some of the ideas of our previous joint efforts. The present work by no means relegates the earlier ones to obscurity. The accompanying Aramaic text, as well as the existence of relevant passages, clauses, phrases, and even single words all in Hebrew characters, lend much value to the latter, while the detailed discussions in the former attest to its independent worth. Second, and far more significant to me, was this opportunity to present a study of Targum Onqelos to the entire Pentateuch. So far, no study exists in English on this official Targum treating its *modus operandum,* taking into consideration the vast relevant Rabbinic literature, comparing the Onqelos reading with that of the Septuagint, Vulgate, Peshitta, the Samaritan Hebrew and Aramaic Bibles, and other ancient versions, not to mention the other extant Targumim. Furthermore, the older standard commentaries in Hebrew have not yet been fully acknowledged by the scholarly world. They include not merely S.D. Luzzatto's classic *Oheb Ger,* and N. Adler's *Netina La-Ger,* works which are familiar to a limited audience of scholars, but also the Yemenite scholar Y. Korach's commentary on Targum Onqelos *Marpe Lashon,* a work rich in interpretive insight. This is of particular relevance in view of the well-known association of the Yemenite tradition with Targum Onqelos.

All of the above features have been incorporated into the Notes throughout the five books of the Pentateuch, together with any relevant finds from Qumran, or other recent discoveries of the Ancient Near East.

First and foremost, I would like to thank Father Martin MacNamara, the project director, and Mr. Michael Glazier, the publisher, for inviting me to participate in this enterprise.

I am also grateful to the Wisconsin Society For Jewish Learning for their continual support of my research.

I thank Professor M. Goshen-Gottstein and the Institute For Advanced Studies of the Hebrew University in Jerusalem for providing me with a Research Fellowship during 1985-6, which gave me the opportunity to interact with scholars in this discipline with whom I formed part of the Targum and Aramaic Studies Group in residence there.

The very laborious task of inputting this manuscript into the computer, as well as the tedious work of checking the cross-references was done by Clare Pfann of Jerusalem, who rose to the challenge at hand with results of the highest quality.

Due credit must also go to my research assistants Sharon Slavin and Christine Gilbert for their meticulous proofreading of the galleys, as well as the preparation of the index.

Last but not least, I gratefully acknowledge the assistance of my wife Sylvia, in proofreading the early computer version of the manuscript, as well as for the patience and encouragement she has given me these past years.

Bernard Grossfeld
Milwaukee, Wisconsin

ABBREVIATIONS

Abot R. Nat	*Aboth de Rabbi Nathan,* ed. S. Schechter. Vienna, 1887.
Afo	Archiv für Orientforschung.
Agg. Ber.	*Aggadath Bereshith,* ed. S. Buber. Krakow, 1903.
ALUOS	Annual of the Leeds University Oriental Society. Leiden.
Ant.	*Antiquities of the Jews*—Josephus. The Loeb Classical Library, ed.
Ber. Rab.	*Midrash Bereshith Rabbati,* ed. C. Albeck. Jerusalem, 1940.
BHM	*Beth Ha-Midrash,* ed. A. Jellinek. Second edition. Jerusalem, 1938.
Biblica	Biblica. Rome.
Cant. Rab.	Canticles Rabbah in *Midrash Rabba al Ḥamishah Ḥumshe Torah veḤamesh Megillot.* Vilna, 1884-7.
CTgA,B,C,D,E,F	*Masoreten Des Westens* by Paul Kahle. Stuttgart, 1930.
Deut. Rab.	*Deuteronomy Rabba,* ed. S. Lieberman. Jerusalem, 1940 (if page numbers are given) also in *Midrash Rabba al Ḥamisha Ḥumshe Torah veḤamesh Megillot.* Vilna, 1884-7.
Ekh. Rab.	Ekha Rabbati, ed. S. Buber. Vilna, 1899.
Esth. Rab.	Esther Rabba in *Midrash Rabba al Ḥamishah Ḥumshe Torah veḤamesh Megillot.* Vilna, 1884-7.
Exod. Rab.	Exodus Rabbah in *Midrash Rabba al Ḥamishah Ḥumshe Torah veḤamesh Megillot.* Vilna, 1884-7.
Frg. Tg.	*The Fragment-Targums to the Pentateuch,* ed. M. Klein. Rome, 1980.
Gen. Rab.	Genesis Rabba acc. to *Bereshith Rabba,* ed. J. Theodor. Jerusalem, 1965.
Hakarmel	Hakarmel. Vilna, 1860-70 (Hebrew Periodical).
HTR	Harvard Theological Review. Cambridge, Mass.

HUCA	Hebrew Union College Annual. Cincinnati.
ICC	International Critical Commentary. Edinburgh, 1901-
IEJ	Israel Exploration Journal. Jerusalem.
JB Jud GL	Jahrbücher für jüdische Geschichte und Literatur. Frankfurt a.M., 1874-92.
JBL	Journal of Biblical Literature.
JHS	Journal of Hebrew Studies. New York, 1969.
JJS	Journal of Jewish Studies. London.
JQR	Jewish Quarterly Review. Philadelphia.
JSOT	Journal for the Study of the Old Testament.
JTS	Journal of Theological Studies. Oxford, London.
Kokhebe Yishaq	Kokhebe Yiṣḥaq. Vienna 1845-1869, 1873 (Hebrew Periodical).
Leq. Tob	*Midrash Leqaḥ Tob,* ed. S. Buber. Lvov, 1878.
Lev. Rab.	Leviticus Rabba acc. to *Wayyiqra Rabba,* ed. M. Margulies. Jerusalem, 1953-60.
Magazin	Magazin für judische Geschichte und Literature. Berlin, 1874-5.
Mek	*Mechilta D'Rabbi Ismael,* ed. H.S. Horovitz and I.A. Rabin. Jerusalem, 1970.
MGWJ	Monatsschrift für Geschishte und Wissenschaft des Judentums.
MHG	*Midrash Haggadol* on Genesis, ed. M. Margulies. Jerusalem, 1946-7; on Exodus, ed. M. Margulies. Jerusalem, 1956.
Mid. Agg.	*Midrash Aggadah,* ed. S. Buber. Vienna, 1893-4.
MRSBY	*Mekhilta de Rabbi Shimon ben Yoḥai,* ed. J.N. Epstein. Jerusalem, 1955.
Num.Rab.	Numbers Rabba in *Midrash Rabba al Ḥamisha Ḥumshe Torah veḤamesh Megillot.* Vilna, 1884-7.
PR	*Pesiqta Rabbati,* ed. M. Friedmann. Vilna, 1880.
PRE	Pirqe Rabbi Eliezer. Jerusalem, 1973 (based on 1544 Venice edition).
PRK	*Pesiqta de Rab Kahana,* ed. S. Buber. Lyck, 1868.
Sam. Tg.	*The Samaritan Targum of the Pentateuch,* ed. A. Tal. Tel-Aviv, 1980-1.
SBL	Society of Biblical Literature.
Sekh. Tob	*Midrash Sekhel Tob,* ed. S. Buber. Lvov, 1900.
Shoh. Tob	*Midrash Shoḥer Tob,* ed. S. Buber. Vilna, 1862.

Sifra	*Sifra debe Rab,* ed. I.H. Weiss. Vienna, 1862.
Sifre (Numbers)	*Siphre D'Be Rab,* ed. H.S. Horovitz. Jerusalem, 1966.
Sifre	*Siphre on Deuteronomy,* ed. L. Finkelstein. New York, 1969.
ST	Studia Theologica. Oslo.
Syr.	*The Syriac Bible.* United Bible Societies, 1979.
Tanh(A)	*Midrash Tanḥuma.* Warsaw, 1875.
Tanh(B)	*Midrash Tanḥuma,* ed. S. Buber. Vilna, 1885.
Tarbiz	Tarbiz. Jerusalem (Hebrew Periodical).
Textus	Textus. Annual of the Hebrew University Bible Project. Jerusalem.
Tg. Neof.	*Neophyti I,* ed. A. Díez Macho. Madrid, 1968-78.
Tg. Onq.	*The Bible in Aramaic: The Pentateuch acc. to Targum Onkelos,* ed. A. Sperber. Leiden, 1959.
Tg. Ps.-Jon.	*Targum Jonathan ben Uzziel,* ed. D. Rieder. Jerusalem, 1984-5.
Tg.Ket.	*The Bible in Aramaic: The Hagiographa,* ed. A. Sperber. Leiden, 1968.
Tg.Neb.	*The Bible in Aramaic: The Former Prophets acc. to Targum Jonathan,* ed. A Sperber. Leiden, 1959; *The Latter Prophets acc. Targum Jonathan,* ed. A Sperber. Leiden, 1962.
VT	Vetus Testamentum. Leiden.
VT Sup	Vetus Testamentum Supplement. Leiden.
Yalq. Makh.	*Yalqut Ha-Makhiri,* ed. S. Buber. Berdichev, 1900.
Yalq. Shim.	*Yalqut Shimoni:Sepher Bereshith,* ed. D. Heimann et al. Jerusalem, 1973; *Sepher Shemoth,* ed. D. Heimann et al. Jerusalem, 1977, 1980.
ZAW	Zeitschrift für die alttestamentlische Wissenschaft. Berlin.

Transcription

Consonant			*Vowel*	
’	א		e	ֶ
b	בּ		ē	ֵ
ḇ	ב		ê	ֵי
g	ג		ī	ִ
d	ד		î	ִי
h	ה		a	ַ
w	ו		ā	ָ
z	ז		o	ָ
ḥ	ח		ŏ	ֳ
ṭ	ט		ă	ֲ
y	י		ĕ	ֱ
k	כּ		ě	ְ
ḵ	כ,	ך	ū	ֻ
l	ל		û	וּ
m	מ,	ם	ō	ֹ
n	נ,	ן	ô	וֹ
s	ס			
‘	ע			
p	פּ			
p̱	פ,	ף		
ṣ	צ,	ץ		
q	ק			
r	ר			
š	שׁ			
ś	שׂ			
t	תּ			
ṯ	ת			

Note

A critical Introduction to all books of Targum Onqelos can be found in *The Targum Onqelos to Genesis,* Volume 6 of this series.

Translation

CHAPTER 1

1. Now these are the names of the sons of Israel who *entered*[1] Egypt with Jacob, each one *entered*[1] with his household. 2. Reuben, Simeon, Levi, and Judah. 3. Issakhar, Zebulun, and Benjamin. 4. Dan and Naphtali, Gad and Asher. 5. Now all the persons, Jacob's offspring, <totalled> seventy persons, as well as Joseph <who> was in Egypt. 6. Then Joseph and all of his brothers, as well as that entire generation died. 7. Now, the Israelites *became numerous*[2] *and prospered,*[3] and became great and exceedingly powerful; and the land was filled with them. 8. Now there arose a new king over Egypt *who did not implement the law of Joseph.*[4] 9. So he said to his people, "Here the Israelite people are more numerous and powerful than we are. 10. Come let us be wise to them lest they become great; then it will be if a war should befall us, they will then be added to our enemies and wage war against us and will ascend from the land." 11. So they appointed over them *cruel supervisors*[5] in order to afflict *them*[6] by

Apparatus, Chapter 1

[a] n, l, and a have: "told them."

Notes, Chapter 1

1The Hebrew employs the root *bw'* "to come," which if denoting "to come in" i.e., "to enter" is rendered in the Targum by the root *'ll*, as in the present case. Where, however, the Hebrew denotes only "coming" i.e., "arriving" the Aramaic root employed in the Targum is *'t'*, for which cf. Exod. 3:1: Num. 13:22; Deut. 32:44.

2See Gen. Chap. 1 n. 9.

3The Hebrew has "and multiplied greatly," employing the root *šrṣ* "to swarm, to teem" normally referring to animals, especially those that crawl as in Gen. 1:20, where the cognate accusative *yšrṣwn* ... *šrṣ* is rendered by the Targum *yrḥšwn rḥš'*. Here, however, the reference is to humans; consequently the Targum in respect for their dignity, employs the root *yld* "to give birth." The Rabbis, on the other hand, make it a definite point to expound on the Hebrew *wayyišrĕṣû* by explaining that the intentional use of this form was meant to convey the image that each Israelite woman gave birth to sextuplets, or twins, or other multiple births, for which cf. the following Midrashim: Tanḥ(A) *Piqqudê* IX; Deut. Rab., p. 15; Exod. Rab. 1:7; PRK X *Wayehi Bĕšallaḥ*, p. 85b; Agg. Ber. X:1, p. 24. The Tgs. Ps.-Jon. and Neof., the Syr., and the Sam. Tg., likewise, employ the root *yld* here.

4The Hebrew has: "who did not know Joseph." The translation of the Targum clearly implies that this Pharaoh could very well have "known" Joseph, but preferred not to go along with him as far as Joseph's reforms were concerned. The exact meaning of this phrase is a matter of dispute in Rabbinic literature as seen from the following discussion in the Talmud (b. Erub. 53a): "Rab and Samuel (debate the subject). One says ['a new king' (Exod. 1:8) means] literally 'new,' while the other says: it means, new decrees were issued by him." The Targum's translation here appears to be in agreement with the latter opinion. The Tgs. Ps.-Jon. and Neof. render this phrase literally then add "and did not follow his laws," which is virtually identical to Tg. Onq. here. In addition to the above-cited Talmud, cf. also Exod. Rab. 1:8; Tanḥ(A) *Šmôṯ* V; Shoḥ. Tob. CV:8, p. 451, and Tanḥ(B) *Šmôṯ* VII, p. 4.

their hard work; and *they*[6] built the treasure house cities for the Pharaoh—Pithom and Raamses. 12. But as much as they afflicted *them*[6] so *they*[6] grew proportionally more numerous and more powerful, so that *the Egyptians*[7] became distressed from before the Israelites. 13. So the Egyptians subjected the Israelites to severity. 14. And they embittered their lives with severe labor, with clay, with bricks, and with all <types of> labor in the field; all the labor to which they subjected them was {done} with severity. 15. Then the king of Egypt *spoke*[8] to the *Jewish*[9] midwives, one whose name was Shiphra, and the other whose name was Puah. 16. And he said, "When you will help the *Jewish*[9] women in their delivery, you shall look upon the birthstool; if it be a son, you shall kill him, but if it be a daughter, let her live." 17. The midwives, however, *were in reverence before*[10] the Lord and {therefore} did not do according to what the king of Egypt *spoke with them,*[a] and they preserved the sons alive. 18. Then the king of Egypt summoned the midwives and said to them, "Why did you do this thing and preserve the sons alive?" 19. So the midwives said to the Pharaoh, "It is because the *Jewish*[9] women are not like the Egyptian women, for they are *shrewd;*[11] they give birth even before the

Notes, Chapter 1 (Cont.)

5The Hebrew has: "taskmasters." This interpretive rendering of the Targum reflects the interpretation of the following Midrashim:

1. *MHG on Exod.*, p. 13: *"śārê missîm* ('taskmasters')—something that melted the hearts of Israel as it says: 'the hills melted (*nmsw*) like wax.'"
2. *Yalqut 'Or Hā-'Apelāh in MS Form* (Torah Shelemah Vol. VIII, p. 27): " *śārê missîm* ('taskmasters') 'cruel supervisors who melted the hearts of Israel.'" The Targum's translation is precisely reflected only in the Syr. while Tgs. Neof. and Ps.-Jon.'s "taskmasters who oppressed them with hard labor" is identical to LXX *επιστάτας τῶν 'έργον* and the Vg's *magistros operum.*

6For Hebrew "it," referring to the nation collectively, the Aramaic refers to the people instead.

7An insertion denoted by the third pers. plural pronoun inherent in the Hebrew "they became distressed."

8The Hebrew has: "said," which, in view of the fact that what he said does not immediately follow, should really be understood as "spoke." Accordingly, it is rendered *mll* in the Targum.

9The Hebrew has: "Hebrew," which, starting with the book of Exodus, is rendered "Jew" in the Targum, while throughout Genesis it is still rendered "Hebrew." This situation has been commented upon by numerous Targum Onqelos scholars, including N. Adler, *Netina La-Ger* in *Sefer Torat Elohim.* Wilna, 1886, to this verse; B. Schefftel, *Bi'ure Onqelos.* Munich, 1888, p. 78; M. Löwenstein, *Nefesh Ha-Ger:* Exodus.Pietrokov, 1908, p. 3; and B.Z.J.Berkowitz, *Leḥem Abirim* in *Leḥem We-Śimla* (Exodus) Wilna, 1854, p. 3. They basically agree that the Targum, beginning with the book of Exodus, is reflecting the name given to them during his own times, during the end of the Second Temple period, or shortly after the destruction of that Temple. The name originated within Jacob's blessing of Judah which is described in the following way by the three Pal. Tgs. and the Rabbis—Gen. Rab. XCVIII:6, p. 1257—"'Judah, you, shall your brethren praise' (Gen. 49:8). ... R. Simeon b. Yoḥai said: All your brethren will be called by your name. A man does not say I am a Reubenite or a Simeonite, but, I am a Yehudi (Jew)." Cf. also Tanḥ (B) *Wayeḥi* XII, p. 219: "All of Israel will call itself by your name—Jews." The only exceptions occur in Exod. 21:2; Deut. 15:12; and Jer. 34:9, 11, where the reference in the Hebrew is to a Hebrew slave male or female. There the Targum renders *bar yiśrā'el* and *bat yiśrā'el* in order to clarify the situation against those who argue that "Hebrew slave" does not mean an Israelite, only someone descended from Abraham (for which cf. further Ibn Ezra on Exod. 21:2).

10See Gen. Chap. 4, n. 1.

11The Hebrew "vigorous" is here interpretively rendered "shrewd," partly paralleling Tg. Ps.-Jon. who has "they are vigorous and shrewd of mind." It may be suggested that this deviation in the Targum

midwives come in to them." 20. And the Lord dealt well with the midwives, and the people became exceedingly numerous and powerful. 21. Now it happened since the midwives *were in reverence before*[10] the Lord that He established families for them. 22. So the Pharaoh ordered all his people as follows: "Every son that is born *to the Jews*[12] throw him into the river, whereas every daughter preserve alive."

CHAPTER 2

1. Then a man from the house of Levi proceeded to take <for a wife> the daughter of Levi. 2. And the woman conceived and gave birth to a son; and perceiving him to be good, she concealed him {for} three months. 3. But as she was not able to conceal him any longer, she procured for him an ark of reed and *covered*[1] it with bitumen and pitch; then she placed the child into it and placed *it*[2] by the bank of the river. 4. And his sister stationed herself from afar, to be aware what would be done to him. 5. Then the Pharaoh's daughter went down to bathe in the river while her maidens were strolling on the banks of the river. When she saw the ark within the rushes, she stretched out her *arm*[3] and took it. 6. When she opened <it> she saw the child and here the young boy

Apparatus, Chapter 2

[a] n omits it, and it is not in the Hebrew.

[b] L and R have: "man."

Notes, Chapter 1 (Cont.)

may be due to the fact that the Hebrew *ḥyh* which could also mean "midwife" (cf. t. B. Bath. VII:2; Cant. Rab. IV:5) in Post-Biblical Hebrew and in Aramaic, as it is the Targumic equivalent for Hebrew *mĕyalédet* throughout this chapter, would here result in a translation that would read "for they are midwives," giving the impression that the Hebrew women were midwives themselves, when, according at least to the Targumist's understanding of the situation, the Hebrew text was just attempting to convey the impression that the Hebrew women were shrewd enough as to be so vigorous and give birth before the midwives arrived on the scene—in a sense they were their own midwives. Accordingly, the Targum preferred to translate the word by the *reason*—"They were shrewd," rather than by the *result*—"they were vigorous."

Alternately, it may be suggested that the Targum's rendering was due to another meaning for Hebrew *ḥyh* "wild beast," which here does not reflect favorably on the Hebrew women. This possibility is discussed in Exod. Rab. 1:16: "'For they are vigorous.' (1:19) [Hebrew *ḥayōṯ*]. If you say the Hebrew women were midwives (*myldwt*) themselves—well, does not even a midwife require the services of another? Hence, this is what they said: These people are like wild beasts which do not require the help of midwives."

[12] The addition "to the Jews," also present in Tgs. Ps.-Jon. and Neof., as well as in Sam. Hebrew and the Sam. Tg. ("to the Hebrews") as well as LXX—*τοῖς ‘Εβραίοις*, was meant to clearly define the Hebrew, where it is implied. Rabbinic tradition, however, contains certain opinions according to which Pharaoh's decree pertained to the Egyptians as well. The following literature pertains directly to the subject:

1. *b. Sot.* 12a "Said R. Jose b. Ḥanina: The Pharaoh issued three decrees ... and last—he

was crying, whereupon she had compassion for him and said, "This one, *he*[a] is one of the *Jewish* [4] children." 7. Then his sister said to the Pharaoh's daughter, "Shall I go and call for you a nursing woman from the *Jews,*[4] that she should nurse the child for you?" 8. So the Pharaoh's daughter said to her, "Go!" Whereupon the young girl went and called the mother of the child. 9. Then the Pharaoh's daughter said to her, "Take this child {away} and nurse it for me and I will give <you> your wages." And the woman took the child and nursed it. 10. And the child grew up and she brought him to the Pharoah's daughter and he became her son; and she called his name Moses, for she said, "Because I drew him out of the water." 11. Now it happened in those days, when Moses had grown up, that he went out to his brethren and witnessed their servitude; and he saw an Egyptian man striking a *Jewish* [4] man, {one} of his brethren. 12. So he turned here and there and saw that there was no *person*[b] <around>, thereupon he struck the Egyptian and concealed him in the sand. 13. Then he went out the second day, and here two *Jewish* [4] men were fighting; so he said to the wicked one, "Why are you striking your companion?" 14. Whereupon he said, "Who made you a leader and judge over us? Did you say you were going to kill me, as you killed the Egyptian?" Then Moses became fearful and said, "Truly the matter is known." 15. When the Pharaoh heard <about> this matter, he sought to kill Moses; so Moses fled from the Pharaoh's presence and dwelt in the land of Midian, staying near a well. 16. Now *the chief of*[5] Midian had seven daughters, and they came and drew water and filled the troughs to water the sheep. 17. Then the shepherds came and drove them away, but Moses arose

Notes, Chapter 1 (Cont.)

decreed against his own people too."

2. Exod. Rab. 1:18 "R. Jose b. Ḥanina said: 'he decreed against his own people too.' And why was this? Because his astrologers told him, 'The mother of Israel's saviour is already pregnant with him, but we do not know whether he is an Israelite or an Egyptian.' Then the Pharaoh assembled all the Egyptians before him and said 'Lend me your children for nine months that I may cast them in the river,' as it is written: 'Every son that is born, you shall cast into the river' (Exod. 1:22). It does not say 'every son who is an Israelite' but 'every son,' whether he be Jew or Egyptian. But they would not agree, saying: 'An Egyptian son would not redeem them; he must be a Hebrew.'" Also Josephus (*Ant.* II, 9, 2, Vol. IV, p. 253) adds "born to the Israelites" (ὑπὸ τῶν Ἰσραηλιτῶν).

Notes, Chapter 2

[1]The Hebrew has: "coated" or "daubed" or "calked"—*wattaḥmĕrāh,* which together with the following *bahĕmār,* creates, in the form of a cognate accusative, an alliteration, a situation the Targum usually resolves as in Gen. 11:3, for which see there ns. 3 and 4.

[2]An insertion supplying the direct object, referring to the ark, which is implied in the Hebrew. The Tgs. Ps.—Jon., and Neof., as well as the Syr., and LXX have it too, while the Vg. has "him" (*eum*) referring to the child.

[3]The Hebrew has *'mṯh,* concerning which there exists the following dispute in the Talmud, b. Sot. 12b—"'and she sent forth her *'mṯh* and took it' (Exod. 2:5). R. Judah and R. Nehemiah (dispute the matter), one said (*'mṯh* means) her hand, and the other said (*'mṯh* means) her servant." The LXX 'ἄβραν is in agreement with the latter opinion, while Ps.-Jon.'s *qrmyd'* ("elbow") favors the former. Tg. Onq. here using *'mh,* as do Tg. Neof. and the Sam. Tg. (J), which could mean either "handmaid" or "forearm," appears to reflect both opinions in the Talmud.

[4]See above Chap. 1, n. 9.

[5]See Gen. Chap. 41, n. 22.

and rescued them, then watered their father's sheep. 18. When they came to their father Reuel, he said {to them}, "Why is this that you have hurried to come <home> today?" 19. So they said, "An Egyptian man rescued us from the shepherds, and he also drew water for us and watered the sheep." 20. Then he said to his daughters, "Where is he then? Why so did you leave the man? Summon him that he may eat bread." 21. And Moses *chose*[6] to dwell with the man, and he gave his daughter Zipporah to Moses {in marriage}. 22. Then she gave birth to a son and he called his name Gershom, for he said, "I was an alien in a strange land." 23. Now it happened in the course of those many days that the king of Egypt died, and the Israelites sighed by reason of the labor *that was hard on them;*[7] so they cried out, and their outcry by reason of the labor ascended *before*[8] the Lord. 24. *Then their outcry was heard before the Lord,*[9] and the Lord remembered His covenant with Abraham, Isaac, and Jacob. 25. *Now the servitude of the Israelites was revealed before the Lord,*[10]*and the Lord promised through His Memra to redeem them.*[11]

CHAPTER 3

1. Now Moses was pasturing the flock of his father-in-law Jethro, the *chief of*[1] Midian, and he led the flock *to a good pasturing spot*[2]*to*[a3] the wilderness, and came to *the mountain on which the glory of the Lord was revealed*[4]—to Horeb. 2. Then an angel of the Lord was revealed to him within a flame of fire from the midst of the bush; and he perceived that here the bush was burning in fire; but the bush was not

Apparatus, Chapter 3

[a] E and G have: "of."
[b] n has: "when it was revealed before the Lord."
[c] n has: "earth."
[d] n has: "taskmasters," as does the Hebrew.
[e] v_a has: "its," as does the Samaritan Hebrew and the Vg., while the Hebrew has "its pains." The LXX and the Syr. have: "their pain."

Notes, Chapter 2 (Cont.)

6The Hebrew has: "consented." The use of *ṣby* "chose" in the Targum to translate Hebrew *y'l* is paralleled here by Tg. Ps.-Jon. and the Syr., and by Tg. Neb. to Judg. 17:11 where the exact sequence—*y'l* followed by the infinitive of *yšb* "to dwell"—occurs. Tg. Neof. here employs the root *šry* "begin" as does Tg. Neb. to Judg. 19:6, and the Tg. to 1 Chron. 17:27, which is in agreement with R. Judah's opinion in Sifre Deut. (IV, p. 12): *"hô'îl mōšēh"* (Deut. 1:5). R. Judah says, "*hô'ālāh* is strictly an expression meaning 'beginning' as its says 'start now (*hô'el nā'*) and lodge all night, and rejoice' (Judg. 19:6) and it says (further), 'And now, (*hô'altā*) you started to bless'" (1 Chron. 17:27). Whereas the Sages say, "*hô'ālāh* is strictly an expression of 'oath,' as it says: 'and Moses (*wayyô'ēl*) swore to dwell with the man' (Exod. 2:21), and it says, 'and Saul adjured the people saying' (1 Sam. 14:24)." The Targum here, oddly enough, follows neither of these two opinions and goes his own way in rendering this somewhat enigmatic Hebrew root by "chose."

7The addition of this clause, also present in Tg. Ps.-Jon. and to some extent in the Syr.—"from the *hard* enslavement," expands on the preceding "from the labor" by further depicting the effect on them.

consumed. 3. So Moses said, "I will now turn and behold this great sight; why then is the bush not burned up?" 4. *When the Lord perceived*[b] that he had turned to see, the Lord called to him from the midst of the bush and said, "Moses, Moses!" Whereupon he said, "Here I am." 5. And He said, "Do not approach hither; loosen your *sandal*[5] from your *foot,*[6] for the place on which you are standing is a sacred *place*."[c] 6. And He said, "I am the God of your father, the God of Abraham, the God of Isaac, and the God of Jacob"; whereupon Moses hid his face, for he was afraid to look *in the direction of*[7] *the glory of the Lord.*[8] 7. Then the Lord said, "The *servitude*[9] of my people who are in Egypt is indeed *revealed before Me,*[10] as is their cry on account of *their hard labor*[d] *heard before me,*[10] for *their*[e] pain *is revealed before me.*[11] 8. *So I*

Notes, Chapter 2 (Cont.)

8See Gen. Chap. 4, n. 1.

9The Hebrew has, "and God heard their outcry." For this change of the Hebrew active to the Aramaic passive with the verb "to hear," see Gen. Chap. 29, n. 9.

10The Hebrew has "God saw the Israelites." The phrase "God saw" is transformed into the passive "was revealed before the Lord," for which see Gen. Chap. 29, n. 8. The Hebrew "God saw the Israelites" is vague. What exactly did God see? Accordingly, the Targum made the natural insertion—"the servitude." Tg. Neof. makes the identical insertion here, while Tg. Ps.-Jon. expands it to "the pain of the servitude." A similar exposition of this verse occurs in Exod. Rab. 1:36—"'And God saw the Israelites' (Exod. 2:25) as it says: 'I have surely seen the affliction of my people'" (*ibid. 3:7*). There the Hebrew for "affliction"—*'ŏn* is rendered *šiʿbûd* ("servitude"), the very same word used here.

11The Hebrew has, "and God took notice of them." This paraphrase in the Targum, also contained in identical form in Tg. Neof., reflects the train of thought from 3:8 below where God's intention to *save* Israel is revealed. Accordingly, the concise *wayyedaʿ* "he took notice of" is expanded and clarified that through His Memra, the Lord has decided that He will take notice of them and redeem them. Also, the factor of anthropomorphism inherent in God "knowing," was responsible for the paraphrase. Cf. similarly Deut. 2:7.

Notes, Chapter 3

1See Gen. Chap. 41, n. 22.

2An insertion to supply a prepositional clause implied in the concise Hebrew text. This insertion was also supplied by Tg. Ps.-Jon. In fact that "good pasturing spot" was within the wilderness as the Targum understood the following preposition—*'ăḥar,* which he renders by *l* or *d* according to the many variants (for which see the Apparatus).

3The Hebrew has "behind," for which see preceding note.

4The Hebrew "the mountain of God" could cause misapprehensions about the omnipresence of God, and is accordingly paraphrased. Tg. Ps-Jon. and Neof. have a similar paraphrase here. Cf. further Exod. 4:20—"the rod of God."

5The MT has the plural, but 33 other Hebrew mss., as well as the Sam. Heb., the LXX, the Vg., and Tg. Ps.-Jon. have the singular.

6The MT has the plural, but 53 other Hebrew mss., as well as the Sam. Heb., and the Tg. Ps-Jon. have the singular here too.

7The Hebrew preposition *'el* is here interpretively rendered to mean "towards" or "in the direction of," functioning as a buffer between man and God, whereas *'el* which could be taken to mean "into," could therefore be misunderstood.

8See Introduction VII D. 2.

9The Hebrew has: "affliction" a general term, which is here particularized into a specific affliction—"servitude." Cf. likewise below Exod. 4:31 and 2 Kgs. 14:26, where the Tg. Neb. renders "servitude" as well.

10See Gen. Chap. 29, n. 8.

11See Gen. Chap. 3, n. 1.

revealed Myself[12] to deliver *them*[f] from the power of *the Egyptians*[g] and to bring *them*[f] up from that land to a land which is good and spacious, to a land *producing*[13] milk and honey, to the land of the Canaanites, (and) Hittites, (and) Amorites, (and) Perizzites, (and) Hivites, and Jebusites. 9. And now, here the cry of the Israelites has come up before me and also the oppression with which the Egyptians have oppressed them *is revealed before me.*[10] 10. So now, come, and I will send you to the Pharaoh and bring out my people, the Israelites from Egypt." 11. Then said Moses *before*[14] the Lord, "Who am I that I should go to the Pharaoh, and that I should bring out the Israelites from Egypt?" 12. So He said, "For *My Memra will support you*[15] and this <will be> to you a sign that I have sent you—when you bring out the people from Egypt, they will worship *before*[14] the Lord on this mountain." 13. Then said Moses *before*[14] the Lord: "Here, I am about to come to the Israelites and say to them, 'The God of your fathers has sent me to you'; if they say to me, 'What is His name?' What should I say to them?" 14. So the Lord said to Moses, *"ʾhyh ʾšr ʾhyh,*[h16] and accordingly, you shall say to the Israelites, *'ʾhyh*[16] has sent me to you.'" 15. And He further said to Moses, "Thus you shall say to the Israelites, 'The Lord God of your fathers, the God of Abraham, the God of Isaac, and the God of Jacob has sent me to you'; this is My name forever, and this is My memorial for every generation. 16. Proceed to assemble the elders of *Israel*[i] and say to them, 'The Lord, God of your ancestors, the God of Abraham, the God of Isaac, and the God of Jacob has *revealed Himself*[10] to me,' saying, 'I do indeed remember you, and that which has been committed against you in Egypt.' 17. And I have said, 'I will bring you up from *the Egyptian servitude*[j] to the land of the Canaanites, (and) the Hittites, (and) the Amorites, (and) the Perizzites, (and) the Hivites, and the Jebusites, to a land

Apparatus, Chapter 3 (Cont.)

[f] b and d have: "it," as does the Hebrew.
[g] a has: "Egypt."
[h] I translates this clause: "I will be, concerning that which I will be." Nachmanides cites an Onqelos version which reads: "I will be with whomever I will be."
[i] I has: "the Israelites" adding *bny*, as do the LXX, the Syr. and the Sam. Hebrew, although MT has only "Israel."
[j] b, c, g, and I have: "the servitude of Egypt."
[k] b, d, and g have "your Memra."
[l] C has: "chanced Himself," as does the Hebrew.
[m] n has: "except."
[n] G, N, i, a, and c have: "the Egyptians."

Notes, Chapter 3 (Cont.)

[12]See Gen. Chap. 11, n. 6.

[13]The Hebrew "flowing" is idiomatic and accordingly rendered into its intended meaning.

[14]See Gen. Chap. 4, n. 1.

[15]See Gen. Chap. 26, n. 2.

[16]The Targum does not translate the Hebrew text; instead he reproduces the Hebrew *in toto.* There are, however, a few Onqelos versions which do render a translation——(1) the printed edition of the Biblica Hebraica (Ixar, 1490) has "I will be, concerning that which I will be." (2) Nachmanides cites a version that reads, "I will be with whomsoever I will be." S. D. Luzzatto, *Ohev Ger* (Second edition. Krakow, 1895, p. 136) cites a version that is virtually identical to that of Nachmanides, which M. Kasher (*Torah Shelema, op. cit.*, VIII, p. 150, n. 176) identifies as that of the Pentateuch edition of Bologna, 1482. Most Onqelos versions, however, do not contain a translation for this enigmatic Hebrew clause, a situation which is not in line with the Mishna (cf. m. Meg. IV:10), according to which only the following Biblical passages are "read but not translated": (1) the story of Reuben (Gen. 35:22);

producing[13] milk and honey.' 18. And they will *listen to you;*[k17] then you and the elders of Israel will come to the king of Egypt and say to him, 'The Lord, God of the *Jews has revealed Himself*[l] to us; so now let us go now a distance of three days in the wilderness and sacrifice *before*[14] the Lord our God.' 19. Now *before me it is revealed*[11] that the king of Egypt will not let you go, *not even*[m] *on account of Him whose strength is powerful.*[18] 20. And I will send forth *the stroke of My power*[19] and strike the Egyptians with all My wonders which I shall perform among them, only afterwards will they send them away. 21. Then I will set this people *compassionately*[20] in the sight of the Egyptians, and when you go, you will not go empty {handed}. 22. But a woman will ask of her neighbor *and of the one close to her*[21] from her house, silver (vessels) and gold vessels, as well as garments; and you will place them on your sons and on your daughters, and {so} *empty out*[22] *Egypt.*"[n]

Notes, Chapter 3 (Cont.)

(2) the second recounting of the Golden Calf incident (Exod. 32:21-35); (3) the Priestly Blessing (Num. 6:24-26) and (4) the David-Amnon affair (2 Sam. 13:1). However, the situation among the other Ancient Versions is far from unanimous. Tg. Neof., the Syr., the Sam. Tg. and the Sam. Heb. leave it untranslated, while Tg. Ps.-Jon. has: "He who spoke and the world was, spoke, and all of it came about"; the LXX has: *ἐγώ εἰμι ὁ* 'Ὤν—"I am the Being"; and the Vg.: *EGO SUM QUI SUM*—"I Am Who I Am."

The third occurrence of Hebrew *'hyh* is still left untranslated in the Targum here in all extant Onqelos versions, while Tg. Neof. has a similar paraphrase to what Tg. Ps.-Jon. had for the first clause—"He who spoke and the world was from the beginning, and is to speak again to it: Be!, and it will be. . . " Tg. Ps.-Jon. here has: "I am he who was and will (continue) to be. . . " The Syr., the Sam. Heb. and the Sam. Tg. leave it untranslated, while the LXX renders ὁ Ὤν—"the being" and the Vg. *QUI EST*—"He Who Is."

17See Gen. Chap. 16, n. 1.

18The Hebrew "by a mighty hand" is anthropomorphic and accordingly circumvented by this paraphrase. See further the following note.

19The Hebrew "My hand" is anthropomorphic and accordingly circumvented. See likewise the preceding note.

20See Gen. Chap. 6, n. 8.

21The Hebrew has "the one who resides" which the Syr. renders literally *twtbt* < *ytb.* The Hebrew, as pointed out by M. Rosenbaum and A. M. Silbermann, *et al. (Pentateuch with Targum Onkelos, Haphtaroth and Rashi's Commentary: Exodus.* New York [Hebrew Publishing Company] 1934, p. 231), is ambiguous: it may mean an Egyptian woman who is a tenant in an Israelite house, or an Israelite woman who resides in the house of an Egyptian woman. They conclude that the latter possibility was more likely, since the Israelites were slaves and not likely to be landlords. Accordingly, the Targum renders "of the one close to her" i.e., a fellow lodger, which is precisely the translation of Tg. Neof. *qrybt twtbt,* and the LXX *συσκήνου*. That the Israelites resided together with the Egyptians is expounded in the following Midrash on this particular phrase—*MRŠBY Bō'—Exod.* XII:36, p. 31: "Rabbi says: When the Israelites were in Egypt, what does it say about them? 'Every woman shall borrow from her neighbor and from the one who resided in her house' (Exod. 3:22), teaching (us) that they resided with them." This "fellow lodger" could very well have been a slave like herself.

22The Hebrew *wnṣṣltm* is here, as well as in Tgs. Neof. and Ps.-Jon., and the Sam. Tg., understood to be derived from the root *nṣl*—"strip" in the *pi'el,* hence the root *ryq* is employed, while the LXX and Vg. as well as the Syr. render "to plunder," a translation which would reflect unfavorably upon the Israelites and is therefore avoided by the Targumim. Cf. Rashi here, who elaborates on this root which he thinks is literally rendered by the Targum.

CHAPTER 4

1. Then Moses replied and said, "But, here, they will not believe me, nor will *they listen to me*[1] for they will say, 'The Lord did not *reveal Himself*[2] to you.'" 2. So the Lord said to him, "What is this *that is in your hand?*"[a] And he said, "A rod." 3. And He said, "Throw it to the ground"; and he threw it to the ground and it became a serpent and Moses fled from its presence. 4. And the Lord said to Moses, "Stretch out your hand and take hold of its tail." So he stretched out his hand and grasped it strongly, and it became a rod in his hand. 5. "In order that they believe that the Lord, the God of their ancestors, the God of Abraham, the God of Isaac, and the God of Jacob *revealed Himself*[2] to you." 6. Then the Lord said further to him, "Now bring in your hand into your bosom"; so he brought in his hand into his bosom; when he brought it out, here his hand was *white*[3] as snow. 7. So he said to him, "Return your hand into your bosom"; and he returned it, then brought it out from his bosom, and here it again was like his <own> flesh. 8. "Now it will be, if they will not believe you, nor listen to the tone of the first sign, then they will listen to the tone of the latter sign. 9. But if they will not even believe both of these signs nor *listen to you;*[1] then you shall take of the water that is in the river and pour <it> onto dry land; and the water which you took from the river will become blood on dry land." 10. So Moses said before the Lord, "Please, Oh Lord, I am not a man of words, not since yesterday, not since *before that <time>*,[4] nor since the time that You spoke with Your servant, for I am heavy of speech and *unintelligible of*[5] expression." 11. Then the Lord said to him, "Who placed a mouth in man, or who set <someone to be> a mute or a deaf person, or a seeing person, or a blind person? Did not I, the Lord? 12. So now go, and *My Memra*[6] will be with your mouth and teach you what you should say." 13. But he said, "Please, Oh Lord, send now through *one who is qualified*[7] to be sent." 14. Then the anger of the Lord grew intensely against Moses and He said, "Has it not *been revealed before Me*[8] that your brother Aaron, the Levite, does indeed speak; in fact he is presently departing to meet you; and when he will see you, he will rejoice in his heart. 15. Now you shall speak *with*[b] him, and put the words in his mouth; and *My Memra*[6] will be with your mouth and his mouth; and I will teach you what you should do. 16. Then he will speak for you *with*[b] the people; so he will be *an interpreter*[9] for you, and you will be *a leader*[10] for him. 17. And this rod you shall take into your hand with which you shall perform the signs." 18. Then Moses proceeded to return to his father-in-law, Yether, and said to him, "I will proceed to return to my brethren who are in Egypt and see if they are still alive"; and Jethro said to Moses, "Go in peace!" 19. And the Lord said to Moses in Midian, "Proceed to return to Egypt, for all the men who sought to kill you are dead." 20. So Moses took his wife and his sons and mounted them on a donkey, returning to the land of Egypt; and Moses took in his hand *the rod with which miracles were preformed by the Lord.*[11] 21. Then the Lord said to Moses as he was proceeding to return to Egypt, "Concentrate on all the wonders which I have placed in your power,

Apparatus, Chapter 4

[a] V omits the relative *d* here and simply has, "in your hand," as does the Hebrew.

[b] I has: "to," as does the Hebrew.

in that you shall perform them before the Pharaoh, while I will strengthen *his resolve*[12] that he will not send away the people. 22. Now you should say to the Pharaoh, 'Thus says the Lord: Israel is My firstborn son.' 23. And I say to you, 'Send away My son, so that he may worship Me; now if you refuse to send him away, here I am prepared to kill your firstborn son.'" 24. Now it happened on the road at a lodging place that an angel of the Lord met him and sought to kill him. 25. Whereupon Zipporah took a flint and circumcised the foreskin of her son *and she*

Notes, Chapter 4

[1]See Gen. Chap. 16, n. 1.

[2]See Gen. Chap. 29, n. 8.

[3]The Hebrew has "leprous." The Targum transforms the Hebrew simile "*leprous* as snow" into the more accurate and realistic simile "*white* as snow" (since snow is not "leprous" but "white") in defining this particular figure of speech. The simile "white as snow" occurs twice—Isa. 1:18 and Ps. 51:9. Similarly in Num. 12:10 and 2 Kgs. 5:27, Tg. Onq. and the Tg. Neb., respectively, observe this transformation. The LXX also appeared uncomfortable with this Hebrew simile by omitting "leprous" in its translation—*καὶ ἐγενήθη ἡ χεὶρ αὐτοῦ ὡσεὶ χιών*—"and his hand became as snow." The other versions—Syr., Vg., Tg. Neof. and the Sam. Tg. render this simile literally, while Tg. Ps.-Jon. has a double reading—"leprous, white as snow."

[4]See Gen. Chap. 31, n. 3.

[5]The Hebrew has: "heavy of," a figure of speech which is resolved by the Targum into its implied meaning. The Aramaic expression was no doubt influenced by Isa. 33:19 where it occurs in the Hebrew text itself. The other ancient versions, likewise, resolved the Hebrew figure of speech but in different ways. Tgs. Neof. and Ps.-Jon. contain two readings: "halting of speech" and "hard of speech," while the Syr., the LXX and Vg. have "slow-tongued."

[6]See Introduction VII D.1.

[7]The Hebrew "send now through whom You will send" appears incomplete in syntax, lacking an object clause, which the Targum, as well as virtually all the other ancient versions, here supplies—Sam. Tg. (A), the Syr., the Vg. have "whom," the Frg. Tg. (V), and Tg. Neof. have "who is qualified," and the LXX has "another able person," while Tg. Ps.-Jon. has "Phineḥas" by name.

[8]See Gen. Chap. 3, n. 1.

[9]The Hebrew "a mouth" is idiomatic, and accordingly rendered into its implied meaning. Tgs. Neof., Ps.-Jon., and the Frg. Tg. (V), as well as the Syr. have the identical term, while the Sam. Tg. (A) has "a speaker." The translation in the Targum is also reflected in the Midrash, for which cf. Exod. Rab. III:17.

[10]The Hebrew *elohim* had to be interpretively rendered, hence "a leader," and this function Moses was to display to the Pharaoh according to the following Midrash—MHG to Exod. p. 71: "'and you will be to him as a god' (Exod. 4:16)—i.e., to the Pharaoh, or perhaps to Aaron, it therefore states—'see, I have designated a god to the Pharaoh' (Exod. 7:1)." The Syr. and Sam. Tg. are literal here, while Tg. Neof. has "as one seeking instruction from before the Lord." Tg. Ps.-Jon. contains Onqelos' translation followed by the paraphrase contained in Tg. Neof., while the Vg. and LXX have "in things pertaining to God."

[11]The Hebrew "the rod of God" could not be rendered literally anymore than could "the mountain of God" (Exod. 3:1, cf. n. 4 there). Just as the latter expression could cause misapprehensions about God's omnipresence, the "rod of God" could likewise cause misunderstanding concerning God's omnipotence. Furthermore, the following Midrash discusses the possession of this particular rod, Tanḥ (A) Šĕmoṯ XXIII ". . . at times it (Scripture) refers to it as 'the rod of God' (Exod. 4:20), at other times it (Scripture) refers to it as 'your rod' (Exod. 17:5)." The paraphrase in the Targum makes the possessor of the rod a relative matter.

[12]Lit. "his heart."

[13]The Hebrew has "and touched his legs with it, "with *wattagga'* a *hiphil* of *ng'*—"to touch." The Targum in translating "and she approached in front of him" evidently read the verb in the *qal* instead, as *wattigga'*, then *lĕraglāw* as a figure of speech meaning "in front of him."

approached in front of him,[13] saying, "*On account of this circumcision blood, let my husband be given <back> to us.*"[14] 26. Then he let go of him, whereupon she said, "*Were it not for this circumcision blood, my husband would have been condemned to death.*"[15] 27. Now the Lord said to Aaron, "Go towards Moses into the wilderness"; and he went and met him at the mountain *upon which the glory of the Lord was revealed,*[16] and he kissed him. 28. And Moses related to Aaron all the matters of the Lord <concerning> which He had sent him, as well as all the signs <concerning> which He commanded him. 29. Then Moses and Aaron proceeded to assemble all the elders of the Israelites. 30. And Aaron spoke all the words which the Lord spoke *with*[c] Moses and performed the signs in the sight of the people. 31. And the people believed and understood that the Lord remembered the Israelites *and that their servitude was revealed before Him.*[17] So they bowed down and worshiped.

CHAPTER 5

1. Thereafter, Moses and Aaron *entered*[a] and said to the Pharaoh, "Thus said the Lord, God of Israel, 'Send away my people, so that they may celebrate a festival *before*[1] me in the wilderness.'" 2. And the Pharaoh said, "*The name of the Lord*[b] *is not revealed to me*[2] *that I should obey his command*[3] to send away the Israelites; *the name of the Lord is not revealed to me,*[4] neither will I send away the Israelites." 3. So they said, "The God of the Jews *revealed Himself*[c] to us; let us now go a three days' distance into the wilderness and sacrifice *before*[5] the Lord our God, lest He meets us *with death or with slaughter.*"[6] 4. Then the king of Egypt said to them, "Why, O Moses and Aaron, are you *idling*[7] the people from their work; go to your labor." 5. The Pharaoh, further, said: "*Here now*[d] the people of the land are many and you are idling them *from their work.*"[e] 6. So the Pharaoh that day commanded the governors of his people and its overseers as follows, 7. "Do not continue to supply straw to the people to cast bricks as yesterday *and earlier;*[8] they should go and rake straw for themselves. 8. And the sum total of bricks which they produced as of yesterday *and earlier*[8] you shall *assign to*[f] them; do not diminish from it, for they are idlers therefore they cry, saying, 'Let us go

Apparatus, Chapter 4 (Cont.)

[c] n has: "to," as does the Hebrew.

Apparatus, Chapter 5

[a] a has: "came," as does the Hebrew.

[b] a has: "what is the name of the Lord," which partially reflects the Hebrew "who."

[c] Sperber's text has the more literal: "has chanced Himself." Cf. above Chap. 3, n. 1.

[d] J and n have: "since," which is an interpretive rendering.

[e] J, G, M have: "from their labor," which is a literal rendering of the Hebrew.

[f] a and l have the literal: "place upon."

[g] M, b, d, and g have: "become heavier," as does the Hebrew.

[h] l has the literal: "and let them do it."

and sacrifice *before*[5] our God.' 9. Let the labor *become more intense*[g] upon the men, and *let them be preoccupied with it,*[h] and not be preoccupied with *idle chatter."*[9] 10. So

Notes, Chapter 4 (Cont.)

[14]The Hebrew has: "You are truly a bridegroom of blood to me." The Targum interprets Zipporah's statement to refer to Moses, whose life was spared after being condemned to die by God for not having circumcised his firstborn son. The term "bridegroom" would then refer to Moses and "blood" to the act of circumcision. This opinion is expressed in the Midrash—Agg. Ber. XVII; 1, p. 36: "Moses, the greatest of prophets, of sages, of the righteous, because he delayed for a while the act of circumcision, the Holy One blessed be He sought to kill him, as it says 'and it came to pass on the way at the lodging . . . that the Lord sought to kill him' (Exod. 4:24). . . " Nevertheless, a difference of opinion exists in the Talmud as to whether "bridegroom" refers to Moses or to the child, for which cf. y. Ned. III:14, p. 38b. The Targum reinforces his interpretation that bridegroom refers to Moses or to the child, for which cf. y. Ned. III: 14, p. 38b. The Targum reinforces his interpretation that bridegroom refers to Moses, by his explicit translation of vs. 26b below. According to Tgs. Neof. and Ps.-Jon. as well as the Frg. Tg. (V, P), the stumbling block to circumcising the child was Jethro, and Hebrew *ḥṯn* would not refer to "bridegroom" (i.e., Moses) but to "father-in-law" (i.e., Jethro).

[15]The Hebrew has "a bridegroom of blood because of the circumcision." See preceding note.

[16]See above Chap. 3, n. 4.

[17]The Hebrew has: "He saw their affliction." See Gen. Chap. 29, n. 8. For the rendering "servitude" as a translation for "affliction," see above Chap. 3, n. 9.

Notes, Chapter 5

[1]See Gen. Chap. 4, n. 1.

[2]The Hebrew has: "who is the Lord." In contrast to Tg. Neof., the Syr., the Sam. Tg., and the Vg., all of which render here literally, the Targum, as well as Tg. Ps.-Jon, offers a free paraphrase that is also employed for the latter part of this verse in translation for "I do not know the Lord," and is reflected in the following Rabbinic tradition in Exod. Rab. V:14—"He (the Pharaoh) said to them (Moses and Aaron), 'Wait a while, till I search my records (wherein was a list of the nations, their kings and gods).' So he went into his palace chamber and scrutinized every nation and its gods, beginning with the gods of Moab, Ammon, and Zidon. He then said to them, 'I have searched for His name throughout my archives, but have not found Him.'" In line with this Rabbinic tradition, one can understand the Targum's translation of "who is the Lord"—"the name of the Lord is not revealed to me," i.e., "I have searched the records and failed to locate His name."

[3]The Hebrew "that I should listen to His voice" is anthropomorphic and here accordingly circumvented by transforming the Hebrew "hear" (i.e., listen) to "accept," and "His voice" to "His command." See also Gen. Chap. 16, n. 1.

[4]The Hebrew has "I do not know the Lord." As one cannot really "know" the Lord, the Targum transforms this clause into the exact statement that he used at the beginning of the verse in accord with the Rabbinic tradition cited there, for which see n. 2 above.

[5]See Gen. Chap. 4, n. 1.

[6]The Hebrew has: "with a plague or with a sword." The Targum, here identical to Tg. Ps.-Jon., merely generalizes the Hebrew figure of speech which states that God will punish the people either by natural death (plague) or by divine execution (sword). The LXX here is identical to the Targum, as it renders *θάνατος ἢ φόνος*—"death or slaughter." Tg. Neof. and the Sam. Tg. have "death" for Hebrew "plague," while the Syr. has "death" for Hebrew "sword." The Vg. is entirely literal here. See further Chap. 9, n. 4 below, for the Targumic treatment of Hebrew *deḇer.*

[7]The Hebrew has: "cause to refrain" which is here, as well as in all Aramaic versions (except Sam. Tg. [J], where "separate" is used) interpretively translated by the root *bṭl* "to cause suspension of," while LXX renders *διαστρέφετε*—"to turn (the people) from" while the Vg. has *sollicitatis*—"to draw (the people) from."

[8]See Gen. Chap. 21, n. 3.

[9]The Hebrew has "deceptive words" which is here rendered by a nonliteral translation "idle chatter." Of the Ancient Versions, only the Syr. *bml' aryqt'* "vain/empty words" and the LXX *λόγος κενοῖς*

the governors of the people and its overseers went out and said to the people as follows, "Thus said the Pharaoh, 'I am no longer giving you straw. 11. You go and take straw for yourselves wherever you can find <it>; yet nothing shall be diminished from your labor.'" 12. So the people were scattered throughout the entire land of Egypt to rake stubble for straw. 13. Now the governors were urging as follows, "Complete your work, the quota for each day, just as you did when straw was *supplied to you.*"[10] 14. Then the overseers of the Israelites, whom the Pharaoh's governors appointed over them, were beaten, saying, "Why is this that you did not complete your quota *to cast brick*[i] as yesterday and *earlier,*[8] also yesterday as well as today?" 15. So the Israelite overseers came and cried before Pharaoh, saying, "Why *is this being done*[j] to your servants? 16. Straw is not being supplied to your servants, and they <still> say to us, 'Make bricks'; and here, your servants are beaten and your people sin against them." 17. So he said, "Idlers! You are idlers, therefore you say, 'Let us go and sacrifice *before*[5] the Lord.' 18. Now then, proceed to work; but straw will not be supplied to you, {yet}; you shall supply the {required} sum total of bricks." 19. So the overseers of the Israelites viewed them as evil for saying, "Do not diminish your daily quota of bricks." 20. Then they met Moses and Aaron standing in front of them as they were departing *from*[k] the Pharaoh. 21. And they said to them, "May the Lord *reveal Himself*[11] to you and *punish*[12] <you>, for you have caused our pride to be deteriorated in the sight of the Pharaoh and in the sight of his servants, by placing a sword into their hands to kill us." 22. So Moses returned *before*[5] the Lord and said, "Why have You dealt wickedly with this people? Why so have You sent me? 23. Since the time that I have come in to the Pharaoh, *this people was wickedly treated;*[l] You have definitely not rescued Your people."

CHAPTER 6

1. Then the Lord said to Moses, "Now you will see what I will do to the Pharaoh; for because of *My*[1] powerful hand he will send them away, and because of *My*[1] strong hand he will expel them from his land." 2. Now the Lord spoke with Moses and said to him, "I am the Lord. 3. *And I have revealed Myself*[2] to Abraham, to Isaac, and to Jacob as El Shaddai but My name 'the Lord' I did not make known to them.

Apparatus, Chapter 5 (Cont.)

[i] h omits "bricks" which is probably implied in *lmrmy*="to cast," as the Hebrew only has *llbn,* for which cf. Gen. 11:3, where the Hebrew *nlbnh lbnym* is rendered *nrmy lbnyn.*

[j] b, g, and l have: "would you do this," as does the Hebrew, while n has: "are you doing this."

[k] G, c, k, and l have the interpretive: "from before."

[l] v, h, l and Ra have the more literal: "he treated this people wickedly."

Apparatus, Chapter 6

[a] n has: "to," as does the Hebrew.

4. Moreover, I have, also, confirmed My covenant with them to give to them the land of Canaan, the land of their sojournings in which they sojourned. 5. And also the outcries of the Israelites, which <are the result> of the Egyptians' subjection of them to hard labor, *have been heard before me,*[3] and I have recalled My covenant to mind. 6. Therefore, say to the Israelites, 'I am the Lord, and I will bring you out of Egypt *from the midst of*[4] *the oppression*[5] of the Egyptian burden; and I will rescue you from their subjection and will redeem you with an *exalted*[6] arm and great judgments. 7. Then I will *bring you close*[7] *before*[8] me as a people and I will be to you a God; then you will realize that I am the Lord, your God, who brought you out *from the midst of*[4] *the oppression*[5] of the Egyptian burden. 8. And I will bring you into the land *which I swore with My Memra*[8] to give it to Abraham, to Isaac, and to Jacob; and I will give it to you <as> a possession; I am the Lord.'" 9. So Moses spoke accordingly *with*[a] the

Notes, Chapter 5 (Cont.)

"vain words" are identical, whereas the remaining translators render literally. Schefftel (*Bi'ure Onqelos, op. cit.,* p. 80), remarks that this is another attempt by the Targumist to tone down unfavorable remarks about Israel, even though these were made by the Pharaoh.

10This insertion, which exists in every one of the Ancient Translations as well as in the Sam. Heb., was meant to supplement the concise Hebrew text which implies it.

11See Gen. Chap. 29, n. 8.

12The Hebrew has: "judge" which is here, and in Tg. Ps.-Jon., interpretively rendered to mean "punish," while Tg. Neof., CTgD, the Syr., the Sam. Tg., as well as the LXX and Vg. have the literal "judge." Löwenstein (*Nefesh Ha-Ger, op. cit.,* p. 13) correctly points out that the preceding word—*'ălêḵem* caused the Targum to deviate here and not render it literally with the root *dyn* "to judge" as he does in Gen. 16:5, where Sarah uses *yišpôt* towards Abraham but where *'al* does not appear in conjunction with it. Löwenstein calls attention to the fact that the Targum here is not in accord with the Midrashic exposition of this statement which understood the word literally—Exod. Rab. V:21—"And they said unto them, 'The Lord look upon you, and judge' (Exod. 5:21)—If you have really come in the name of the Lord, then let Him *judge* between us and Pharaoh; but if you have come of your own accord, then let the Lord judge between us and you."

Notes, Chapter 6

1Lit. "a."

2See Gen. Chap. 29, n. 8.

3See Gen. Chap. 29, n. 9.

4The Hebrew has "from under" which is figurative, and accordingly rendered interpretively by the Targum "from the midst." Tg. Ps.-Jon. is identical here, whereas the LXX, Vg., Tg. Neof. m., and Syr. have simply "from"; Sam. Tg. (J), CTgD, and Tg. Neof. are literal here.

5An insertion also present in Tg. Ps.-Jon., and, as "yoke," in Tg. Neof. and CTgD. Cf. B. Schefftel, *Bi'ure Onqelos, op. cit.,* p. 80, who explains it as the equivalent of an implied Hebrew *láḥaṣ* ("oppression") and justifies its use here.

6The Hebrew "outstretched" is anthropomorphic and accordingly circumvented by this rendering.

7The Hebrew has: "take you." As the following preposition "to" is rendered "before" by the Targum (for which see Gen. Chap. IV, n. 1), the Hebrew "take" could no longer be translated literally (as it is in the Syr., Sam. Tg., LXX, and Vg. where no such adjustment of the preposition exists). Accordingly, the Targum chose a verb that would be compatible with the preposition "before"—which turned out to be "to bring close." Tg. Ps.-Jon is here entirely identical to the Targum. See also Gen. Chap. 15, n. 7.

8The Hebrew has lit. "I raised My hand" which is anthropomorphic as well as being an idiomatic phrase for the art of swearing. The Targum accordingly circumvents the anthropomorphism and figure

Israelites, but they did not *listen to*[9] Moses because of the mental anguish *and from the labor which bore down upon them.*[10] 10. Then the Lord spoke with Moses as follows, 11. "Go in and speak to the Pharaoh, king of Egypt, that he send away the Israelites from his land." 12. Whereupon, Moses spoke before the Lord as follows, "Here the Israelites do not listen to me, then how will the Pharaoh listen to me when I am *heavy of speech?*"[11] 13. Then the Lord spoke with Moses and *to*[b] Aaron and gave them orders concerning the Israelites and the Pharaoh, king of Egypt, to bring out the Israelites from the land of Egypt. 14. These are the heads of their families: The sons of Reuben, the firstborn of Israel: Ḥanok and Pallu, Ḥezron and Karmi; these are the offspring of Reuben. 15. And Simeon's sons: Jemuel, and Jamin, and Ohad, and Jakhin, and Zohar, and Shaul, the son of a Canaanite woman; these are the offspring of Simeon. 16. And these are the names of Levi's sons according to their generations: Gershon, Kehath, and Merari; now the years of Levi's life <totaled>, 137 years. 17. Gershon's sons: Livni and Shim'i, according to their generations. 18. And Kehath's sons: Amram, and Yiṣhar, and Hebron, and Uzziel; now the years of Kehath's life <totaled>, 133 years. 19. And Merari's sons: Mahli, and Mushi; these are the offspring of *Levi*[c] according to their generations. 20. Now Amram took for himself Yokheved, *his father's sister,*[d12] for a wife, and she gave birth for him to Aaron, and Moses; and all the years of Amram's life <totaled>, 137 years. 21. And Yiṣhar's sons: Qorah, and Nefeg, and Zikhri. 22. And Uzziel's sons: Mishael, and Elṣafan, and Sithri. 23. Now Aaron took for himself Elisheva, daughter of 'Aminadav, as a wife, and she gave birth for him to Nadav, and Avihu, and Ele'azar, and Ithamar. 24. And Qorah's sons: Asir, and Elqanah, and Aviasaf; these are the offspring of Qorah. 25. Now Ele'azar, son of Aaron, took for himself from the daughters of Putiel, a wife, and she gave birth for him to Pinḥas. These are the heads of the Levite families according to their generations. 26. It is Aaron and Moses to whom the Lord said, "Bring out the Israelites from the land of Egypt according to their hosts." 27. They are the ones who spoke to the Pharaoh, king of Egypt, in order to bring out the Israelites from Egypt; it is Moses and Aaron. 28. Now it came about on the day that the Lord spoke with Moses in the land of Egypt, 29. that the Lord said to Moses as follows, "I am the Lord. Speak to the Pharaoh, king of Egypt, all that I have spoken *with*[a] you." 30. But Moses said before the Lord, "Here I am heavy of speech, and how will the Pharaoh listen to me?"

Apparatus, Chapter 6 (Cont.)

[b] R, U, and v have: "and with."
[c] i and l have: "the Levites."
[d] n has: "daughter."

Apparatus, Chapter 7

[a] n has: "over," which is interpretive.
[b] a and l have: "the Egyptians."
[c] a has: "with."
[d] n has: "wonder," as does the Hebrew.

Notes, Chapter 6 (Cont.)

of speech by translating it with its intended meaning and introducing the Memra, for which see Introduction VII D. 1.

[9]Lit. "accept from," for which see Gen. Chap. 16, n. 1.

[10]The Hebrew has "and from the hard labor." The Targum here transforms the Hebrew adjective "hard" into a relative clause—"which bore down on them." Of interest here is the translation of the Tg.

CHAPTER 7

1. Then the Lord said to Moses, "See here, I have appointed you as a leader towards the Pharaoh, while your brother Aaron shall be your *interpreter*.[1] 2. You shall speak all that I have commanded you, while your brother Aaron shall speak to the Pharaoh that he send away the Israelites from his land. 3. Whereas I will harden the Pharaoh's heart, so that I may multiply My signs and wonders in the land of Egypt. 4. But the Pharaoh will *not listen to you*[2] so that I will deliver *the stroke of My power*[3] *at*[a2] Egypt and will bring out my hosts, my people—the Israelites, from the land of Egypt with great judgments. 5. Then the Egyptians will realize that I am the Lord when I shall raise *the stroke of My power*[3] over *Egypt*[b] and bring out the Israelites from their midst." 6. So Moses and Aaron did as the Lord commanded them; so did they do. 7. Now Moses <was> 80 years old and Aaron <was> 83 years old when they spoke to the Pharaoh. 8. Then the Lord spoke *to*[c] Moses and *to*[c] Aaron, as follows, 9. "When the Pharaoh will say to you, as follows, 'Produce *a sign;*[d] then you shall say to Aaron,

Notes, Chapter 6 (Cont.)

Ps.-Jon. "and from the difficult idol worship that they were involved in" (lit. "that was in or on their hands"). The Aramaic expression for idol worship is *pûlḥānā' nûkrā'āh,* lit. alien worship, which is a literal translation of the Post-Biblical Hebrew *'ăḇôdāh zārāh.* Here, the word *pûlḥānā'* means "worship" but it can also mean "labor" and be the Aramaic equivalent for Hebrew *'ăḇôdāh.* One could very well reason, in view of the great similarity that exists between the translations of Onqelos and Ps.-Jon. that the word *nûḵrā'āh* could quite conceivably have originally been present in the text of Onqelos as well, but during its revision was dropped. The Onqelos text would thus have originally read *umippûlḥānā' nûḵrāh dhawēh qašyā'* (reading with A and E) *'ălêhôn"*—"from the idol worship that was difficult for them." What this reconstructed Onqelos text and Tg. Ps.-Jon.'s translation relate is the notion that it was difficult for the Israelites to break away from their worship of idols in which they must have been quite deeply entrenched. This type of a situation is precisely reflected in the following Midrashic exposition—Exod. Rab. VI:5—"It was so difficult for them to abandon idol worship. Thus does Ezekiel explain when he says: 'Cast away every man the detestable things of his eyes, and defile not yourselves with the idols of Egypt' (Ezek. 20:7). But see what is written: 'They did not every man cast away the detestable things of their eyes, neither did they forsake the idols of Egypt (*ibid.* vs. 8)." On the relationship of Tg. Ps.-Jon. with Onqelos see G. J. Kuiper's work—*The Pseudo-Jonathan Targum and its Relationship to Targum Onkelos.* Studia Ephemerides "Augustinianum" 9. Rome (Institutum Patristicum "Augustinianum") 1972, pp. 5, 99-107 where the author concludes that Tg. Ps.-Jon. received its authoritative redaction in Targum Onqelos.

11The Hebrew has: "uncircumcised of lips" which is idiomatic, and accordingly rendered by the already-used expression of Exod. 4:10. The other Aramaic versions also make appropriate changes in their translations of this Hebrew figure of speech. Tg. Neof. m. and Tg. Ps.-Jon. have "hard of speech;" Tg. Neof., "halting of speech;" the Syr., "a stutterer." The LXX has "not eloquent" (*δέ 'άλογὸς έιμι*) while the Vg. is literal.

12See Lev. Chap. 10, n. 2.

Notes, Chapter 7

1The Hebrew has: "prophets." The Targum renders this term interpretively in the manner of Exod. 4:16 where it is expressed in the Hebrew as "mouth" and likewise rendered "interpreter" in the Targum. In ancient times the "prophet" was actually the "interpreter" of the word of God and His actual "mouth" (piece). Of the ancients, only Tg. Neof. has "interpreter"; the others all render literally here.

2Lit. "accept from you." See Gen. Chap. 16, n. 1.

3See above Chap. 3, n. 18.

'Take your rod and cast it before the Pharaoh; it will <then> become a serpent.'" 10. So Moses and Aaron *went in*[e] to the Pharaoh and did precisely as the Lord commanded, and Aaron cast his rod before the Pharaoh and it became a serpent. 11. Now the Pharaoh also summoned the wise men and the magicians, and they too, *the magicians of Egypt,*[f] did likewise through their secret arts. 12. So each one cast his rod and they became serpents, but Aaron's rod swallowed up their rods. 13. Nevertheless, the Pharaoh's heart *was hardened,*[4] and he did not listen to them, as the Lord had said. 14. Then the Lord said to Moses, "The Pharaoh's heart *has become heavy;*[g] he refuses to send away the people. 15. Go to the Pharaoh in the morning; here he goes out to the water, and you shall station yourself before him on the bank of the river, and the rod, which turned into the serpent, you should take into your hand. 16. Then you should say to him, 'The Lord, God of *the Jews,*[5] has sent me to you, saying, "Send away my people that they may worship me in the wilderness, but here you *have not listened*[6] till now." 17. Thus says the Lord, "Through this you will realize that I am the Lord. I am, hereby, about to strike with the rod that is in my hand, the waters of the river and they will turn into blood. 18. *And the fish*[7] which are in the river will die and the river will become malodorous, and the Egyptians will labor in vain to drink the water of the river."'" 19. Then the Lord said to Moses, "Say to Aaron, 'Take your rod and raise your hand over *the Egyptian waters,*[h] over their rivers, over their canals, and over their lakes, and over all the gatherings of their waters and they will become blood, and blood will be throughout the land of Egypt, as well as *in wooden vessels and in stone vessels.*[8]'" 20. So Moses and Aaron did precisely as the Lord commanded, and he raised the rod and struck the water of the river in sight of the Pharaoh and in sight of his servants, and all the waters of the river turned into blood. 21. *And the fish*[7] of the river died, and the river became malodorous; now the Egyptians were not able to drink the water from the Nile; and there was blood throughout the whole land of Egypt. 22. Now the *Egyptian magicians*[i] did likewise with their secret arts, and the Pharaoh's heart *was hardened*[4] and he did not listen to them as the Lord had said. 23. Then the Pharaoh turned and came into his palace, and did not pay attention even to this. 24. So all the Egyptians dug around the Nile<to find > water to drink, for they were unable to drink the water *that was in the Nile.*[j] 25. Now seven days were complete since the Lord struck the Nile. 26. Then the Lord said to Moses, "Go in to the Pharaoh and say to him, 'Thus said the Lord, "Send away My people that they may worship Me. 27. *Now*[k] if you are going to refuse to send <them> away, here I am about to strike everyone of your borders with frogs. 28. And the Nile *will produce frogs in abundance,*[9] and they will come up and enter your palace, your bedchamber, and (upon) your bed, and (into) your servants' houses, and (among) your people, and (into) your ovens, and (into) your kneading troughs. 29. And upon you, and upon your people, and upon your servants will the frogs ascend."'"

Apparatus, Chapter 7 (Cont.)

[e] k has: "came," as does the Hebrew.
[f] L, R, and c have: "the Egyptian magicians."
[g] J, g, and l have: "is heavy," as does the Hebrew.
[h] Sperber's text has: "the waters of Egypt."
[i] Sperber's text has: "magicians of Egypt."
[j] a has: "of the Nile."
[k] l has: "For."

Apparatus, Chapter 8

[a] D has: "the waters of Egypt" which reflects the Hebrew more accurately.

CHAPTER 8

1. Then the Lord said to Moses, "Say to Aaron, 'Raise up your rod over the rivers, over the canals, and over the lakes; and bring up the frogs over the land of Egypt.'" 2. So Aaron raised his hand over *the Egyptian waters,*[a] and the *frogs*[1] ascended and covered the land of Egypt. 3. Then the magicians did likewise with their secret arts, and brought up the frogs over the land of Egypt. 4. Now the Pharaoh summoned Moses and Aaron and said, "Pray *before*[2] the Lord that He remove the frogs from me and from my people, then I will send away the people that they may sacrifice *before*[2] the Lord." 5. Then Moses said to the Pharaoh, "*Ask for a mighty deed, set an appointed time*[3] when I should pray on behalf of you, and your servants, and your people to

Notes, Chapter 7 (Cont.)

[4]The Hebrew has: "hardened." In view of the verb *ḥzq* being an intransitive verb, the Targum employs the *ithpa'al* form to express this character.

[5]See above Chap. 1, n. 9.

[6]See Gen. Chap. 16, n. 1.

[7]The Hebrew *dāgāh* is the collective term for fish, which is here rendered interpretively in the plural to refer to all the species of fish. All the ancients have the plural form as well.

[8]The Hebrew "in wood (vessels) and stone (vessels)" implies "vessels"—a term which the Targum actually adds, as do Tg. Ps.-Jon, the LXX *τοῖς ξύλοις*, and the Vg. *vasis,* while Tg. Neof., CTgD, the Sam. Tg., and the Syr. render the Hebrew literally.

[9]The Hebrew has: "will swarm frogs" which is here interpretively rendered, as it is in the Tg. Ps.-Jon., and the Vg. *ebulliet;* the LXX has *ἐξερεύξεται*—"discharge, "the Syr. *nrḥš*—"bring forth," while Tg. Neof. is literal, by reproducing the Hebrew root *šrṣ*—"swarm."

Notes, Chapter 8

[1]The Hebrew has the singular, which is reflected only in Sam. Tg. (J), while Tg. Neof., Sam. Tg. (A), the Syr., and the Vg., like the Targum, have the plural. Tg. Ps.-Jon. expands it to "the plague of the frogs," but plural nevertheless, while the LXX first renders *καὶ 'ανήγαγε τοὺς βατράχους*—"and brought up the *frogs,*" thus the plural, then inserts *καὶ 'ανεβιβάσθη ὁ βάτραχος*—"and the *frog* was brought up," here singular. According to Rabbinic tradition, originally one frog existed, which emerged from the Nile and produced many frogs, as seen from the Talmud, b. Sanh. 67b—"'And the frog came up, and covered the land of Egypt' (Exod. 8:2). R. Eleazar said: It was one frog, which bred prolifically and filled the land. . . . R. Akiba said: There was one frog which filled the whole of Egypt [by breeding]. But R. Eleazar b. Azariah said to him: Akiba! What have you to do with Aggadah? Cease your words, and devote yourself to Leprosies and Tents. One frog croaked for the others and they came." Cf. also Exod. Rab. X:4, as well as Tanḥ (A) *Wā*'ērā' XIV.

[2]See Gen. Chap. 4, n. 1.

[3]The Hebrew has: "you may glorify yourself over me." As pointed out on many occasions in Genesis, the Targum was particularly concerned for the dignity of the Patriarchs and Israel. Accordingly anything disparagingly said of them was reworded or toned down. The present situation is just such a case. Here Moses asks the Pharaoh to glorify himself over Moses. This was a statement that could not be rendered literally (as did Tg. Ps.-Jon.—"pride yourself on my account"); instead it was paraphrased in such a way as to suggest its meaning indirectly. Accordingly, the Targum first translates: "Ask for a mighty deed." Moses says to the Pharaoh: "Ask for the impossible, ask for something so great that I would not be able to grant, whereupon you would be able to boast yourself in triumph over me" (Tg. Neof. and the Frg. Tg. [V, P] paraphrase differently with "give me a sign and trust me"). The Targum then adds "set an appointed time" (an addition also present in the Syr., the LXX, and the Vg.) as a lead-in to what follows in the Hebrew "when I should pray for. . . ."

remove the frogs from you and from your houses; only *those that are in the Nile*[b] will remain." 6. So he said, "Tomorrow!" And he said, "According to your word, so that you may realize that there is none like the Lord our God. 7. Then the frogs will be removed from you, and from your houses, and from your servants, and from your people; only *those that are*[c] in the Nile will remain." 8. So Moses and Aaron departed *from*[d] the Pharaoh and Moses *prayed*[4] *before*[2] the Lord on account of the frogs, which He had set against the Pharaoh. 9. Then the Lord did according to Moses' word and the frogs died out of the houses, out of the courtyards, and out of the fields. 10. And they collected them heaps <atop> of heaps and *they were malodorous through the land.*[e] 11. When the Pharaoh realized that there was relief, he made heavy his heart, and did not *listen to them*[5] as the Lord had said. 12. Then the Lord said to Moses, "Say to Aaron, 'Raise your rod and strike the dust of the earth and it shall become vermin throughout the land of Egypt.'" 13. So they did accordingly, and Aaron raised his hand with its rod and struck the dust of the earth, and it became vermin in man and beast; all of the dust of the earth became vermin throughout the land of Egypt. 14. Now the magicians did likewise with their secret arts to bring out the vermin but were not able to, and the vermin was in man and beast. 15. So the magicians said to the Pharaoh, "*It is a plague from before the Lord*";[6] yet the Pharaoh's heart hardened, and he did not *listen to them,*[5] as the Lord had said. 16. Then the Lord said to Moses, "Arise early in the morning and station yourself in front of the Pharaoh; here he is going out to the water and you shall say to him, 'Thus says the Lord, "Send away My people so that they may worship Me. 17. For if you do not send away My people, here I am about to *send*[f] against you, and against your servants, and against your people, and against your houses a mixture of wild beasts; and *the houses of Egypt*[g] will become filled with the mixture of wild beasts, as well as the ground upon which they are. 18. And on that day I will set apart the land of Goshen where my people *dwell,*[h] in that there will not be there the mixture of wild beasts, so that you may realize that I am the Lord *ruling*[7] in the midst of the earth. 19. And I will set up a redemption *for My people, but upon your people I will bring the plague.*[8] Tomorrow will be this sign."'" 20. So the Lord did so and a *powerful*[9] mixture of wild beasts came into the Pharaoh's palace and into the *houses*[10] of his servants, while throughout the land of Egypt, the earth *was destroyed*[i] on account of the mixture of wild beasts. 21. Then the Pharaoh summoned Moses and Aaron and said, "Go and sacrifice *before*[2] your God in the land." 22. And Moses said, "It is not proper to do so, because *we are taking the* (*very*) *cattle which the Egyptians worship to sacrifice*[11] (them) *before*[2] the Lord our God; here we will be sacrificing *the cattle which the Egyptians worship and they would be seeing* (*it*); *would they not intend*

Apparatus, Chapter 8 (Cont.)

[b] d has: "in the Nile."
[c] D has: "in the Nile."
[d] J, c, k, and l have: "from before."
[e] l has: "and the land was malodorous," as does the Hebrew.
[f] l has: "incite," which is interpretive.
[g] J, U, a, b, and g have: "the houses of the Egyptians."
[h] E has the literal: "stand."
[i] a has: "will be destroyed," a literal rendering of the Hebrew, which has to be understood in the perfect as seen from the LXX, the Sam. Heb. and the Syr. renderings, all of which translate as if there existed a *waw consecutive*.
[j] c has: "he told," which makes more sense in the syntax.
[k] B, D, and R add: "also," as does the Syr. and the LXX.

to stone us?![11] 23. We shall go a distance of three days into the wilderness and shall sacrifice before the Lord our God as *He will tell*[j] us." 24. And the Pharaoh said, "I will send you away and you shall sacrifice *before*[2] the Lord your God in the wilderness, only do not go too far; *pray*[k] for me." 25. So Moses said, "Here I will be departing from you and praying *before*[2] the Lord that He should remove the mixture of wild beasts from the Pharaoh, from his servants, and from his people tomorrow; only let the

Notes, Chapter 8 (Cont.)

4The Hebrew has "cried out." The translation "prayed" employed by the Targum, also present in Tgs. Neof. and Ps.-Jon., as well as in the Syr. is interpretive. The Midrash Sekh. Tob. (Exod., p. 45) reflects this interpretation: "'Then Moses and Aaron departed from the Pharaoh' (Exod. 8:8). They went outside the city preferring not to pray within the city which is full of idolatrous abominations." The Sam. Tg., LXX, and the Vg. render the Hebrew literally. The association of Hebrew *ṣ'q* with prayer is already made by the Rabbis in the Mishna—Ber. IX:3 (also b. Ber. 54a). ". . . but to cry out (*ṣô'ēq*) over the past is to utter a vain *prayer.*"

5Lit. "accept from them," for which see Gen. Chap. 16, n. 1.

6The Hebrew "it is a finger of God" is anthropomorphic and accordingly circumvented. The particular choice of the word "plague" as the equivalent for "finger" recalls the following Rabbinic opinions on the matter—

1. *Mek. Bĕšallaḥ Mĕsektā' dwayeḥî* VI, ed. Horovitz and Rabin, p. 114—"Rabbi Jose the Galilean said: Whence do we deduce that whereas the Egyptians were smitten in Egypt with ten plagues, they were smitten with fifty plagues at the Sea? What is said in reference to Egypt? Then the magicians said to the Pharaoh, 'This is the *finger* of God' (Exod. 8:15). But at the Sea it says, 'Israel saw the great *hand,* etc.' (Exod. 14:31). With how many *plagues* were they *smitten* with the *finger*? Hence you may deduce that they suffered ten plagues in Egypt and fifty plagues at the Sea."

2. *PRE* XLVIII—"Rabbi Ishmael said: The five fingers of God's right hand are all dedicated to redemption. With his little finger He showed Noah how to make the Ark . . . *With the next He smote the Egyptians. . . .*"

3. Midrash Aggadah (Exodus, p. 137)—"Wait for him, *He has so far only smitten you with a finger,* when He will smite you with the hand, you will then be afraid, as it says: 'the great hand which God displayed against Egypt' (Exod. 14:31)."

7An insertion, also present in Tg. Ps.-Jon. and reflected in the following Midrash (Sekh. Tob: Exod., p. 48): "'In order that you may realize that I am the Lord in the midst of the land' (Exod. 8:18). So that you should not say that My presence is in heaven and not on earth. Rather the entire earth is filled with His Glory, May He be blessed, as well as His presence; and just as I rule in heaven, I *rule* on earth."

8The Hebrew has: "between My people and (between) your people." This re-division of the verse, also present in Tg. Ps.-Jon., was first and foremost necessitated by the difficulty involving the beginning of the verse, specifically the meaning of the Hebrew *pdûṯ*. The LXX, Vg., and Syr. all translate "distinction" which would assume *pdûṯ* to be a corruption of *plûṯ* • *plh* as in vs. 18 above. As a result, the following sequence *bên . . . bên*—"between" would make good sense, whereas *pdûṯ* "redemption" does not fit in syntactically with *bên . . . bên.* The Targum, reading *pdûṯ* accordingly translates *bên* as "for," and ends the first clause with "My people," thus "I will set up redemption for My people." He then renders the second *bên* by *w'al*—"but upon," continues with "your people," then adds "I will bring a plague," an addition that is reflected in the Midrash-Exod. Rab. XI:2 "'I will put a division or redemption between My people and your people' (Exod. 8:19). This teaches that Israel too deserved to be smitten with this plague, but God made the Egyptians their ransom."

9The Hebrew "heavy," is here interpretively rendered.

10Lit. house. The LXX has the plural, as does the Vg. and Tg. Neof.

11The Hebrew has: "for we shall be sacrificing the abominations of the Egyptians." This paraphrase, which also exists in Tg. Ps.-Jon. who further adds that these are the sheep which the Egyptians worship, is reflected in Exod. Rab. XI:3 "'And Moses said it is not right to do so' (Exod. 8:22), because the

Pharaoh not continue *to lie*[12] in not sending away his people to sacrifice *before*[2] the Lord." 26. Then Moses departed *from*[l] the Pharoah and prayed *before*[2] the Lord. 27. And the Lord did according to Moses' word and He removed the mixture of wild beasts from the Pharaoh, from his servants, and from his people; not a single one was left. 28. But the Pharaoh made heavy his heart even this time and did not send the people away.

CHAPTER 9

1. Then the Lord said to Moses, "Go in to the Pharaoh and *speak with*[a] him, 'Thus said the Lord, the God of *the Jews:*[1] "Send away My people, so that they may worship *before Me.*[2] 2. For if you are going to refuse to *send <them>away,*[b] and up to now you have held on to them, 3. here, *a plague from the Lord*[3] will be upon your *livestock*[c] which are in the field, upon the horses, upon the camels, upon the cattle, and upon the sheep, a very *great*[d] *death.*[4] 4. And the Lord will distinguish between the Israelite livestock and the Egyptian livestock, so that not a single one of all those <belonging> to the Israelites will perish."'" 5. So the Lord set an appointed time, as follows, "Tomorrow the Lord will do this thing in the land." 6. And the Lord did this thing on the following day, whereupon all Egyptian livestock perished, while not a single one of the Israelite livestock perished. 7. Then the Pharaoh sent <to have this matter investigated> and here not even a single Israelite livestock had perished, and the Pharaoh's heart became heavy, and he did not send the people away. 8. So the Lord said to Moses and Aaron, "Take handfuls of dust of the furnace, and Moses should scatter it toward heaven *in sight of*[e] the Pharaoh. 9. And it will become fine dust over the entire land of Egypt, and it will be upon man and upon beast as boils teeming with postules throughout the land of Egypt." 10. So they took the dust of the furnace, and standing before the Pharaoh, Moses scattered it toward heaven, and it became boils teeming with postules upon man and (upon) beast. 11. Now the magicians were unable to stand before Moses because of the boils, for the boils were upon the magicians and upon all the Egyptians. 12. And the Lord hardened the Pharaoh's heart and he did not

Apparatus, Chapter 8 (Cont.)

[l] G and c have: "from before."

Apparatus, Chapter 9

[a] i_a has: "say to" while n has "to" instead of "with" as well. The Hebrew reads "to him."

[b] i_a adds: "My people," not in the Hebrew.

[c] n has: "cattle."

[d] l has: "intense," which is the usual Targumic equivalent for the Hebrew "heavy," used here.

[e] G has: "before."

[f] d and g add: "ruling" here. In 8:18 above a similar addition to the Hebrew text exists in the Targum, for which cf. n. 7 there.

[g] k omits it.

listen to them, as the Lord had spoken to Moses. 13. Then the Lord said to Moses, "Arise early in the morning and station yourself before the Pharaoh and say to him, 'Thus said the Lord, God of *the Jews,*[1] "Send away My people that they may worship *before Me.*[2] 14. For this time I am about to send all my plagues upon your heart, and upon your servants, and (upon) your people; so that you shall realize that there is no one like *Me*[f] throughout the land. 15. For now <the time> *is approaching for Me*[g] that I indeed send *the stroke of My power,*[5] and smite you and your people with *death* [4] that you be destroyed from earth. 16. For truly because of this have I preserved you in order

Notes, Chapter 8 (Cont.)

Egyptians worshipped cattle as gods" as well as in MHG (Exod., p. 128):"'We shall be sacrificing the abominations of the Egyptians' (Exod. 8:22). Scripture informs us that the Egyptians worshipped the Constellation of Ram, and neither slaughtered nor ate any small cattle. Therefore it says elsewhere: 'for every shepherd is an abomination to the Egyptians.' (Gen. 46:34)."

[12]The Hebrew *hōtēl*—"to make sport of"—is here interpretively rendered, "to lie," a translation that is identical to that of every other Ancient Version. The same holds true for Gen. 31:17. A Halakhic Midrash commenting on Deuteronomy Chapter 13 which deals with a false prophet, likewise makes the connection between the meaning "to lie" and the Hebrew *hōtēl* by citing the present verse, for which cf. *Midrash Tannaïm zum Deuteronomium,* ed. D. Hoffmann. Berlin, 1909, p. 111. Also relevant in this context is the following comment in the late Midrash Sekhel Tob (on Gen. 31:7, p. 157): "'and your father made sport of me,' *htwl*—this refers to one who suspends words of truth into deceit in order to make sport of a person, as in (1 Kgs. 18:27) 'and Elijah made sport of them,' in that he made sport of the prophet of Baal . . . similarly Exod. 8:25 . . . Isa. 30:10 . . . and Job 17:2 . . . ," where this root occurs.

Notes, Chapter 9

[1]See above Chap. 1, n. 9.

[2]See Gen. Chap. 4, n. 1.

[3]The Hebrew has: "the hand of the Lord" which is anthropomorphic, and accordingly circumvented. The particular choice of the word "plague" as the equivalent for "hand" was governed by the same criterion as was that for the word finger in Exod. 8:15, for which see n. 6 there.

[4]The Hebrew has "plague" which is literally rendered in the Vg. (*pestis*), the Syr. (*mwṯn'*), and Sam. Tg. (*mwṯn*), while the Targum, as well as Tgs. Ps.-Jon. and Neof., renders interpretively "death," as does the LXX (*θάνατος*). It appears that the Targum basically uses *mwṯ* ("death") as the equivalent for Heb. *déḇer* when that word is used to denote "death" in general as in Exod. 5:3; 9:15; Num. 14:12; and Deut. 28:21 (the single exception being Lev. 26:25 where *mwṯn'*—"plague" is used.) In the present verse where the reference is to the cattle-plague, murrain, there may have been an additional reason for *mwt* "death" having been used, as there exist specific references in certain Midrashic texts which correlate "death" with this particular plague, as follows:

1. Yelamdenu (Kasher, *Torah Shlemah, op. cit.,* 9, p. 80, #7)—"Said the Holy One blessed be He: Let the *death-dealing pestilence* exact retribution from the Egyptians, who sought to destroy a people who incur *death* for the Unity of My name, as it says 'for Your sake are we killed all day' (Ps. 44:23)."
2. *Sekhel Tob.* (Exod. p. 50)—"'A very grievous murrain' (Exod. 9:3). What does 'very grievous' imply? Do not think that some cattle died while others only sickened and then recovered. For it says, 'a very grievous murrain,' which means that the *Angel of Death* laid a heavy hand on them and killed them all right away, for 'very grievous' implies that it was unusually severe."

Otherwise (with the exception of Lev. 26:25), the Targum used *mwṯānā'*—"plague" for Hebrew *négep* (Num. 17:11, 12) and *magēp̱āh* (Num. 14:37; 17:13, 14, 15; 25:8, 9, 18; 26:1) almost exclusively (*mwṯā'* is used for *négep̱* only in Exod. 12:13; 30:12; and Num. 8:19).

[5]See above Chap. 3, n. 18.

to show My strength, and in order that they should talk about *the power of*[6] My name throughout the land. 17. Until now you have *suppressed My people*[7] in order not to send them away. 18. Here I am about to bring down tomorrow at this time a very powerful[8] hail; there has never been one of its kind in Egypt from the day it was founded till now. 19. So now send for and *gather*[9] in your *livestock*[c] and all that is yours in the field; every man and beast that may be found in the field and was not gathered in to the house, upon them the hail will descend and they will perish."'" 20. Whoever of the Pharaoh's servants that is in reverence of the word of the Lord *would gather in*[10] his <own> servants and *livestock*[c] into the houses. 21. But whoever did not pay attention to the word of the Lord left his servants and his beast in the field. 22. Then the Lord said to Moses, "Raise your hand toward heaven and there will be hail throughout the land of Egypt; upon man, and upon beast, as well as upon all plants of the field." 23. So Moses raised his rod toward heaven and the Lord gave <forth> thunder and hail, and fire descended onto earth, and the Lord caused hail to rain down upon the land of Egypt. 24. And there was hail and fire flaming through the hail very *intensely;*[8] there had never been hail of its kind throughout the land of Egypt from the time it became a nation. 25. Now throughout the land of Egypt the hail struck all that was in the field from man to beast; and all the plants of the field did the hail strike, and all the trees of the field did it smash. 26. Only in the land of Goshen where the Israelites were, there was no hail. 27. Then the Pharaoh sent for and summoned Moses and Aaron and said to them, "I am guilty this time; the Lord is righteous, but I and my people are the guilty ones. 28. Pray *before*[2] the Lord *and <let there proceed> from Him much relief, that there not be <any longer> upon us any cursed thunder as these from before the Lord,*[11] nor hail; then I will send you away and you will not continue *to be detained.*"[12] 29. Then Moses said to him, "As I depart from the city I will be spreading out my hands *in prayer*[13] *before*[2] the Lord; the thunder will cease, nor will there be any more hail, so that you may realize that the earth is the Lord's. 30. But as for you and your servants, I know that as yet you have not *humbled yourselves*[14] from before the Lord God."[h] 31. Now the flax and the barley were blighted, because the barley was ripening and the flax was in bloom. 32. But the wheat and the spelt were

Apparatus, Chapter 9 (Cont.)

[h] y omits it, as does LXX[B] and the Sam. Heb.

[i] h has: "to the earth" which reflects the Hebrew.

Notes, Chapter 9 (Cont.)

[6]An insertion which is unique to the Targum (Tgs. Ps.-Jon. and Neof. have "the holy name"). M. Löwenstein (*Nefesh Ha-Ger, op. cit.*, p. 21) correctly points out that the present infinitive *sappēr* does not refer to the Pharaoh but should be understood in the passive—"that My name *be related* throughout the land." The passive sense of this verb is also reflected in the Sam. Tg., the LXX, and the Vg., as well as the Syr. and by all the Targumim. The addition of "the power of" just reflects God's activity within Egypt which is always qualified by this term, as seen in Exod. 3:20; 7:4, 5 for "my hand" is rendered "the stroke of My power."

[7]The Hebrew has: "exalt yourself against My people." The translation "suppress" in the Targum for the Hebrew *mistôlēl* is similar to the Vg.'s *retines*—"hold back." However, the Targum is closer to the interpretation of the following Midrash of this term, Exod. Rab. XII:1—"'You still exalt yourself

not blighted because they were late in ripening. 33. Then Moses departed the city from the Pharaoh and spread out his hands *in prayer*[15] *before*[2] the Lord. Whereupon the thunder and hail ceased, and the rain *which had descended*[16] did not reach *the earth.*[i] 34. As the Pharaoh saw that the rain and hail and thunder had ceased, he continued to sin, and he as well as his servants made heavy their hearts. 35. So the Pharaoh's heart was hardened, and he did not send away the Israelites as the Lord had said through Moses.

Notes, Chapter 9 (Cont.)

against My people' (Exod. 9:17)—this means that He made them like a highway (*mĕsillāh*) on which everybody *trod*. . . ." In contrast, Tgs. Neof. and Ps.-Jon. render "boast yourself" while the Syr. and the Frg. Tg. (V) have "hold on firmly to," and the LXX "determined with regards to" is similar in respect.

[8]See apparatus, note d.

[9]The Hebrew has "brought into safety," which is here interpretively rendered "gathered" which according to the Targum was the general connotation of the Hebrew *hiphil* form of *'wz* in this context—"to bring into safety." Tgs. Neof. and Ps.-Jon. translate this verb by this same Aramaic root *knš*—"gather in," while the Syr. uses *ḥml* with this identical meaning. The LXX and Vg. likewise translate "gather in." Of interest here is the Midrash Leq. Tob. (Exod., p. 41): "'Bring to safety' (Exod. 9:19)—gather in, similarly Isa. 10:31 and Jer. 6:1."

[10]The Hebrew has "made to flee," the *hiphil* from the root *nws,* which the Targum here, as in the preceding verse, renders interpretively in a general sense—"to gather in" as does the Tg. Ps.-Jon. (same root—*knš*), the Syr. (same root as in preceding verse—*ḥml*) and the LXX, while Tg. Neof., the Sam. Tg. (using Aramaic *ʿrq,* the usual equivalent for Hebrew *nws*), and the Vg. translate it literally—"caused to flee."

[11]The Hebrew has: "there has been enough of." The Targum attempted to deal with the concise Hebrew phrasing—*wĕrab̲ mihyôt̲ qōlōt̲ 'Elōhîm*—in the following manner:

1. *wĕrab̲* is rendered "much" (*saggî*) which he precedes with the jussive clause "let there be (=proceed)" which actually exists in the Tg. Ps.-Jon. This is followed by an object clause "relief (as in 8:11 above) from Him." By this paraphrasing the Targum separated *wĕrab̲* from the following *mihyôt̲* to which it was connected in sense, and made it an independent clause. He then interpreted *mihyôt̲* to be a negative infinitive (in the manner of *biltî*) adding the suffixed preposition *'ălanā'* to complete the prepositional clause. The Hebrew "thunder" is more precisely defined as "cursed thunder" thus separating it from its genetive—God, so as to avoid the sequence "cursed" and "God." Finally, he inserts "as these" and extends the isolated word "God" into a prepositional phrase with the standard *qdm,* for which see Gen. Chap. 4, n. 1.

[12]The Hebrew has "to stand" which is idiomatic, and accordingly, interpretively rendered into its intended meaning. Tg. Ps.-Jon. is identical here although Tg. Neof. and the Sam. Tg. are literal here.

[13]This insertion is reflected in Exod. Rab. XII:5—"'As I depart the city' (Exod. 9:29), from here it is evident that Moses did not wish *to pray* inside Egypt because it was full of abominable idols." Tg. Ps.-Jon. likewise adds this term.

[14]The Hebrew has: "you do not yet fear." The Hebrew syntax is somewhat difficult here. The Tg. Neof. m. contains a similar paraphrase though slightly augmented—"that until the plagues reached you, you did not humble yourselves." The other Ancients are all literal here.

[15]This insertion is similar to that of vs. 29 above and is separately reflected in the Midrash—Exod. Rab. XII:7—"'And Moses went out of the city from the Pharaoh' (Exod. 9:33). Though he was still in the city's boundary, he delayed not in *praying* for them, but 'spread forth his hands unto the Lord' (*ibid.*) and He accepted his *prayer.*"

[16]The insertion of this relative clause was meant for clarity.

CHAPTER 10

1. Then the Lord said to Moses, "Go in to the Pharaoh for I have made heavy his heart and the heart of his servants, in order to demonstrate these signs of Mine among them. 2. And in order that you may recount *before*[1] your children and grandchildren *the miracles which I performed*[2] in Egypt and My signs which I demonstrated among them, so that you may realize that I am the Lord." 3. Then Moses and Aaron *went in*[a] to the Pharaoh and said to him, "Thus says the Lord, God of *the Jews,*[3] 'Until when will you refuse to humble yourself before Me? Send away My people that they may worship *before*[4] Me. 4. For if you <still> refuse to send away My people, here I am about to bring locusts into your border(s). 5. And it will obscure *the view of the sun from the earth*[5] so that one will not be able to see the earth; and it will devour the remaining residue that is left for you from the hail, and it will devour every tree which is growing for you in the field. 6. And your houses, and the houses of your servants and the houses of all the Egyptians will be filled, which neither your fathers, nor your fathers' fathers have seen from the day of their existence on earth until this day.'" Then he turned and departed *from*[b] the Pharaoh. 7. Then the Pharaoh's servants said to him, "Until when will this one be an obstacle for us? Send away the men that they may worship *before*[4] the Lord their God. Do you not yet know that Egypt is ruined?" 8. Whereupon Moses and Aaron were returned to the Pharaoh and he said to them, "Go and worship *before*[4] *the*[c] Lord your God. Who precisely is going?" 9. So Moses said, "With our young ones and with our elders will we go, with our sons and with our daughters, with our sheep and with our cattle will we go, for it is for us a feast *before*[4] the Lord." 10. Then he said to them, "*The Memra of the Lord shall now*[d] *support you*[6] as I will send away you and your little ones. *Realize the evil that you are contemplating on doing; it is not your intention to repent* <from it>.[7] 11. Not so; let, now, the men go and worship *before*[4] the Lord, for that is what you are seeking"; and he expelled them *from before*[e] *the*[f] Pharaoh. 12. Then the Lord said to Moses, "Raise your hand over the land of Egypt and bring about the locust that it may ascend over the land of Egypt and devour every plant of the *field,*[g] all that the hail left over." 13. So Moses raised his rod over the land of Egypt, and the Lord led an east wind through the land throughout that day and night; by morning, the east wind had carried in the locust. 14. Now the

Apparatus, Chapter 10

[a] a has: "came."
[b] g and k have: "from before."
[c] c has: "before the."
[d] a, b, c, g, and k have the literal: "so," while l has: "thus."
[e] v and l have: "from."
[f] l adds: "the presence (lit. 'face') of."
[g] Sperber's text has: "earth," which literally reflects the Hebrew.
[h] a and l have: "the Egyptians."

Notes, Chapter 10

[1]See Gen. Chap. 23, n. 2.

[2]The Hebrew has: "I made a mockery of" or "dealt ruthlessly with," which is somewhat anthropomorphic, and is accordingly circumvented. Schefftel (*Bi'ure Onqelos, op. cit.*, p. 82) correctly points out that the Hebrew root *ʿll* involved here is usually rendered literally in the Targum when

locust ascended over the entire land of Egypt and came to rest within every border of *Egypt;*[h] <it was> very *intense;*[8] never before had there been locust like it, nor will there ever be again. 15. And it obscured *the entire view of the sun from the earth,*[5] thus darkening the earth; and it devoured every plant of the earth and all the fruits of the

Notes, Chapter 10 (Cont.)

pertaining to other than God as in Num. 22:21; Judg. 19:25. When referring to God, however, it is usually paraphrased, as in 1 Sam. 6:6, where the Hebrew has "when I mocked them" pertaining to the Egyptians, the Tg. Neb. renders "when I punished them." In the present verse the paraphrase—"the miracles which I performed," was especially designed to fit into the framework of this part of the verse which is followed by "and my signs," and the signs-miracles couplet is very widespread, for which cf. Exod. 7:3; Deut. 4:34; 6:22; 7:19; 13:3; 26:8; 29:2; 34:11; Jer. 32:20, 21; Ps. 135:9; Neh. 9:10; Isa. 8:18. Tg. Ps.-Jon. is here identical to the Targum and the following Midrash on this word reflects the same thought, Leq. Tob (Exod., p. 44): ". . . Another interpretation: I inflicted the plagues upon them by *My great deeds,* as it says—'He is terrible in His deeds *('alîlāh)* toward the children of men' (Ps. 66:5)."

[3]See above Chap. 1, n. 9.

[4]See Gen. Chap. 4, n. 1.

[5]The Hebrew has: "the surface of the earth." The Targum here adds "the sun," so what was obscured was not the surface of the earth but the surface of the sun which illuminates the earth. This addition, not made by any other of the Ancients, is also present in vs. 15 below, as well as in Num. 22:5. In his commentary (*Nefesh Ha-Ger, op. cit.,* p. 23), M. Löwenstein observes that it was in fact the illumination of the sun which was obscured, since the earth itself is in essence darkness, and only illuminated by the sun. This, according to him, is clear from vs. 15 below—"and it covered the surface of the entire earth and the earth became dark," indicating that the word 'surface' refers to the sun which shines upon the earth, since the earth itself is in essence darkness, consequently 'and it became dark' could not refer to the earth which by nature is dark. An interesting suggestion was made by G. A. Rendsburg, in his paper, "The Egyptian god Ra in the Bible," presented to the Annual Meeting of the Society of Biblical Literature, December 1984, that a veiled reference to the legendary eye of the Egyptian god Ra is made here. He points out that the three last plagues involve darkness or occur at night, and are therefore to be viewed as attacks on Ra specifically, as well as on Egypt as a whole.

[6]See Gen. 26, n. 2.

[7]The Hebrew has: "realize that evil faces you." This passage is very abstract and even somewhat idiomatic. Accordingly, the Targum paraphrase "the evil" (which is literal) adding "that you are contemplating on doing," which is reflected in the Midrash (Exod. Rab. XIII:5)—"What is the meaning of 'Evil is before you'? Realize, therefore, that what you are planning—to flee [and not to return]"), "it is not your intention" (lit. it is not opposite [written on] your face, the Hebrew has "it is opposite your faces," i.e., it is written all over your faces). The Targum adds—"to repent" i.e., from it, from what you are planning in your hearts. This interpretation is partially based on that of Nachmanides on this verse who enumerates three distinct versions of Targum Onqelos for this clause. These follow with appropriate references to them in Sperber's edition:

1. "realize, that the evil that (L and b in Sperber's apparatus) you are contemplating on doing will return (k and l in Sperber's apparatus) against you (u, and b omits the negative *lēṯ*). Nachmanides explains: "the evil that you are contemplating to do will return towards you (lit. your faces) to testify against you that you want to flee."
2. "realize, that the evil that you are contemplating on doing (is destined) to return (the infinitive as in Sperber's main text) against you." Nachmanides here relates the Midrash Exod. Rab., cited above, to Onqelos.
3. "realize, that the evil that you are contemplating to do, it is not your intention (with the negative *lēṯ* as in Sperber's main text) to repent from it." Nachmanides explains: "it is not recognizable on your facial expressions (that you intend) to remove the evil that is in you for your facial expression testifies against you."

[8]See above Chap. 9, Apparatus, note d.

trees which the hail had left over, and there did not remain green on the trees, nor plant in the field throughout the land of Egypt. 16. Then the Pharaoh hurriedly summoned Moses and Aaron and said, "I have been guilty *before* [4] the Lord your God and to you. 17. And now, truly forgive now my guilt and pray *before* [4] the Lord your God that He remove from me only this death." 18. So Moses departed from the Pharaoh and prayed *before* [4] the Lord. 19. Then the Lord transformed <the wind> into an exceedingly strong west wind, which carried away the locust and cast it into the sea of reeds; not a single locust was left within any border of *Egypt.*[i] 20. But the Lord hardened the heart of the Pharaoh, and he did not send away the Israelites. 21. Then the Lord said to Moses, "Raise your hand toward heaven and there will be darkness over the land of Egypt, *after the darkness of the night has departed.*"[j][9] 22. So Moses raised his hand toward heaven, and there was total darkness throughout the land of Egypt {for} three days. 23. No one saw his fellow man, nor did anyone rise from his place {for} three days; whereas the Israelites had light in their places of residence. 24. Then the Pharaoh summoned *Moses*[k] and said, "Go and worship *before* [4] the Lord, only *leave*[10] {behind} your sheep and cattle, even your little ones may go with you." 25. So Moses said, "You must also place into our hands *sanctified sacrifices*[11] and burnt-offerings that we may serve *before* [4] the Lord our God. 26. Even our livestock shall go with us; *nothing*[12] of it shall remain behind, because from it we take *to worship*[l] *before*[4] the Lord our God; as for us, we *do*[m] not know how to worship *before* [4] the Lord until we come there." 27. But the Lord hardened the heart of the Pharaoh, and he became unwilling to send them away. 28. And the Pharaoh said to him, "Go away from me; watch yourself from ever seeing my face again, for {on} the day you will see my face, you will die." 29. Whereupon Moses said, "You have spoken *well.*[13] I shall never see your face again."

Apparatus, Chapter 10 (Cont.)

[i] l has: "the Egyptians."
[j] a has: "and the darkness of the night will pass away."
[k] l adds: "and Aaron," but MT does not have it; yet 2 Hebrew mss. have it, as do the Sam. Heb., the LXX, and the Vg.
[l] i has: "to sacrifice."
[m] k has: "did."

Apparatus, Chapter 11

[a] i, a, b, g, and n have: "Egypt."
[b] l has: "this," as does the LXX and the Vg.
[c] V has: "among the Egyptians."
[d] Sperber's text has: "the," while J, U, b, and c have "his."

Notes, Chapter 10 (Cont.)

[9]The Hebrew has "even darkness that may be felt." The Targum, here virtually paralleled by Tg. Ps.-Jon., understood the Hebrew *wĕyāmeš* not to be derived from *mšš* ("feel," "touch") but from *mwš* "depart," "pass away," hence he employs the Aramaic *'dy* "pass away." The word "darkness" is expanded to "darkness of the night" the idea being that darkness overlapped into the day even after the darkness of the night had passed away. Tg. Ps.-Jon. in fact is more explicit here—"at daybreak, after the darkness of the night first departed." The following two Midrashim reflect in their exposition of this passage the two possible roots that could be at the base of the Hebrew *weyāmeš*:

1. Exod. Rab. XIV:1—"'Even darkness that may be felt' (Exod. 10:21). How thick was this

CHAPTER 11

1. Then the Lord said to Moses, "One more plague will I bring upon the Pharaoh and upon *the Egyptians,*[a] after which he will send you away from here; and when he sends (you) away he will totally and thoroughly expel you from here. 2. Say now *before*[1] the people that they should borrow each man from his friend and each woman from her friend silver vessels and gold vessels." 3. So the Lord set *the people*[b] *favorably*[2] in the sight of the Egyptians; also the man Moses <was viewed as> very great in the land of Egypt in the eyes of the Pharaoh's servants and in the eyes of the people. 4. And Moses said, "Thus said the Lord: 'About midnight I will *reveal myself*[3] *within Egypt.*[c] 5. Then every firstborn in the land of Egypt will die, from the firstborn of the Pharaoh *who is destined to sit*[4] on *the throne of his*[d] *kingdom*[5] to the firstborn

Notes, Chapter 10 (Cont.)

darkness? Our sages conjectured that it was as thick as a *denar,* for when it says 'even darkness that may be felt,' it means a darkness that had substance" (*mmš* from *mšš*).

2. *Leq. Tob.* (Exod., p. 46)—"The word *weyāmeš* has the sense of *lō'yāmêš* in the text: 'the pillar of cloud by day and the pillar of fire by night *lō'yāmêš* (did not depart) from before the people' (Exod. 13:22). That is to say, following the normal darkness of night came this special Egyptian darkness, and the two darknesses were fused into one. This came without any previous warning."

Notice the similarity between the later Midrash and Tgs. Onq. and Ps.-Jon.

[10]The Hebrew "stay in place" is here interpretively rendered. Likewise Tg. Ps.-Jon. renders "should stay by me," and Tg. Neof. "should stay here." The Syr. has "leave" as does the Sam. Tg. (J), the Vg., and the LXX, while the Sam Tg. (A) has "should stay."

[11]The Hebrew "sacrifices" is extended by the Targum into "sanctified sacrifices" an interpretive rendering, which is reflected according to one opinion in the Talmud—b. Zeb. 116b—"Sacrifices (Exod. 10:25)—One scholar maintains that Noahides offered peace-offerings." Accordingly, all mankind, including the Israelites before the Revelation at Sinai, is designated as Noahides. Furthermore, peace offerings were considered sacred sacrifices and the Targum is here in apparent agreement with that opinion of the Mishna—m. Zeb. V:7—"the peace-offering is a sacrifice of lesser sanctity." Cf. further Y. Behaq, "*Gemārā' Wĕtargûm,*" *Hakarmel* 8 (1870-71):110-111, 117, 183, 189-190.

[12]The Hebrew "not a hoof" is a figure of speech which is here interpretively rendered into its intended meaning.

[13]The Hebrew "so" is idiomatic and interpretively rendered.

Notes, Chapter 11

[1]See Gen. Chap. 4, n. 1.

[2]Lit. "compassionately," for which see Gen. Chap. 6, n. 8.

[3]The Hebrew "I will go out" is an anthropomorphism which is here circumvented as in Gen. 11:5, 7 for which cf. ns. 6, 7, where the Hebrew has God "going down." Cf. the Midrash Leq. Tob (Exod., p. 48f.) who cites Isa. 26:21; 42:13; Hab. 3:13; and Zech 14:3 as additional examples, then concludes "that is meant by 'I will go out' (Exod. 11:4). He revealed Himself in Egypt in His great overwhelming glory."

[4]The Hebrew "who sits" applies to the reigning Pharaoh, whereas the firstborn of the Pharaoh although being the crown prince is "destined to sit" on the throne, hence the paraphrase in the Targum. Tgs. Ps.-Jon. and Neof. paraphrase similarly, as does Midrash Leq. Tob (Exod., p. 49).

[5]The extension of Hebrew "his throne" to "the throne of his kingdom" in the Targum is also accomplished by Tgs. Ps.-Jon. and Neof. and reflects a common Biblical Hebrew phrase, for which cf. Deut. 17:18; 2 Sam. 7:13; 1 Kgs. 1:46; 9:5; Hag. 2:22; Esther 1:2; 5:1; 1 Chr. 28:5, 2 Chr. 7:18; 23:20.

of the maid who is *in*[e] the *mill*[f] house, as well as every firstborn of the beast. 6. And there shall be great wailing throughout the land of Egypt; there had never been of its kind, and there will never be of its kind. 7. Whereas as far as the Israelites were concerned, no dog *shall do any harm with its tongue by barking*[6] at man or at beast, in order that you should realize that the Lord has differentiated between the Egyptians and (between) the Israelites. 8. Then all of these servants of yours will come down to me and *beg of me*[g7] saying, 'Leave! You and the people that is with you'; and after that I will leave." So he departed *from*[h] the Pharaoh in great anger. 9. And the Lord said to Moses, "<Still> the Pharaoh will not *listen to you,*[8] in order that <I continue> to multiply My wonders in the land of Egypt." 10. Now Moses and Aaron performed all these wonders before the Pharaoh, while the Lord hardened the heart of the Pharaoh, and he did not send away the Israelites from his land.

CHAPTER 12

1. Then the Lord said to Moses and to Aaron in the land of Egypt as follows, 2. "This month is for you the beginning of the months; it is the first for you as far as the months of the year are concerned. 3. Speak to the whole community of *Israel*[a] saying: On the tenth of this month they should take for themselves, each one a lamb per family, one lamb for each household. 4. Now if a household *is too small*[b] *to be counted for a lamb,*[1] then he and his nearest neighbor should take <one> according to the *number*[2] of persons; in accordance with what each person eats, they should be counted for each lamb. 5. It should be for you a lamb without blemish, a male, *a year old,*[3] from the sheep or from the goats you may take <it>. 6. And it shall be in a state of confinement by you until the fourteenth day of this month, when the entire community of the congregation of Israel shall slaughter it at twilight. 7. Then they shall take of its blood and place <it> on the two doorposts and on the lintel, upon the houses wherein they shall eat it. 8. And they shall eat the flesh on that same night roasted by fire; along with unleavened bread and bitter herbs they shall eat it. 9. You shall not eat of it *when it is*[c]

Apparatus, Chapter 11 (Cont.)

[e] b, g, k, and l have the literal: "behind."
[f] c has: "prison" as in Exod. 12:29.
[g] b has: "seek me out."
[h] n has: "from before."

Apparatus, Chapter 12

[a] i has: "Israelites," as do many Hebrew mss. other than MT, the Sam. Heb., the LXX, the Syr., and the Vg.
[b] D and a have: "will become too small," while K and b have: "will be too small." which are closer to the Hebrew. l has: "members of the household" and puts this verb into the imperfect plural—"will become too few."
[c] b and g omit *kad* here, which is implied in the Hebrew.
[d] a and c have: "the Egyptians."

raw, even not[4] if thoroughly boiled in water; but rather roasted by fire, its head with its leg and with its inner parts. 10. Neither shall you leave over any of it till morning; now whatever was left of it till morning you must burn with fire. 11. Now this is how you must eat it—your loins should be girded, your sandals on your feet, and your rods in your hand; and you should eat it in haste; it is the Passover *before*[5] the Lord. 12. *Then I will reveal Myself*[6] in the land of *Egypt*[d] on that same night and I will slay every firstborn in the land of Egypt from man to beast; and against all *the abominations*[7] of the Egyptians I will execute judgment; I am the Lord. 13. So the blood will be for you as a sign upon the houses where you are; and when I will see the blood *I will spare*[8]

Notes, Chapter 11 (Cont.)

[6]The Hebrew has: "no dog will whet/move his tongue" which is a figure of speech implying that not only will the dog not do any harm, but that it would not even bark. The Targum accordingly paraphrases the Hebrew by explaining its implication. The Tg. Ps.-Jon. paraphrases similarly, while Tg. Neof. simply rephrases "will not bark with its tongue," whereas the Syr. totally rephrases into "no one shall be harmed, not even a dog shall bark," and the Vg. paraphrases *non mutiet canis*—"no dog shall make the least noise."

[7]The Hebrew has "and they will bow down to me," which has a connotation of worship, resulting in Moses uttering exclamations of grandeur unbefitting his personality, which is described by none other than God as "now that man Moses was very humble, more than any man on the face of the earth" (Num. 12:3). In fact, the LXX and Vg. render this verb precisely with this connotation, the former *καὶ προσκυνήσουσί με*—"and do me reverence," the latter *et adorabunt me*—"and shall worship me." The Targum, as do Tgs. Ps.-Jon. and Neof. (the latter—"will ask about my welfare"), render interpretively "will seek me out."

[8]Lit. "accept from you," for which cf. Gen. Chap. 16, n. 1.

Notes, Chapter 12

[1]This insertion is in line with the Mekhilta which uses the technical expression "they *count* themselves (i.e., form themselves into a group) for the Paschal lamb, for which cf. Mek. *Mes. Pisḥā'* III, p. 11. Tg. Neof. inserts "is too few in *number*," while Tg. Ps.-Jon. elaborates further—"from the number of ten, enough for the requirement for the eating of." The insertion is also linguistically identical with the end of this verse—"they shall be counted for the lamb."

[2]The Hebrew *mḵst* is here rendered in agreement with the Mekhilta (*Pisḥā'* III, p. 12) "*mḵst* means nothing else but *number.*"

[3]This rendering is reflected in the Mekhilta (*ibid.* IV, p. 12) "I would think only a year old, how do we know that its entire year is meant?" R. Ishmael and R. Jose Ha-Galili then proceed to show that the entire year is meant by way of a conclusion, *a minori ad majus.*

[4]This insertion, which is implied in the Hebrew, is also added in Tgs. Ps.-Jon., Neof., the Syr., the LXX, and the Vg. and is expressly stated in the Mek. (*ibid.* VI, p. 20)—"*nā'* refers exclusively to something raw,... or 'thoroughly boiled,' this condemns eating it either raw or boiled."

[5]See above Gen. Chap. 4, n. 1.

[6]The Hebrew has: " Then I will pass through," which is an anthropomorphism and is circumvented as in Gen. 11:5, 7 for which cf. ns. 6 and 7, where the Hebrew has God "going down."

[7]The Hebrew has: "gods." For this Targumic translation, see Introduction VII A. 3.

[8]This translation for Hebrew *upāsaḥtî* is in agreement with Rabbi Jonathan's opinion in the Midrash where the following debate is recounted as to the meaning of this word—Mek. *ibid* VII, p. 25—"'*Upāsaḥtî 'ălêkem*' (Exod. 12:13). Rabbi Josiah says: Do not read *upāsaḥtî* (I will protect) but *upāsa'tî* (I will step over). God skipped over the houses of His children in Egypt, as it is said: 'Hark! My beloved! Behold, He comes leaping upon the mountains,' and it continues: 'Behold, He stands behind our wall, etc.' (Cant. 2:8-9). Rabbi Jonathan says: '*Upāsaḥtî 'ălêḵem*". This means you alone will I protect (*ḥws,*

you; and there will not be against you any *destructive death*[9] when I carry out executions in the land of Egypt. 14. Now this day shall be for you a memorial, and you should celebrate it as a festival to the Lord for your <future> generations; you should celebrate it as an everlasting ordinance. 15. {For} seven days you should eat unleavened bread; but on the first day you should renounce leaven from your houses, for whoever eats leaven from the first day through the seventh day, that person will be cut off from Israel. 16. And on the first day <have> a sacred convocation, and on the seventh day you should have a sacred convocation; do not engage in any kind of work on them, except that which is eaten by every person, that alone may be prepared for you. 17. And you should observe <the festival of> unleavened bread, for on that same day I brought your hosts out of the land of Egypt, and you should observe this same day for your <future> generations as an everlasting ordinance. 18. *In Nisan,*[10] on the fourteenth day of the month, in the evening you should eat unleavened bread until the evening of the twenty-first day of the month. 19. {For} seven days no leaven shall be found in your houses, for whoever eats leaven, that person shall be cut off from the community of Israel whether he be an alien or native born of the land. 20. You are not to eat any kind of leaven; wherever you live you should eat unleavened bread." 21. Then Moses summoned all the elders of Israel and said to them, "Draw out and take for yourselves from the young sheep for your families and slaughter the paschal lamb. 22. And you should take a bundle of hyssop and dip <it> in blood that is in the *basin,*[11] then *sprinkle*[12] from the blood of the *basin*[11] towards the lintel and two doorposts; and as for you, not one of you should go out {from} the door of his house till morning. 23. Then the Lord will *reveal Himself*[6] to strike the Egyptians *and He will see*[13] the blood on the lintel and upon the two doorposts, so the Lord *will spare*[8] the doorway and will not permit the destroyer to enter your houses {in order} to strike {you}. 24. Now you should observe this event as an everlasting ordinance for you and your descendants. 25. And when you enter the land which the Lord will give you as He has spoken, then you should observe this ritual. 26. And when your children will say to you, 'What does this ritual <mean> to you?' 27. Then you should say, 'It is the Passover sacrifice *before*[5] the Lord who passed over the Israelite houses in Egypt and spared our homes when He struck down the Egyptians'"; and the people bowed down and worshiped. 28. So the Israelites proceeded to do precisely what the Lord commanded Moses and Aaron, accordingly they did. 29. Now it happened at midnight that the Lord slew every firstborn in the land of Egypt—from the Pharaoh's firstborn *who is destined to sit*[14] *on the throne of his kingdom*[15] to the firstborn of the captive that is in *the prison*[16]—as well as every firstborn of the beast. 30. Then the Pharaoh and all his servants and all the Egyptians arose that night and there was a great wailing in Egypt,[e] for there was not a house *there*[f] without someone *dead.*[g] 31. And he summoned Moses and Aaron *at*[h] night and said, "Proceed to depart from amongst my people both you and the Israelites and go worship the Lord as you have been saying. 32. Take your sheep as well as your cattle as you have spoken, and go *pray for me*[17] as well." 33. Now

Apparatus, Chapter 12 (Cont.)

[e] l has: "the entire land of Egypt," as does the LXX.
[f] L omits, the Hebrew does not have it.
[g] b, d, g, and l add: "there," the Hebrew has it.
[h] b, d, g, a, and l omit, the Hebrew only implies it.
[i] v, b, d, L, and a have: "the Egyptians."

the Egyptians were urging the people to hurry in order to send them away from the land, for they said, "We are all about to die." 34. So the people carried off *their*[18] dough before it had yet leavened, *that which was still left in the kneading trough,*[19] bound with their clothes upon their shoulders. 35. And the Israelites did according to the word of Moses and borrowed from *Egypt*[i] silver and gold vessels, as well as clothing. 36. While the Lord set the people *favorably*[20] in the sight of the Egyptians and they lent them, and they (thus) emptied out[21] Egypt. 37. So the Israelites journeyed from Ramses to

Notes, Chapter 12 (Cont.)

the same root the Targum uses to translate *upāsaḥtî* in this verse), but I will not protect the Egyptians...."

Furthermore, the following statement is even more explicit about this meaning—Mek. *ibid.* p. 24—"*Pesîḥāh* means to spare (your) lives, as it says: 'As birds hovering, so will the Lord of Hosts protect Jerusalem; He will deliver it as He protects it, He will rescue it as He passes over [*psḥ*] (Isa. 31:5).'" Tgs. Ps.-Jon. and Neof. m. employ the root *ḥws*—"to protect," the LXX renders σκεπάσω—"protect," while Tg. Neof. and the Sam. Tg. have *psḥ* the identical root of the Hebrew, and the Vg. translates *transilo*—"pass over." Of interest is the Syr. *'pṣḥ* < *pṣḥ* (for Hebrew *psḥ*) "I will make (you) glad."

[9]See above Chap. 9, n. 4.

[10]The Hebrew "first" is here defined as the first month of the year, namely—"Nisan." This definition, also in Tg. Ps.-Jon., as well as in the Tg. Neb. to Ezek. 45:21, was made by the Targum, according to B.Z.J. Berkowitz (*Simlat Ger in Leḥem We-Simla,* Wilna, 1854, p. 23), because he understood the Hebrew to refer to the name of the month rather than to the first month *per se,* which he would have rendered literally as he does in Lev. 23:5, where the Hebrew text specifically says "first month," or Gen. 8:14 ("second month").

[11]The Hebrew *sāp* is here rendered *mn',* precisely the very term used by R. Aqiba in explaining this verse, as seen from the Mekhilta (*ibid.* XI, p. 37) "'*bassāp*' (Exod. 12:22)—*sap* means threshold exclusively ... these are the words of R. Ishmael, while R. Aqiba says: *sap* means vessel (*mn'*) exclusively."

[12]The Hebrew has: "and make it touch" which is literally rendered in the LXX—'αμφοτέρων "touch," from the root *ng'*. The Targum, as do Tg. Ps.-Jon. and the Sam. Tg. (J), renders it interpretively to mean "sprinkle" (<*ndy*), as does the Syr. (but from *rss*), and the Vg. *aspergite,* while Tg. Neof. simply renders "place." This interpretive rendering in the Targum may be related to the Mek. (*ibid.,* XI, p. 38)—"Scripture says here '... and sprinkle towards the lintel and the two side-posts with the blood' (Exod. 12:22). There must be a dipping for every sprinkling."

[13]It is peculiar not to see here an anthropomorphic circumvention of this verb pertaining to God in the Targum.

[14]See above Chap. 11, n. 4.

[15]See above Chap. 11, n. 5.

[16]See Gen. Chap. 40, n. 8.

[17]The Hebrew has: "bless me." This interpretive rendering, paralleled in Tg. Neof. and in slightly longer form in Tg. Ps.-Jon.—"pray for me that I should not die," is in agreement with the interpretation of the Mek. (*ibid.* XIII, p. 45): "... 'and bless me also' (Exod. 12:32)—*Pray for me* that this visitation may cease from me."

[18]The Hebrew "its" refers to "people" collectively, while the Targum, as well as Tgs. Ps.-Jon., Neof., the Syr. and the LXX, all understood it to refer to "people" in the plural sense, thus translating "their."

[19]The Hebrew has: "their kneading-troughs." The Targum in adding "that which was still left" apparently is here translating Hebrew *miš'arōṯām* as a form derived from the root *š'r* "to remain, leave over," as well as rendering it literally into "kneading-troughs." This double rendering of one word is peculiar to Onqelos, whereas Tg. Ps.-Jon. contains only the first one; Tg. Neof. renders the second one in its main text while the first one is found in Tg. Neof. m.

[20]Lit. "compassionately," for which see Gen. Chap. 6, n. 8.

[21]See above Chap. 3, n. 21.

Succoth, about six hundred thousand men on foot, besides children. 38. Also *numerous aliens*[22] went up with them, as well as sheep, and cattle, a great amount of *livestock.*[j] 39. And they baked the dough which they brought out from Egypt <into> unleavened cakes for *it was not leavened,*[k] since they were expelled from Egypt and could not be detained; even provisions they could not make for themselves. 40. Now the residence <time> of the Israelites during which they lived in Egypt was four hundred and thirty years. 41. And it happened at the end of the four hundred and thirty years on that very same day, all the hosts of the Lord departed from the land of Egypt. 42. It was *nights*[l] *of vigil*[m] before the Lord to bring them out of the land of Egypt; therefore this very night before the Lord should be one of vigil for the Israelites, for their <future> generations. 43. Then the Lord said to Moses and *to*[n] Aaron, "This is the ordinance of the Passover—*no Israelite who becomes apostasized*[23] may eat of it. 44. But every male servant purchased with money you must circumcise him, after which he may eat of it. 45. A temporary resident and a hired worker may not eat of it. 46. It should be eaten in one *group;*[24] do not bring outside any of the flesh from the house, nor should any bone be broken in it. 47. The entire community of Israel *should celebrate it.*[o] 48. Now when an alien who resides with you temporarily shall <want to> celebrate the Passover *before*[5] the Lord, he must <first> circumcise for himself every male; only then may he draw near and celebrate it and be like a native of the land; no uncircumcised one may eat of it. 49. There should be one law for *natives*[p] and *aliens*[q] who *reside*[r] among you." 50. Then all the Israelites did precisely as the Lord had commanded Moses and Aaron, accordingly they did. 51. Now it happened on that very same day that the Lord brought out the Israelites from the land of Egypt by their hosts.

Apparatus, Chapter 12 (Cont.)

[j] n has: "cattle."
[k] n has: "there was no."
[l] So also in Sperber's main text, while A, B, and E have the singular.
[m] l has the plural, as does the Hebrew.
[n] i omits it, as it is only implied in the Hebrew.
[o] l has: "should occupy themselves with it."
[p] L, R, and c have singular, as does the Hebrew.
[q] R, U, and c have the singular, as does the Hebrew.
[r] b, d, and g, as well as l have the singular as does the Hebrew.

Apparatus, Chapter 13

[a] a has: "they should," which is interpretive of the Hebrew *hw'*.
[b] n has the singular here, as does the Hebrew.
[c] E, v, and a have the singular, as does the Hebrew.

Notes, Chapter 12 (Cont.)

[22]The Hebrew "a mixed multitude" is here more precisely defined in the Targum, as well as in Tgs. Ps.-Jon. and Neof., as consisting of "numerous aliens." In various Midrashim these "aliens" are even more accurately defined:

1. MRŠBY *Bō'* XII:38, p. 33— "'and also a mixed multitude went up with them' (Exod. 12:38)— this teaches that also proselytes and slaves went up with them."
2. Tanḥ (A) *Bĕha'ălôtḵā* XXVII—"'and the mixed multitude that was among it' (Num. 11:4)— R. Simeon b. Menasya and R. Simeon b. Abba: One says these were the proselytes that went up with them from Egypt who joined the Israelites when they left Egypt."

[23]The Hebrew has: "no stranger." The Targum interpretively renders "no Israelite who became

CHAPTER 13

1. [Then the Lord spoke to Moses as follows,] 2. "Sanctify to me every firstborn, *every first offspring (of the womb)*[1] among the Israelites whether of man or of livestock; *it*[a] belongs to Me." 3. And Moses said to the people, "Remember this day that you departed from Egypt, from a place of slavery; because the Lord brought you out from here with a mighty hand: no leavened bread should be eaten. 4. This day, in the month of Abib, you are departing. 5. Now it shall be when the Lord will bring you in to the land of the *Canaanites, and the Hittites, and the Amorites, and the Hivites, and the Jebusites*[b] which He swore to your ancestors to give to you, a land *producing*[2] milk and honey, that you perform this ceremony during this month. 6. <For> seven days you should eat unleavened bread, and on the seventh day is a festival to the Lord. 7. Unleavened bread should be eaten for seven days; no leavened bread is to be visible to you, nor shall any yeast be visible to you within any of your borders. 8. Now you should tell your son on that day as follows, '<It is> because of that <which> the Lord did for me when I departed from Egypt." 9. Now this shall be for you as a sign upon your hand and a memorial between your eye(s) so that the law of the Lord should be in your mouth; because the Lord brought you out of Egypt with a mighty hand. 10. And you should observe this ordinance in its season *from season to season.*[3] 11. Now it shall be when the Lord will bring you in to the land of the Canaanites[c] as He has sworn to you

Notes, Chapter 12 (Cont.)

apostasized," in contrast to Tg. Neof.'s "no gentile," and Tg. Ps.-Jon. who contains a combination of both Neof. and Onqelos—"no gentile or Israelite who became apostasized." The Mekhilta ruling agrees with Tg. Ps.-Jon.—Mek. *ibid.* XV, p. 53—"'No stranger should eat thereof' (Exod. 12:43)—meaning both an apostate Jew and a gentile." However, whereas the Mekhilta de Rabbi Ishmael deduces both apostate Jew and gentile from this verse, the Mek. de Rabbi Sim. b. Yoḥai deduces only the former one from this verse, in agreement with Onqelos, while deducing the latter from Exod. 12:48—*MRŠBY Bō'* XII:43, p. 35.

[24]The Hebrew has: "house" which is here interpretively rendered in complete agreement with the following Midrash—Mek. *ibid.*, p. 54—"'In one house shall it be eaten' (Exod. 12:46)—Scripture here means in one *group.* You interpret it to mean in one group, perhaps 'in one house' is to be taken literally? When it says: 'Upon the houses wherein you shall eat' (vs. 12 above), we learn that it may be eaten in one house. Hence, what does Scripture mean by saying here 'in one house it shall be eaten?' Scripture means in one *group.*" Cf. further b. Pes. 86a-b.

Notes, Chapter 13

[1]The Hebrew has: "whatever first opens the womb, "i.e., the first offspring of the womb. The Targum here renders a translation for Hebrew *péṭer* in two words *ptaḥ* "the opening," i.e., the first, and *waldā'* "offspring," leaving *réḥem*—"womb"—untranslated but implied in the translation, since the normal translation for *réḥem* is either Aramaic *m'y* for which cf. Jer. 20:17; Ps. 22:11, 58:4; Job 31:15; or *rḥm* Hos. 9:14; Job 3:10, 10:18, 24:20, 38:8; Prov. 30:16, and even once as *bṭn*—Jer. 20:18, but never as *waldā'*, which is the equivalent for "offspring." The two cases of 1 Sam. 1:5, 6 indicate only that *wld* is used as a paraphrase rather than a translation for Hebrew *rḥm.*

[2]See above Chap. 3, n. 12.

[3]The Hebrew *miyyāmîm yāmîmāh* "from year to year" is here rendered in accordance with R. Aqiba's opinion expressed in b. Erub. 96a and b. Men. 36b—"this law was stated exclusively for Passover." R. Aqiba being of the opinion that the verse means—celebrate a Passover from year to year in its proper season.

and to your ancestors, and gives it to you, 12. that you should deliver *every first offspring* (*of the womb*)[1] *before* [4] the Lord, and *every first offspring*[5] of livestock which you have, the males, you should consecrate to the Lord. 13. Now every *firstborn*[d] among donkeys you should redeem with a lamb and if you do not redeem <it> then strike it mortally; and every firstborn of man among your sons you shall redeem. 14. Now it shall be when your son will ask you *in times to come,*[6] 'What is <the meaning of> this?' You should say to him, 'With a mighty hand did the Lord bring us out of Egypt, from a place of slavery. 15. Now it happened that when the Pharaoh stubbornly refused to send us away, that the Lord killed every firstborn in the land of Egypt from the firstborn of man to the firstborn of beast; therefore I sacrifice to the Lord every *first offspring* (*of the womb*)[1] of the males, while every firstborn of my sons I redeem.' 16. And it shall be as a sign upon your hand *and as phylacteries*[7] between your eyes, for with a mighty hand did the Lord bring us out of Egypt." 17. Now it happened when the Pharaoh sent away the people that the Lord did not *lead*[8] them on the road <through> the land of the Philistines though it was near, for the Lord said, "Perhaps the people *might panic*[9] when confronted by war and return to Egypt." 18. So the Lord led the people around via the road of the wilderness toward the Reed Sea; and the Israelites went up from the land of Egypt *armed for war.*[10] 19. And Moses brought up Joseph's bones with him; for he had made the Israelites swear an oath as follows, "The Lord *will surely remember*[e] you and then you must bring up my bones with you from here." 20. So they set out from Succoth and encamped at Ethan at the edge of the wilderness. 21. Whereas the Lord led them in front—by day in a pillar of cloud *to lead them*[f] on the road, and at night in a pillar of fire to illuminate for them, so that they could go by day and by night. 22. Neither did the pillar of cloud by day, nor the pillar of fire by night depart *from*[g] before the people.

Apparatus, Chapter 13 (Cont.)

[d] a has: "first offspring" as does the Hebrew, while b, d, and g have the awkward: "first firstborn."

[e] a and l have: "remembers."

[f] n has: "to let them rest" deriving the Hebrew *lnḥtm* from *nwḥ* rather than from *nḥh.*

[g] d omits with the Hebrew.

Apparatus, Chapter 14

[a] E and d have: "them."

Notes, Chapter 13 (Cont.)

[4]See Gen. Chap. 4, n. 1.

[5]The Hebrew has "that which first opens the womb of newly born beasts" (*péṭer šéger*).

The Targum here omits translating *šéger,* as do Tg. Neof. and the Syr. C. Heller (*Peshitta in Hebrew Characters with Elucidatory Notes:* Part II Exodus. Berlin, 1929, p. 87) points out that the Peshitta omitted translating one of the terms due to the synonymous meaning of the two terms which resulted in an unnecessary repetition. The same may well be true for Tgs. Onq. and Neof. as well. The Targum Ps.-Jon., however, translates it—"and every first offspring of the livestock that which its mother cast forth (*dmšgryh*)."

[6]Lit. "tomorrow."

[7]The Hebrew has *tōṭapōt*—"frontlet." In translating this word as "phylacteries," the Targum, as also Tg. Ps.-Jon., is in agreement with the halakhic interpretation of this entire verse, which interpreted "sign" to

CHAPTER 14

1. [Then the Lord spoke to Moses as follows,] 2. "Say to the Israelites that they turn back and encamp in front of the entrance of Hiratha, between Migdol and the Sea, in front of Baal Zephon directly opposite *it,*[a] you should encamp by the Sea. 3. Then the Pharaoh will say concerning the Israelites, 'They are *wandering around*[1]

Notes, Chapter 13 (Cont.)

refer to the *Tephillin* (phylactery) of the hand and "frontlet" to the *Tephillin* of the head. Of the numerous Rabbinic texts that make this interpretation, only the Mekhilta is hereby cited, with the remaining ones documented:

Mek. *Mesekta de Pisha* XVII, p. 66f.—"'and it shall be a sign unto you upon your hand'—One roll containing all four scriptural sections. For the following argument might have been advanced: The Torah says: Put phylacteries upon the head, put phylacteries upon the hand. Just as the one put on the head contains four sections on four separate rolls of parchment, so the one put on the hand should also contain four separate rolls of parchment ... Scripture says 'frontlet' here (Exod. 13:16), 'frontlet' (Deut. 6:8), 'frontlets' (Deut. 11:18) thus four separate rolls are mentioned."

Cf. Mek. *ibid.*XVIII, p. 74; MRŠBY *Bō'* XIII:9, 10, pp. 40ff.; 16, p. 44; b. Men. 34b; 37a-b; Sekh. Tob: Exod., p. 155, 158; MHG: Exod., p. 231f., 239f; Leq. Tob: Exod., P. 74f., 78.

[8]The Hebrew *nḥm* is here interpretively rendered in exactly the same way as understood in the Mekhilta (*ibid.* Introduction, p. 75); "this term *nḥwm* here means exclusively 'leading.'"

[9]The Hebrew has: "change their mind" which is here interpretively rendered and may very well be associated with the following Aggadic tradition, in view of Tg. Ps.-Jon.'s rendering—'if they will see this, they will become afraid and return to Egypt." This concluding statement in the Tg. Ps.-Jon. is preceded by an Aggadic supplement that is also contained in Mek. *Mesekta deWayehî Běšallaḥ* I, p. 76f—"Another interpretation: 'For God said: Lest the people change their mind when they see war ...' (Exod. 13:17). This refers to the war of the Ephraimites, as it is said: 'And the sons of Ephraim: Shuthelaḥ—and Bered was his son ... whom the men of Gath that were born in the land slew' (1 Chr. 7:20-21)—two hundred thousand children of Ephraim. And it also says: 'The children of Ephraim were archers, handling the bow, they turned back in the day of battle' (Ps. 78:9). Why? Because 'they did not keep the covenant of God and refused to follow His law' (*ibid.* 78:10), that is, because they ignored the stipulated term, because they violated the oath" (the term stipulated for their deliverance from Egypt and the oath imposed upon them not to attempt to leave Egypt before the time fixed by God).

According to one Aggadic tradition, there was an exodus from Egypt sometime before the Exodus under the leadership of Moses took place. This first exodus under the leadership of the sons of Ephraim is, according to the Midrash, referred to in 1 Chronicles and alluded to in Ps. 78:9. The Ephraimites failed and the undertaking resulted in disaster for them and their followers. Other Rabbinic sources are PRE XLVIII: Exod. Rab. XX:11; Cant. Rab. to I:7, end of *Sidra Qamma.* In view of this Aggadic tradition and Tg. Ps.-Jon's rendering of the Hebrew "lest they change their mind" = "if they will see this (the slaughtered bodies of their Ephraimite brethren) they will become afraid and return to Egypt (Ps.-Jon.), Tg. Onq's rendering "perhaps the people might panic" may very well refer to the Gath massacre without the Aggadic supplement that is present in Tg. Ps.-Jon.

[10]The Hebrew *ḥămûšîm* is here rendered interpretively similar to the way it is explained in the Mekhilta (*ibid.*, p. 77) to interpret it—"*waḥămûšîm* (Exod. 13:18), the term *ḥămûšîm* means nothing else but *mzwynyym*—'armed for war,'" the Aramaic *zwn* employed by the Mekhilta and the Aramaic *zrz* by the Targum.

Notes, Chapter 14

[1]The Targum employs the term *m'rblyn* < *'rbl* which closely resembles *m'wrbbyn* < *'rbb* in the following Mekhilta (*ibid.* I, p. 84) "Another explanation *nĕḇûḵîm* (Exod. 14:3) means *m'wrbbyn* 'wandering around' exclusively."

the land in confusion, the wilderness has enclosed them.' 4. And I will harden the Pharaoh's heart and he will pursue them. Then I will become glorified by the Pharaoh and by his entire *camp,*[b] in that the Egyptians will realize that I am the Lord." So they did accordingly. 5. Then it was related to the king of Egypt that the people *had gone;*[2] so the Pharaoh and his servants had a change of heart toward the people, and they said, "What is this <that> we have done—that we have released the Israelites *from our service?"*[c] 6. So he harnessed his chariot and took along his people. 7. And he took along six hundred of the choice chariots as well as all the <other> *Egyptian chariots,*[d] and *warriors*[3] appointed over all of them. 8. Whereas the Lord hardened the heart of the Pharaoh, king of Egypt, and he pursued the Israelites; while the Israelites went forth *defiantly.*[4] 9. Then the Egyptians—all the chariot horses of the Pharaoh and his horsemen as well as his *camp,*[e] pursued them and overtook them as they encamped by the sea near the entrance of Hiratha {which is} opposite Baal Zephon. 10. Now the Pharaoh approached, and as the Israelites raised their eyes here the Egyptians were on the move behind them, and they became very terrified; so the Israelites cried out to the Lord. 11. And they said to Moses, "Is it because there are no graves in Egypt that you have led us to die in the wilderness? What is this that you have done to us to bring us out of Egypt? 12. Is this not the matter we discussed with you in Egypt saying: *Leave us alone*[f] *that we may serve*[g] the Egyptians; for it is better for us that we should serve the Egyptians than we should die in the wilderness." 13. So Moses said to the people, "Do not be terrified. Be prepared and you will witness the redemption that the Lord will perform for you this day; for *in that*[h] you have been seeing the Egyptians today, so you will never ever see them again. 14. *The Lord*[i] will wage war for you, but you remain still." 15. Then the Lord said to Moses, "*I have accepted your prayer;*[5] say to the Israelites that they move forward. 16. As for you, take your rod and raise your hand over the sea and split it, so that the Israelites come into the midst of the sea on dry ground. 17. As for Me, I am about to harden the heart of the Egyptians so that they will come in after them; then I will be glorified through the Pharaoh and through his entire camp, through his chariots and through his horsemen. 18. Then the Egyptians will realize that I am the Lord, when I become glorified through the Pharaoh, through his chariots and through his horsemen." 19. Whereupon, the angel of the Lord who was in the lead ahead of the Israelite camp set out and *came*[j] behind them, while the pillar of cloud moved from in front of them and set down behind them. 20. Then it came between the Egyptian camp and the Israelite camp *and the cloud became darkness for the Egyptians but illumination for the Israelites all night,*[6] so that they did not approach each other all night. 21. So Moses raised his hand over the sea, whereupon the Lord *churned*[7] the sea with a strong east wind all night and turned the sea into dry land; thus the sea was split. 22. Now the Israelites came into the midst of the sea on dry

Apparatus, Chapter 14 (Cont.)

[b] k has the more literal: "army."
[c] B, E, b, and d have: "from serving us," which is more interpretive.
[d] a and b have: "chariots of Egypt."
[e] b and d have: "army," as does the Hebrew.
[f] E has: "cease from us," as does the Hebrew.
[g] I has: "to serve."
[h] b, d, g, and k have: "just as," so do the Sam. Heb. and 6 Hebrew mss. in contrast to MT.
[i] h adds: "through His Memra."
[j] I has the more literal: "went."
[k] R has: "camp of Egypt."

ground, while the waters were for them <as> walls on their right and on their left. 23. And the Egyptians in pursuit came into the midst of the sea behind them, every one of the Pharaoh's horses, his chariots, and his horsemen. 24. Then it happened during the morning watch that the Lord looked down upon the Egyptian camp from the pillar of fire and cloud and confounded the *Egyptian camp.*[k] 25. And He removed the *wheels*

Notes, Chapter 14 (Cont.)

[2]The Hebrew has: "fled," which is questioned in the following Midrash—Mek. (*Mesekta' Wayehi Bešallaḥ* II, p. 86)—"'that the people fled' (Exod. 14:5)—and were they really fleeing? Has it not already been said: 'On the morrow after the Passover the Israelites departed defiantly' (Num. 33:3)? Why then does it say that 'the people fled?'" On the question of the general treatment of the root *brḥ* "to flee" by the Targum and further examples where *'zl* ("to go") is employed in translation for it see, B. Grossfeld, "The Relationship between Biblical Hebrew *brḥ* and *nws* and their Corresponding Aramaic Equivalents in the Targum—*'rq, 'pk, 'zl:* A Preliminary Study in Aramaic-Hebrew Lexicography." *ZAW* 91 (1979): 107-123, esp. pp. 109-113. The Tg. Ps.-Jon. contains a double reading—"that the people of Israel *went away,* that the people *fled,*" while the Syr. is identical to Onqelos.

[3]The Hebrew *šlšm* here rendered *gbryn* by the Targum is similarly explained in the Mekhilta (*ibid.,* p. 89); "*šlšym* means nothing else but 'warriors' (*gbwrym*)."

[4]The Hebrew has lit. "with a high hand" i.e., boldly, which is obviously a figure of speech, here reworded into an Aramaic figure of speech lit. "with an uncovered head(s)", precisely the very expression occurring in the Mek (*ibid.* II, p. 90). Here, Tg. Neof. renders identically, whereas Tg. Ps.-Jon. is literal, as are the other Ancients. The two other times this expression occurs (Num. 15:30; 33:3), the Targum renders similarly.

[5]The Hebrew has: "why do you cry unto Me?" In order to understand the Targum's translation here, it is imperative that the translations of Tgs. Neof. and Ps.-Jon. as well as the Frg. Tg. be listed side by side with that of Onqelos in conjunction with the Hebrew:

MT:	"Why do you cry unto Me?"
Frg. Tg. (P, V); Neof.:	"How long will you stand and pray before Me? Your prayer has been heard before Me; however the prayers of My people took preference over yours."
Ps.-Jon.:	"Why do you stand and pray before Me? Here, the prayers of My people took preference over yours."
Onq.:	"I have accepted your prayers."

The above comparative table indicates that the Frg. Tg. and Tg. Neof. have the most complete text of God's reply to Moses. Tg. Ps.-Jon. appears to lack the middle statement "Your prayer has been heard before Me," and, consequently, sounds contextually incomplete. Tg. Onq., on the other hand, having only the middle statement, though slightly reworded, sounds even more incomplete and, consequently, appears as an awkward translation for the Hebrew statement.

The Syr. has "why do you pray to me?" which is similar to the Targum in respect to rendering the Hebrew *ṣ'q* ("cry out") by *ṣly* "pray," for which cf. Exod. 8:8 and n. 4 there.

[6]The Hebrew "thus there was the cloud with the darkness, and it lit up the night" is syntactically difficult. The Targum makes two insertions which divides this passage in the following manner: "there was the cloud with the darkness" is to be understood as "the cloud became darkness"; here the Targum inserts "for the Egyptians." For contrast, the Targum then adds—"but for the Israelites," simultaneously fitting it into the sense of what follows in the Hebrew—"it lit up the night." Here the Targum separates the last phrase, connecting "lit up" with the preceding insertion, thus forming the contrasting phrase—"but illumination for the Israelites," and rewording "the night" into "all night." Tgs. Neof. and Ps.-Jon. likewise paraphrase this difficult passage, only more elaborately as does the Frg. Tg. This interpretive reading is also reflected in the Mekhilta (*ibid.* IV, p. 101) "the cloud for Israel and the darkness for Egypt, Israel was in illumination, Egypt in darkness."

[7]Lit. "led."

of their chariots thus causing them[8] to drive them with difficulty. So the Egyptians said, "Let *us*[l9] flee from the Israelites, for it is the power of the Lord that is waging their battles against *Egypt.*"[m] 26. Then the Lord said to Moses, "Raise your hand over the sea that the waters may return over the Egyptians, over their chariots, and over their horsemen." 27. So Moses raised his hand over the sea and the water returned to its *normal state*[10] at morning time, and the Egyptians were fleeing towards it, so the Lord drowned the Egyptians in the midst of the sea. 28. As the water returned, it covered the chariots and the horsemen as well as the entire camp of the Pharaoh which had come into the sea after them; not one of them remained. 29. Whereas the Israelites went through the midst of the sea on dry land, while the waters were for them <as> walls on their right and on their left. 30. On that day the Lord delivered Israel from the hand of the Egyptians, and the Israelites saw the Egyptians <lying> dead upon the shore of the sea. 31. When the Israelites perceived *the power of*[11] the mighty hand which the Lord had manifested against *the Egyptians,*[n] the people were in reverence of the Lord and trusted in *the Memra of*[12] the Lord and in *the prophecy of*[13] His servant Moses.

Apparatus, Chapter 14 (Cont.)

[l] i, n, and l have the literal: "me."
[m] a has: "the Egyptians."
[n] L, i, and b have: "Egypt."

Apparatus, Chapter 15

[a] c has the imperfect form, as does the Hebrew. Cf. the Mekhilta de Rabbi Ishmael (*Bešallaḥ Mesek̲tā' dešîrāh* I, p. 116) which discusses the conjunction *'āz* as prefacing either a perfect or imperfect form of the verb.
[b] n has the singular.

Notes, Chapter 14 (Cont.)

[8]The Targum pluralizes the idiomatic Hebrew singulars here.

[9]The Hebrew singular referring to Egypt collectively is here pluralized in agreement with the translation "Egyptians" in the Targum.

[10]Lit. "strength." The Hebrew *'êtānô* is here rendered *toqpēh* precisely the way it is understood in the Mekhilta (*ibid.* VI, p. 110).

[11]Insertion to tone down the anthropomorphism, also present in the Frg. Tg. (P) and in the Tg. Ps.-Jon.

[12]See Introduction VII D. 1.

[13]An insertion, also in Tgs. Ps.-Jon., Neof., and the Frg. Tg. (P), intended to avoid any misapprehension of the people displaying any faith in a human being, even one like Moses, rather their faith was in his prophecy which consisted of all he had been telling them up to this time. Y. Behaq (*Tosefot uMillu'im.* Wilna, 1898, p. 3) compares this translation to 2 Chr. 20:20—" ... Believe in the Lord your God ... believe in His prophets."

Notes, Chapter 15

[1]See Gen. Chap. 4, n. 1.

[2]The Hebrew has the singular referring to Moses, whereas the Targum interprets it as a plural, referring to Moses and the Israelites, who are mentioned in the first half of the verse. All the Pal. Tgs. have the plural here as well; the Syr., the Sam. Tg., and the Sam. Heb. have the plural but render the Hebrew by only one term in contrast to all the Targumim which have—"let us offer praise and acclamation." The plural form in the Targum was, according to the author of *Nefesh Ha-Ger* (*op. cit.*, p. 34), intentionally used to reflect the view of Rabbi Aqiba whose school of thought was followed by Onqelos as the latter was a disciple of Rabbis Eliezer and Joshua, themselves pupils of Rabbi Aqiba (cf. B. Meg. 3a). The latter's view

CHAPTER 15

1. Then Moses and the Israelites *sang*[a] this song of praise *before*[1] the Lord, saying
as follows, "Let *us offer praise and acclamation*[2] *before*[1] the Lord for He is *exalted*
above the exalted;[b3] *now His glory is that*[4] the horse and its rider has He cast into the
2. *My strength*[5] and my song of praise concern *the reverence of*[6] the Lord; *He said*
through His Memra[7] that He would be a deliverer to me; this is my God *and I shall*
build (for) Him a sanctuary,[8] the God of my *ancestors*[9] and I shall *worship before*[1]
Him.[10] 3. The Lord is *the Lord of victory in battles,*[11] the Lord is His name. 4. The

Notes, Chapter 15 (Cont.)

is stated in the Talmud b. Sot. 30b—"On that day Rabbi Aqiba expounded: At the time the Israelites ascended from the *Yam Suf,* they desired to utter a song; and how did they render the song? Like an adult who reads the Hallel (for the congregation) and they respond after him with the leading word (the heads of chapters). (According to this explanation) Moses said: "'I will sing unto the Lord,' and they responded, 'For He has triumphed gloriously'; Moses said: 'For He has triumphed gloriously,' and they responded, 'I will sing unto the Lord.'" The use of this doublet—*nĕšabbaḥ wĕnôdê* producing a sort of verbal *hendiadys*—"let us offer acclamatory praise" is a common devise in the Targum as the combination of these two particular verbs *ydy* and *šbḥ* occurs elsewhere as in Dan. 2:23; Ps. 106:47; 1 Chr. 16:35, and in the Tg. to 1 Chr. 29:13 as well as in b. Nid. 31a. The author of *leḥem 'abîrîm* (*op. cit.*, p. 28) comments on the Targum translation of Hebrew *šîr* ("song") by *šbḥ* ("praise"), that every form of the Hebrew roots *šîr, rnn,* and *hll* are rendered *šbḥ* in the Targum.

[3]The Hebrew has: "highly exalted." The Targum is here identical to the Talmudic exposition of this phrase by Resh Laqish—b. Hag. 13b—"Resh Laqish said: What is the meaning of the passage 'I will sing unto the Lord, for He is highly exalted' (Exod. 15:1)? It means a song to Him *who is exalted above the exalted.*" Likewise, the Mekhilta (*ibid.* II, p. 121), "Another explanation 'for He is highly exalted' (Exod. 15:1)—He is exalted above the exalted."

[4]An insertion, serving as a lead-in to the following statement.

[5]The Targum using *tqpy* is identical to the Mekhilta (*ibid.* III, p. 126), "Another explanation—*'zy* (Exod. 15:2) means *tqpy* exclusively."

[6]An insertion, serving as a buffer between Moses and God, thus avoiding the equation of the Hebrew "the Lord is my strength and my song" which, in the Targumist's perception, contained disrespectful overtones that may be misunderstood by the people.

[7]An insertion, for which cf. Introduction VII D. 1.

[8]The Hebrew "and I will enshrine him" is irreverential, and accordingly paraphrased to explain that this "enshrining" consists of building a shrine—a sanctuary—for Him. This train of thought is also reflected in the Mekhilta (*ibid.* III, p. 127)—"'And I will enshrine Him' (Exod. 15:2). Rabbi Ishmael says: And is it possible for a man of flesh and blood to enshrine his Creator? . . . Rabbi Jose, the son of the Damascene, says: I will make for Him a beautiful Temple. For the word ***nawēh*** designates the Temple, as in the passage: 'and laid waste His habitation' (Ps. 79:7). And it also says: 'Look upon Zion, the city of our solemn gatherings; your eyes shall see Jerusalem, a peaceful habitation (*nāwēh*)' (Isa. 33:20)."

[9]The Hebrew is singular, which the Targum pluralizes in agreement with the Mekhilta (*ibid.*, p. 128f.)—"'my father's God and I will exalt Him' (Exod. 15:2). The community of Israel said before the Holy One, blessed be He: Not only for the miracles which You have performed for me will I utter song and praise before You, but for the miracles which You have performed for my *fathers* and for me . . . ."

[10]The Hebrew has: "and I will exalt Him." The Hebrew *wa'ărōmĕmenhû* is derived from *rwm* "to lift up," which lends an anthropomorphic overtone to this verb, and is accordingly circumvented by the use of "worship" as a substitute verb.

[11]The Hebrew "the Lord is a warrior" does not reflect very well on God and is accordingly paraphrased. The Mekhilta (*ibid.*, p. 131) also alludes to this difficulty—"'The Lord is a warrior' (Exod. 15:3)—Is it possible to say so?"

Pharaoh and his army has He cast into the sea, and the choice of his warriors has He drowned in the Sea of Reeds. 5. The deep waters covered them; they descended to the depths like a stone. 6. Your right hand, O Lord, is majestic with power; Your right hand, O Lord, shattered the enemy. 7. Then with the abundance of Your *power*[12] You *shattered*[13] those who rose up *against Your people.*[14] You sent Your wrath; it consumed them *like fire*[15] does stubble. 8. And by *the command of Your mouth,*[16] the waters *ingeniously stood up*[17] like a wall of running waters, the deep waters congealed in the heart of the sea. 9. So that the enemy said, 'I shall pursue, I shall overtake, I shall divide the spoils; my desire shall become satiated from them; I shall draw my sword, my hand shall destroy them.' 10. *You spoke through Your Memra,*[18] the sea covered them, they sank like lead in mighty waters. 11. *There is no one*[c] *besides You; You are God, O Lord, there is no god,*[d] *but You*[e19] majestic in sanctity, revered through praises, performing *wonders.*[20] 12. You raised Your right hand; the earth swallowed them. 13. You led forth with Your kindness this people which You redeemed; You *led it forth*[f] with Your power to Your sacred residence. 14. Nations had heard and trembled; panic had seized *them*[21]—those who dwell in Philistia. 15. Then the *chiefs of Edom*[g] were terrified, terror seized the *mighty ones of Moab,*[h] all those who dwell in Canaan

Apparatus, Chapter 15 (Cont.)

[c] J and y_b have: "god."
[d] b, g, and n have: "one beside You, O God."
[e] n omits.
[f] B, v, a, b, c, k, and l have: "carried it."
[g] a and b have: "Edomite chiefs."
[h] a and b have: "Moabite chiefs."
[i] h adds: "the brooks of."
[j] n omits.
[k] v, a, b, and g have: "endures."

Notes, Chapter 15 (Cont.)

[12]The Hebrew has "splendor" which is here interpretively rendered by the Targum as "power," similarly in the Syr., whereas the Pal. Tgs. Ps.-Jon., Neof., and the Frg. Tg. (P) render literally. Yet, the translation "power"—*twqpā'* occurs quite frequently in translation for Hebrew *gĕ'ôn* ("splendor") cf. Tg. Neb. to Isa. 13:11; Jer. 13:8; Ezek. 32:12; Amos 6:8; Hos. 5:5; Nah. 2:3; Zech. 10:11.

[13]The Hebrew has: "destroy" (*hrs*) which in its numerous occurrences throughout the Biblical text is never rendered "to shatter" (*tbr*) except here, the standard root, *pqr* is the literal term used in all its occurrences except for Proverbs where *ʿqr* "uproot" occurs, no doubt, due to the Peshitta character of that Targum. The exclusive use of *tbr*—"to shatter" here may be related to the nature of the object of this verb— "those who stand up against you," i.e., your enemies, as well as Exod. 23:24 where *hrs* in the Hebrew appears in conjunction with *šbr* "to shatter." Tg. Neof. m. and the Frg. Tg. (P) employ the same root here. Cf. similarly Deut. 33:11, where a contextually similar passage containing the Hebrew *mḥṣ* is likewise rendered *tbr* "shatter" in the Targum.

[14]The Hebrew has: "against you," which the Targum transforms into "against your people" in agreement with the Mekhilta (*ibid.* VI, p. 134f.)—"'And in the greatness of your splendor, you destroyed those who rose up against you' (Exod. 15:7). You have shown yourself exceedingly great against those who rose up against you. And who are they that rose up against you? They that rose up against your children. It is not written here: 'You overthrow those that rose up against *us,*' but: 'You overthrow those that rose up against *you.*' Scripture thereby tells us, that if one rises up against Israel it is as if he rose up against Him by whose word the world came into being." Similarly Tgs. Ps.-Jon., Neof., and the Frg. Tg., all of which have "the enemies of Your people."

[15]An insertion to elaborate on the simile—"like stubble," but implied in the Hebrew.

[16]The Hebrew "with a blast of Your nostrils" is anthropomorphic and here only partially resolved by the Targum who substitutes "mouth" for "nostrils" unlike Tgs. Ps.-Jon. and Neof. as well as the Frg. Tg. (P) who have complete resolution—"and by a command from before You, O Lord" (the last two words, only in Tgs. Neof. and the Frg. Tg.).

were shattered.[22] 16. Fear and dread will fall upon them, through the greatness of Your power they will fall silent as stone until Your people, O Lord, will cross *the*[i] *Arnon,*[j] until this people that you have *redeemed*[23] will cross *the Jordon.*[j] 17. You will bring them in and *encamp*[24] them on the mountain of your inheritance (*in*) *the place which You, O Lord, have established for the site of Your Divine Presence,*[25] the sanctuary, O Lord, which Your hands have established. 18. *The Lord, His kingdom is*[k] *for ever*

Notes, Chapter 15 (Cont.)

[17]The Hebrew "were piled up" is based on the root *ʿrm,* which could also mean "shrewd." It is the latter meaning that the Targum chose to translate by the Aramaic equivalent *ḥkm,* an equivalence which was used by the Targumist in Gen 3:1 (mss. M and i in Sperber), by Tg. Neb. to Josh. 9:4; 1 Sam. 23:22; and the Tg. Ket. to Job 5:12; 15:5. In the present verse, the choice of this particular meaning is also reflected in the following Rabbinic text on this passage:

Mekhilta (*ibid.,* p. 137)—"'The waters became shrewd' (Exod. 15:8). The measure with which they measured out You did measure them. They said: 'Come let us deal *shrewdly* with them' (Exod. 1:10). You, too, put *shrewdness* into the water, and the water fought against them, inflicting upon them all kinds of punishments. In this sense it is said: 'And with the blast of Your nostrils, the water became shrewd.'"

"Another interpretation: '. . . the waters were piled up.' He piled them up in stacks (pile upon pile)."

The second interpretation in this Midrash is reflected in the translations of Tgs. Ps.-Jon., Neof., and the Frg. Tg. (P)—"the waters were made to be piles upon piles," and in the Syr. and Sam. Tg. ("the waters piled up").

[18]The Hebrew "You blew with Your wind" is grossly anthropomorphic and accordingly circumvented by use of the Memra. Oddly enough, only this Targum paraphrases the anthropomorphism completely—as the 3 Pal. Tgs. have "You blew with a wind from before You," which hardly avoids the issue.

[19]The Hebrew "Who is like unto You, O Lord, among the mighty? Who is like unto You" is here rephrased from an interrogative statement into a declaratory one, to avoid any misapprehension that could arise from the question, especially the word *bāʾēlîm*—"among the mighty," which could also be rendered "among the gods" and imply the concept of monolatry. In fact that phrase is thoroughly reworked into "there is no god but You." Here again this Targum is the most radical of all the Targumim in dealing with this difficulty. The Pal. Tgs. are virtually literal here.

[20]The Hebrew has the singular which is idiomatic and, accordingly, translated in the plural. See Gen. Chap. 21, n. 7.

[21]An insertion supplying the direct object of the verb "seize" in the form of a pronominal suffix, although it follows in the form of the compound noun—"those who dwell in Philistia." This insertion, also existing in the Frg. Tg. (P), CTgG., as well as in the Syr. and the Tgs. Ps.-Jon. and Neof. in the form of an independent objective pronoun, is in essence a *casus pendens,* a common phenomenon in Aramaic.

[22]The Hebrew "melted away" is a figure of speech and thus interpretively rendered. Tgs. Neof. and Ps.-Jon. reword this figure of speech differently—"their hearts melted within all the inhabitants of the land of Canaan." Instructive here is the Frg. Tg. (P) which is virtually identical to the above rendering of the other Pal. Tgs., the exception being the word "melted" instead of which it has "were shattered," the very term used here in Tg. Onq. The Syr. and Sam. Tg. are here identical with the Targum.

[23]The Hebrew has: "acquired." The rendering "redeemed" is matched by Tg. Neof., the Frg. Tg. (P, N), CTgG, and the Syr., while the Frg. Tg. (V), the Sam. Tg. (J), and Tg. Ps.-Jon render literally. The Hebrew *qānîtā* < *qnh* could mean "purchase" as well as "acquire," the Targum felt it necessary to translate it interpretively employing the verb "redeem" in agreement with the Talmudic (cf. b. Sanh. 98b) exposition of this verse which relates it to their two entries into the land—at the time of Joshua and after the Babylonian Exile, in both cases they experienced a redemption—one from Egypt, the other from Babylon.

[24]The Hebrew "plant" is figurative and accordingly rendered into its implied meaning. Only the Frg. Tg. (P) and Tg. Neof. render here interpretively— "give them an inherited possession," while all the other Ancients translate literally.

[25]The Hebrew has: "(in) the established place which You, O Lord, have made for Your dwelling, in the Sanctuary, O Lord." The Targum here renders "Your dwelling" as "the site of Your Divine Presence" reflecting Rabbinic exposition of this phrase—

and ever."[26] 19. For the Pharaoh's horses with his *chariots*[20] and his horsemen had entered the sea, and the Lord returned the waters of the sea upon them; whereas the Israelites went in the midst of the sea on dry ground. 20. Then Miriam the prophetess, the sister of Aaron, took a *tambourine*[l] in her *hand,*[m] and all the women followed her with tambourines and dancing. 21. And Miriam responded to them <by saying>, "Let us *offer praise and acclamation*[2] to the Lord for He is *exalted above the exalted;*[n3] *now His glory is that* [4] the horse and its rider has He cast into the sea." 22. So the Israelites set out from the Sea of Reeds and departed for the wilderness of *Hagra*[27] and they went <for> three days in the wilderness without finding water. 23. And they came to Marah, but were unable to drink the waters of Marah because they were bitter; therefore its name was called Marah. 24. So the people grumbled against Moses, saying, "What shall we drink?" 25. Thereupon he *prayed* [28] to the Lord and the Lord instructed him about a piece of wood and he cast <it> into the water whereupon the water became sweet; there He made for him an ordinance and a law, and there He tested him. 26. And He said, "If you will indeed obey *the Memra of*[29] the Lord your God and do what is proper *before Him,*[o] and you will listen to His commandments and observe all His precepts; (then) *all the afflictions*[p20] which I placed upon the Egyptians I will not place *them*[q] upon you, for I am the Lord your healer." 27. So they came to Elim where there were twelve springs of water and seventy palm trees, and they encamped there near the water.

Apparatus, Chapter 15 (Cont.)

[l] b has the plural.
[m] M has the plural.
[n] b, g, and n have the singular as does n in vs. 1.
[o] b and g have the literal: "in his sight."
[p] a has: "every evil."
[q] b and g omit.

Apparatus, Chapter 16

[a] b, g, and n have: "according to the Memra of the Lord."
[b] E has: "before."
[c] h has: the "Memra of the Lord."
[d] J and k add: "before Him."
[e] a has: "the decree of the Memra."
[f] b and g have: "before the Lord."
[g] v, a, and n have "to," as does the Hebrew.

Notes, Chapter 15 (Cont.)

1. *Mekhilta* (*ibid.* X, p. 150)—"'The established place for Your dwelling' (Exod. 15:17). Corresponding (*maḵôn*—'established place' should be read as *mĕḵuwān*) to Your dwelling place. His terrestrial throne (the earthly Temple) corresponds to His celestial throne (the heavenly Temple). Thus it says 'The Lord is in His holy temple; the Lord, His throne is in heaven' (Ps. 11:4); but again, 'I have surely built You a house of habitation, *maḵôn* (= *mĕḵuwān*) corresponding to Your dwelling in eternity' (1 Kgs. 8:13)."

2. *y. Ber.* IV:5, p. 8c—"One who is reciting the Prayer (the 18 Benedictions) should direct his mind to the Holy of Holies. Rabbi Ḥiyya the Elder said: To the Holy of Holies in the celestial Temple above. Rabbi Simeon b. Ḥalafta said: To the Holy of Holies below. Said Rabbi Pinḥas: They do not disagree, for the Holy of Holies below corresponds to the Holy of Holies above."

[26]The Hebrew has: "the Lord shall reign for ever and ever." The Pal. Tgs. contain elaborate Aggadic paraphrases, which Tg. Onq. may have originally contained before its revision. The following is the Frg. Tg. (V)—"*The Lord*—When the Israelites saw the miracles and marvels that the Holy One, blessed be He, performed for them at the edge of the Sea, may His name be blessed forever and ever, they offered glory, and praise as well as exaltation to their God, the Israelites responded, saying to one another: Come let us place a crown upon the head of the Redeemer, Who causes things to pass away, but does not Himself pass

CHAPTER 16

1. Then they set out from Elim, and the entire community of the Israelites came to the Wilderness of Sin which is between Elim and (between) Sinai, on the fifteenth day of the second month since their departure from the land of Egypt. 2. And the entire community of the Israelites grumbled against Moses and (against) Aaron in the wilderness. 3. So the Israelites said to them, "If only we had died *before*[1] *the Lord*[a] in the land of Egypt when we were sitting around *pots*[2] of meat, when we were eating bread and were satiated; rather you have brought us to this wilderness in order to kill out this entire community through famine." 4. Then said the Lord to Moses, "Here I am about to *send down*[3] bread to you from heaven, that the people could go out and gather each day's quota daily, in order that I may test them whether they will follow My Law or not. 5. Now it will be on the sixth day that they prepare what they will bring in—twice as much as they would gather every other day." 6. So Moses and Aaron said to all the Israelites, "In the evening you will know that it was the Lord who brought you out of the land of Egypt. 7. Then, in the morning you will perceive the Lord's glory, when your grumblings *against*[b] *the Lord*[c] *are heard,*[d4] and what are we that you grumble against us?" 8. And Moses said, "<This shall be> when the Lord will give you meat to eat in the evening and bread to satiation in the morning; and when your grumblings which you are grumbling against Him *are heard before the Lord;*[4] and what are we? Your grumblings should not be {directed} against us but against *the Memra*[e] *of the Lord.*"[5] 9. Then Moses said to Aaron, "Say to the entire community of the Israelites 'Draw near before the Lord, for your grumblings *have been heard before Him.*'"[f] 10. And it happend when Aaron spoke *with*[g] the entire community of the Israelites that they turned {their attention} to the wilderness, and here the Lord's glory *was revealed*[6] in a cloud. 11. [Then the Lord spoke to Moses as follows,] 12. "The

Notes, Chapter 15 (Cont.)

away; Who replaces things, but is Himself not replaceable; Who is king of kings in the world, and the crown of kingship is also His *for the World to Come, and* it is His *for ever and ever.*"

[27]See Gen. Chap. 16, n. 13.

[28]The Hebrew has: "cried out." The translation "prayed" in the Targum reflects the Mekhilta (*ibid.* I, p. 155)—"'And he cried out unto the Lord' (Exod. 15:25). From this you learn that the righteous are not hard to complain to. By the way, you also learn that the *prayer* of the righteous is short." See also above Chap. 8, n. 4.

[29]See Gen. Chap. 22, n. 14.

Notes, Chapter 16

[1]The Hebrew "by the hand of" is anthropomorphic and accordingly circumvented by *qdm.*

[2]See Gen. Chap. 21, n. 7.

[3]The Hebrew "rain" in verbal form is a figure of speech and accordingly rendered into its intended meaning. Cf. also Gen. 7:4 and Exod. 9:18 where the verb occurs with respect to rain and hail, respectively, and is likewise rendered "send down" in the Targum.

[4]See Gen. Chap. 29, n. 9.

[5]See Introduction VII D. 1.

[6]See Gen. Chap. 11, n. 6.

grumblings of the Israelites *have been heard before me;*[4] speak to them as follows, 'At twilight you shall eat meat, and in the morning you shall eat bread to satiation, and you will realize that I am the Lord your God.'" 13. Now it came about in the evening that the quail ascended and covered the camp; then in the morning *the descended dew*[7] encircled the camp. 14. Then *the descended dew*[7] rose up, and here upon the surface of the wilderness was a very thin scale-like substance, very thin, *heaped*[h8] like frost on the ground. 15. When the Israelites saw <it> they said to one another, "What is it?" For they did not know what it was. So Moses said to them, "It is the bread which the Lord has given you to eat. 16. This is the matter that the Lord commanded, 'Gather of it each one according to his eating <habits>, an Omer per person, according to the number of your persons, you should take, everyone for whoever is in his tent.'" 17. So the Israelites did accordingly, *and they gathered,*[i] some much, some little. 18. And when they measured <it> by the Omer, the one who gathered much did not {actually} have much, and he who gathered little did not {actually} feel deprived; each one {actually} gathered according to his eating <habits>. 19. Then Moses said to them, "No *one*[j] is to *leave*[k] of it until morning." 20. But they did not listen to Moses and the men left of it until morning, and it was teeming with worms and turned odorous; whereupon Moses became angry with them. 21. So they gathered it every morning, each one according to his eating <habits>; *and whatever was left of it upon the field*[9] melted when the sun grew hot <affecting> it. 22. Then on the sixth day, they gathered twice as much bread, two Omers per person; and all the leaders of the community came to tell Moses. 23. So Moses said to them, "That is {precisely} what the Lord has said, 'Tomorrow is a <day of> rest, a sacred Sabbath to the Lord; that which you would bake, bake, and that which you would boil, boil; and whatever is left over, lay away for yourselves to be kept until morning.'" 24. And they laid it away until morning as Moses commanded, and it did not become odorous, nor were there any worms in it. 25. Then Moses said, "Eat it today for today is the Sabbath Day to the Lord; today you will not find it in the field. 26. Six days you shall gather it, but on the seventh day is the Sabbath; there will not be <found> any on it." 27. However, on the seventh day some of the people *did* go out to gather, but did not find <anything>. 28. So the Lord said to Moses, "For how long will you refuse to observe My commandments and My Laws? 29. Realize that the Lord gave you the Sabbath, therefore He is supplying you with a double portion of bread on the sixth day. Each *one*[l] should stay in his place; no one is to leave his place on the seventh day." 30. So the people rested on the seventh day. 31. And *Israel*[m] called its name Manna, it being like a white coriander seed, its taste was like something *grill-baked*[10] in honey. 32. Then Moses said, "This is the matter that the Lord commanded, 'Fill an Omer of it {so as} to preserve it for your <future> generations, so that they may see the bread which I fed you in the wilderness, when I brought you out of the land of Egypt.'" 33. So Moses said to Aaron, "Take a bottle and place into it an Omer's full of Manna and put it aside for the Lord to preserve it for your <future> generations."

Apparatus, Chapter 16 (Cont.)

[h] v, b, h, l, and Ra have: "like powdered chalk" read *kĕgûr*, as in Isa. 27:9.

[i] k adds: "of it," not in the Hebrew.

[j] E and a have: "man."

[k] b and n have the interpretive "conceal."

[l] b and g have: "man."

[m] a has: "Israelites" (*bny* instead of *byt*, as does the Hebrew).

[n] n has: "their coming to."

34. Just as the Lord had commanded Moses so did Aaron put it aside in front of the Testimony to preserve <it>. 35. And the Israelites ate the Manna {for} forty years until *they came into*[n] the inhabited land; they ate the Manna until *they came to*[n] the outer limits of the land of Canaan. 36. Now the Omer is a tenth of *three se'ahs.*[11]

CHAPTER 17

1. Then the entire Israelite community set out from the Wilderness of Sin for their {planned} encampments according to *the Memra of*[1] the Lord; when they encamped at Rephidim, there was no water to drink for the people. 2. So the people contended with

Notes, Chapter 16 (Cont.)

[7]The Hebrew has: "a layer of dew." As the dew was perceived as descending from heaven—Num. 11:9 "and when the dew descended upon the camp," and 2 Sam. 17:12 "as the dew fell upon the earth"—the Targum accordingly renders the Hebrew by fem. const. form of the nominal form from *nḥt* "to descend." Tg. Ps.-Jon. renders similarly.

[8]An insertion to further describe the state in which they found the Manna—"heaped" i.e., pile upon pile. The *dgr*, here used in the Passive Participle *pĕʿîl* is precisely the one used in Exod. 8:10 above to describe just such a situation.

[9] An insertion to expand on the concise *wĕnāmās* "and it melted" referring the "it" to whatever was left of it in the field. Adler (*Netina La-Ger, op. cit.,* on this verse) comments that in his manuscript of the Targum, this insertion is missing. M. Löwenstein (*Nefesh Ha-Ger, op. cit.,* p. 41) states that the Targum was motivated to make this insertion by the contextual difficulty apparent in this verse—21a says "they gathered it every morning each one according to his eating (habits)" while 21b reads "when the sun grew hot it melted," the "it" appears to refer back to what each gathered every morning. If so, what did they have left to eat? The Targum therefore inserts—that what melted was "whatever was left of it upon the field." He then cites the following relevant Mekhilta (*Mesek̲ta dĕwayyissaʿ* IV, p. 168)—"'And as the sun waxed hot' (Exod. 16:21). After four hours of the day. You interpret it to mean after four hours of the day. Perhaps it is not so, but means after six hours? When it says 'in the heat of the day' (Gen. 18:1) this means after six hours of the day. Then how must I interpret the expression "As the sun waxed hot?' After four hours of the day."

[10]The Hebrew has "wafer" which the Targum renders by the Greek LW *'isqrîṭôn* <'εσχαρίτης "something baked on the roast" (cf. S. Krauss, *Griechische und Lateinische Lehnwörter im Talmud, Midrasch und Targum.* Berlin, 1899, r.p. Hildesheim [Georg Olms Verlagsbuchhandlung], 1964, Vol. II, p. 97). The Targum is here in agreement with Rabbi Joshua's interpretation in the Mekhilta (*ibid.*VI, p. 171)—"'And the tase of it was like wafers made with honey' (Exod. 16:31). Rabbi Joshua says: Like a stew and a sort of dumpling (*'isqrîṭê*)."

[11]The Hebrew has: "an ephah" which the Targum renders into its smaller component—"three seahs" in agreement with Rabbi Ḥisda's statement in the Talmud—b. Men. 77a: "'The *ephah* and the *bath* shall be of one measure' (Ezek. 45:11), as the *bath* is three *se'ahs* so the *ephah* is three *se'ahs.*" The Tgs. Neof. and Ps.-Jon. translate similarly.

Notes, Chapter 17

[1]The Hebrew "the command," lit. "the mouth," is anthropomorphic and accordingly circumvented by use of the Memra for which cf. Introduction VII D. 1.

Moses and said, "Give us water that we may drink"; and Moses said to them, "Why are you contending with me, what for are you *testing*[a] *before*[2] the Lord?" 3. But the people thirsted for water, and the people grumbled against Moses and *said,*[b] "Why so did you bring us up out of Egypt to kill us and our children, and our cattle through thirst?" 4. So Moses *prayed*[3] to the Lord as follows, "What can I do for this people? It will not be long before they will stone me." 5. Whereupon the Lord said to Moses, "Pass in front of the people and take with you some of the elders of Israel; and the rod with which you struck the Nile, take in your hand and go. 6. Here I am about to stand there before you by the rock at Horeb, and you shall strike the rock and water will emerge from it, and the people will drink"; so Moses did accordingly in the sight of the elders of Israel. 7. nd he called the name of the place *Nisetha and Mazutha*[4] because the Israelites contended, and because they tested the Lord saying, '*Is the Divine Presence of*[5] *the Lord*[c] among us or not?" 8. Then Amalek came and waged war against Israel at Rephidim. 9. So Moses said to Joshua, "Select {some} men for *us,*[d] then go out and wage war against Amalek; tomorrow I will be standing on top of the hill with the rod, *through which miracles were performed by the Lord,*[6] in my hand." 10. And Joshua did precisely as Moses told him to wage war against Amalek, while Moses, Aaron, and Hur ascended to the top of the hill. 11. Now it happened that when Moses would raise his hands Israel would prevail, and when he lowered his hands Amalek would prevail. 12. But Moses' hands grew heavy so they took a stone and placed it under him and he sat on it, while Aaron and Hur *were supporting*[e] his hands one from this <side> and one from that <side>; and his hands remained *spread out in prayer*[7] until sunset. 13. So Joshua smashed Amalek and his people by means of the sword. 14. Then the Lord said to Moses, "Write this memorial in a document and place <it> *before*[8] Joshua, that I will totally erase the memory of Amalek from below the heaven." 15. So Moses built an altar *and worshiped upon it before the Lord*[f] *Who performed miracles for him.*[9] 16. And he said, "*By oath it was pronounced by the Awe-inspiring One whose Divine Presence is upon the throne of glory*[g] *that it is destined that war will be waged*[h] *before*[i] *the Lord*[10] against Amalek *in order to destroy them*[11] *for eternal generations.*"[12]

Apparatus, Chapter 17

[a] k has: "contending."
[b] i and l have: "they said."
[c] n has: "does the Divine Presence dwell."
[d] a has: "yourself," as does the LXX and the Syr.
[e] b and l have: "supported" while a adds: "him."
[f] n has: "God."
[g] l has: "His glory."
[h] n has: "to wage war."
[i] c, d, h, and n have: "from before."

Apparatus, Chapter 18

[a] E and h have: "released her" employing *pṭr* as against *šlḥ* of the Hebrew.

Notes, Chapter 17 (Cont.)

[2]See Gen. Chap. 4 n. 1.

[3]See above Chap. 8, n. 4.

[4]i.e., "Testing and Striving," literal translations of the Hebrew.

[5]The Hebrew has "the Lord" which the Targum renders here for the first time "the Divine Presence, i.e., *šeḵînā'*, of the Lord," for which cf. G. F. Moore, "Intermediaries in Jewish Theology: Memra, Shekinah, Metatron." *HTR* 15 (1922):41-85.

CHAPTER 18

1. Now Jethro, the *chief of*[1] Midian, Moses' father-in-law, heard of everything that the Lord did for Moses and (for) His people Israel in that He had brought Israel out of Egypt. 2. So Jethro, Moses' father-in-law took Zipporah, Moses' wife, after he had *sent her away,*[a] 3. as well as her two sons, the one whose name was Gershom, for he

Notes, Chapter 17 (Cont.)

[6]See above Chap. 4, n. 11.

[7]The Hebrew "steady—lit. faithfulness in a moral sense,—is somewhat figurative here and accordingly rendered interpretively to mean "spread out in prayer," the most obvious translation suggested by the context of this passage. Cf. *Gesenius' Hebrew Grammar,* Second Edition. Oxford, 1910, p. 452, #141d, where this clause is considered a bold combination in order to emphasize very strongly the unconditional relation between the subject (here—"his hands") and the predicate (here—"were steady").

[8]See Gen. Chap. 23, n. 2.

[9]The Hebrew has: "and he called its name—'the Lord is my banner,'" which out of deference to God had to be paraphrased, since calling God "my banner" could be taken to be too personal and too informal. The paraphrasing would involve the phrase "and he called," which is here associated with the altar and consequently with "prayer" and "worship." Accordingly, as in Gen. 12:8; 22:14; 33:20, the phrase could be rendered either as "and he prayed" (12:8), or "and he prayed and worshiped" (22:14), or "and he worshiped" (33:20). The Targum opted for the last alternative, then translated the Hebrew *ns*—"banner" by its alternate meaning "miracle"—paraphrasing, "Who performed miracles for him" in line with vs. 9 above where the Hebrew "God's rod" is similarly rendered. Cf. further Gen. Chap. 12, n. 7.

[10]The Hebrew has: "for a hand is upon the throne of the Lord," which is enigmatic and obscure in meaning. The Targum thus paraphrases this passage to refer to:

1. God pronouncing an oath, as "hand" is commonly associated with oath, cf. Gen. 14:22; 24:2; 47:29 and the Mekhilta (*Bešallaḥ Mesek̲ta' dĕ 'Amāleq* II, p. 186f, Rabbi Eleazar of Modiʿim and Rabbi Eliezer's statement on this passage).
2. "the throne of the Lord" is paraphrased into "Whose Divine Presence is upon the throne of glory" to avoid attributing any particular possessions to God, as "the rod of God" (as vs. 9 above, for which cf. Chap. 4, n. 11 above), or the "mountain of God" (Exod. 3:1, for which cf. Chap. 3, n.4).
3. "the throne" is expanded into "the throne of glory" (a similar but not identical expression occurs in Exod. 11:5; 12:29, for which cf. Chap. 11, n. 5) in agreement with R. Eleazar of Modiʿim's and R. Eliezer's statement in the Mekhilta (*ibid.*) whose relevant passages are cited in full in n. 12 below.
4. "the Lord will be at war," an anthropomorphism, is circumvented by paraphrase and introduction of *qdm*—"before," hence—"that it is destined that war will be waged before the Lord."

[11]An insertion, recalling vs. 14b above, and serving as a link between the preceding and what follows.

[12]The Hebrew has: "from generation to generation" which is figurative, and interpretively rendered to mean "eternal generations." B.Z.J. Berkowitz (*Ḥalifot Semalot.* Wilna, 1874, p. 64f.) correctly points out that here the context deals with erasing a memory, thus if it is erased from one generation it is automatically erased from all future generations, hence eternally. In contrast, Exod. 3:15, where the subject is to keep a memory alive the Hebrew also having the sequence [*lĕ*] *dōr dōr* "[from] generation to generation"), the Targum renders literally, since there the memory has to be kept alive actively each generation rather than being an automatic phenomenon.

The relevant Mekhilta passage is: "And He said: 'for a hand is upon the throne of the Lord, the Lord will be at war with Amaleq from generation to generation' (Exod. 17:16). R. Joshua says: 'From generation' this means (from) the life of this world, 'generation' this means (from) the life of the future world . . . R. Eleazar of Modiʿim says: From the generation of Moses and from the generation of Samuel . . . . R. Eliezer says: From the generation of the Messiah which are (really) three generations. . . ."

Notes, Chapter 18

[1]See Gen. Chap. XLI, n. 22. This interpretive translation is in agreement with that of R. Eliezer Hamodai in Mek̲hilta (*Yitro Mesekta de'Amaleq* I, p. 190) in whose opinion Jethro was some sort of ruler.

said, "I was an alien in a foreign country." 4. And the other's name <was> Eliezer, for the God of my *father*[b] *supported me*[2] and saved me from the sword of the Pharaoh. 5. So Jethro, Moses' father-in-law, and his sons, and his wife came to Moses in the wilderness where he was encamped, *at the mountain where the glory of the Lord had appeared.*[3] 6. And he said to Moses, "I, your father-in-law Jethro *have come*[c] to you, as well as your wife with her two sons." 7. So Moses went out to meet his father-in-law, and bowed down and kissed him, and they asked each other about <their> welfare and (they) came in to the tent. 8. And Moses told his father-in-law all that the Lord had done to the Pharaoh and *to the Egyptians*[d] for Israel's sake, every hardship that had befallen them along the way and <how> the Lord saved *them.*[e] 9. Whereupon Jethro rejoiced over every good thing that the Lord had done for Israel in that He saved them from the hand of *the Egyptians.*[f] 10. And Jethro said, "Blessed be the Lord Who saved you from the hand of the Egyptians and from the hand of the Pharaoh, Who saved the people *from (being) under*[g] Egyptian domination. 11. Now I realize that *the Lord is great and that there is no God beside Him;*[4] for by the <very> thing through which *the Egyptians had schemed to punish Israel, by it they were punished."*[5] 12. Then Jethro, Moses' father-in-law, offered burnt offerings and *sanctified sacrifices*[6] to the Lord, and Aaron as well as all the elders of Israel came to eat bread with Moses' father-in-law before the Lord. 13. Then it came about on the next day that Moses sat down to act as a judge for the people, while the people stood around Moses from morning till evening. 14. When Moses' father-in-law saw all that he was doing to the people, he said, "What is this thing that you are doing to the people; why is it that you are sitting alone while all the people are standing around you from morning to evening?" 15. So Moses said to his father-in-law, "For the people come to me *to seek instruction from the Lord.*[7] 16. When they have *a judgment case*[8] *they come*[h] to me and I render a decision between a man and his fellow man and inform them of the statutes of the Lord and of His laws." 17. Whereupon Moses' father-in-law said to him, "What you are doing is not the proper thing. 18. You will surely tire yourself out, as will this people, for the matter is too burdensome for you; you will not be able to do it by yourself. 19. Now listen to me and I will advise you; then the *Memra of the Lord will support you*[2]*—be a seeker of instruction from the Lord*[9] for the people and then bring *the matters*[i] to the Lord. 20. Then enjoin them the statutes, and the laws, and inform them of the course they are to follow and the {type of} deed they are to do. 21. And you should seek out from all the people men of valor, God-fearing ones, honest men who detest *accepting*[10] money; then appoint them as leaders of thousands, leaders of hundreds, leaders of fifties, and leaders of tens. 22. And they should judge the people at all times; then every major matter they should bring to you, while every minor matter they {themselves} should decide; so they will lighten <the burden> from you by bearing <it> with you. 23. If you will do this thing, as the Lord commands you, then you will be able to stand up, and

Apparatus, Chapter 18 (Cont.)

[b] n adds: "His Memra."
[c] V, v, a, and c have: "am coming," while A has: "he has come."
[d] B and l have: "Egypt."
[e] b, d, g, a, and k have the third person singular form of the pronoun.
[f] g has: "Egypt."
[g] n has: "from the midst of the oppression of."
[h] A has the singular as does the Hebrew, which is grammatically difficult. The LXX has the plural.
[i] n has: "their matters" as do the LXX and the Syr. while the Hebrew equals Tg. Onq. Vat. 448.
[j] a has: "before" which is interpretive.

also this entire people will *go*[11] to its home satisfied." 24. Then Moses *listened to*[12] *the word of*[13] his father-in-law and did according to everything he said. 25. So Moses selected men of valor from all of Israel and appointed them as heads over the people—leaders of thousands, leaders of hundreds, leaders of fifties, and leaders of tens. 26. And they judged the people at all times; the difficult matter they would bring *to*[j] Moses, while every minor matter they {themselves} would decide. 27. Then Moses sent his father-in-law away, and he went to his {own} land.

CHAPTER 19

1. In the third month since the Israelite departure from Egypt on that very day they came to the Wilderness of Sinai. 2. After setting out from Rephidim they came to

Notes, Chapter 18 (Cont.)

[2]n has the augmented paraphrase "His Memra supported me" for which cf. Gen. Chap. 26, n.2.

[3]See above Chap. 3, n. 4.

[4]The Hebrew "the Lord is greater than all the gods" implies a belief in monolatry which the Targum sought to avoid by splitting this clause into two—"the Lord is great" and "there is no god beside Him," which is a profession of pure monotheism. For a similar paraphrase to avoid the concept of monolatry, see above Chap. 15, n. 19.

[5]The Hebrew "for by the thing in which they acted presumptuously against them" is difficult and vague in its brevity. The Targum here paraphrases in agreement with the following Midrash: Mekhilta *ibid.* I, p. 195—"'Yea for the very thing with which they acted presumptuously against them' (Exod. 18:11) . . . For with the very thing with which the Egyptians *schemed to destroy Israel, God punished them.*"

[6]See above Chap. 10, n. 11.

[7]See Gen. Chap. 25, n. 5.

[8]The Hebrew has "a matter" which is here interpretively rendered as "a judgment case." Tg. Ps.-Jon. renders similarly, as does Tg. Neof. with *'ēseq dîn*—"a matter of judgment," as well as the LXX with *'αντιλογία*—"dispute," and the Vg.'s *disceptatio* "controversy."

[9]"Before, lit. facing, God" which has anthropomorphic overtones as one cannot face God, not even Moses (cf. Exod. 33:20) and this is accordingly circumvented by the same paraphrase used in vs. 15 above.

[10]This insertion, also present in the Tg. Ps.-Jon. but implied in the Hebrew, is reflected in the Mekhilta (*ibid.* IV, p. 198) "'Hating unjust gain' (Exod. 18:21), those who when sitting in judgment hate *to accept* money."

[11]The Hebrew has: "come" (*bw'*), which is here, as well as in Gen. 20:13, rendered interpretively by the Aramaic *nhk*—"go." In his Hebrew edition of the Peshitta (*Peshitta in Hebrew Characters with Elucidatory Notes: Part I Genesis.* Berlin, 1927, p. 40, ns. 1 and 2), C. Heller takes note of such a confusion, also existing in the Syr., for which he cites Gen.32:6; 42:5, 12; Exod. 11:1; Num. 13:27; Deut. 12:29; 17:9; 2 Kgs. 7:10; Ezek. 11:16; Neh. 2:7, where the Hebrew *bw'* is rendered *'zl.* He also cites the reverse situation where Hebrew *hlk* ("go") is rendered *'ty* ("come") in the Syr., for which cf. Gen. 14:24; 24:12; 26:26; 43:65; Num. 22:37; and Eccl. 9:7. He also cites Moshe Ibn Ezra, who, in his work *Širat Yiśrā'ēl* (Leipzig, 1924, p. 200), points out that the Hebrew verb *hlk* denotes "going as well as coming." In the present case, Tg. Onq. is the only Aramaic version translating "go;" Tg. Ps.'Jon. translates literally using *'ty,* Tg. Neof., the Sam. Tg. and the Syr. likewise are literal, using *'ll* instead. In Gen. 20:13, Sperber lists *'ll* as a variant (in *n*), while Tg. Ps.-Jon. has *nhk,* in contrast to Tg. Neof., the Sam. Tg. and the Syr., all of which have "come" (*'ll*).

[12]Lit. "accepted," for which see Gen. Chap. 16, n. 1.

[13]See Gen. Chap. 3, n. 9.

the Wilderness of Sinai and encamped in the wilderness; and Israel encamped there alongside the mountain. 3. Then Moses ascended towards *the Lord*[a] and the Lord called to him from the mountain, saying, "So you should say to the House of Jacob and tell the Israelites: 4. You have seen what I did *to the Egyptians,*[b] how I carried you *like*[1] on eagles' wings *and drew you close to My worship.*[2] 5. So now, if you will really *listen*[3] *to My Memra*[4] and will observe My covenant, then you will be *more beloved before Me*[5] than all the nations, for the entire earth is Mine. 6. And you will be to Me *kings,*[c] priests, and a holy nation; these are the words which you shall speak to the Israelites." 7. Then Moses came and summoned the elders of the people, *and set before them in an orderly manner*[6] all these words which the Lord had commanded him. 8. Whereupon all the people as one replied by saying, "All that the Lord says we shall do"; and Moses brought back the words of the people to the Lord. 9. Then the Lord said to Moses, "Here I am about to *reveal Myself*[7] to you within the thickness of a cloud, in order that the people should hear when I speak with you and trust in you forever as well"; and Moses related the words of the people to the Lord. 10. Whereupon the Lord said to Moses, "Go to the people and *prepare*[8] them today and tomorrow; let them wash their clothes. 11. Then let them be ready for the third day, for on the third day the Lord *will reveal Himself*[9] within sight of the entire people on Mount Sinai. 12. And you should border off the people round about, saying, 'Beware for yourselves *from*[10] ascending the mountain or <even> from *approaching*[11] its border; whosoever *approaches*[11] the mountain shall surely be killed. 13. Not a hand is to touch it, for he will surely be stoned or surely be shot, be it man or beast, he will not live'; only at the protracted sound of the horn are they permitted to go up to the mountain." 14. Then Moses descended from the mountain to the people and *prepared*[8] the people, and they washed their clothes. 15. And he said to the people, "Be ready for the third day. Do not {sexually} approach a woman." 16. Now it came about on the third day when it was morning, that there was thunder and lightning and a dense cloud over the mountain, while the sound of the horn was very strong; whereupon all the people who were in the camp trembled. 17. Then Moses brought out the people from the camp towards *the Memra of*[4] the Lord, and they were stationed *at the foot of*[12] the mountain. 18. Now Mount Sinai was entirely encircled by smoke because the Lord *had revealed Himself*[9] upon it with fire; and its smoke billowed up like smoke from a furnace, while the whole mountain trembled fiercely. 19. Meanwhile the sound of the horn continued to become exceedingly strong; Moses spoke, and *from before the Lord*

Apparatus, Chapter 19

[a] n has: "the Memra of the Lord."
[b] v, k, and l have: "to Egypt," while a has: "in Egypt."
[c] a has: "kingdoms of," which is closer to the Hebrew.

Notes, Chapter 19

[1]With this insertion (also in Tg. Ps.-Jon., CTgF, and the Frg. Tg. [P,V], the Syr., and the LXX), the Targum transforms the Hebrew metaphor into a simile, a figure of speech more easily understood by the people.

he was answered by a voice.[13] 20. Then the Lord *revealed Himself*[9] on Mount Sinai, at the summit of the mountain; and the Lord summoned Moses to the summit of the mountain and Moses ascended. 21. And the Lord said to Moses, "Go down; warn the people not to break through to the Lord in order to see, for many of them will <then>

Notes, Chapter 19 (Cont.)

[2]The Hebrew has: "and brought you to Me." which the Targum paraphrases to avoid direct contact between God and man, hence instead of being drawn close to God, Israel is brought close to the worship of God.

[3]Lit. "accept," for which see Gen. Chap. 16, n. 1.

[4]See Introduction VII D. 1.

[5]The Hebrew has: "My treasured possession," which is a figure of speech and, accordingly, rendered interpretively "more beloved before Me," in agreement with the Aggadic interpretation of the following Midrashim:

1. *Mekhilta Yitro Mĕsektā' dĕbĕḥôdeš* II, p. 208—"'treasured possession' (Exod. 19:5). Just as a man's treasure is *beloved* by him, so you will be *beloved* to Me."
2. *Pesiqtā Rabbātî Yĕhûdāh WeYisrā'ēl* XI, p. 46a—"R. Joshua of Siknin said in the name of R. Levi: Israel is called the treasure of the Holy One, blessed be He, as it is written, 'You shall be My own treasure' (Exod. 19:5) . . . Even as one's proper treasure is better loved by a man than all else which he lay claim to, so is Israel better *loved* by the Holy One, blessed be He, than all other nations. . . ."

This Targumic rendering for Hebrew *sĕgullāh* is also used in Deut. 7:6; 14:2; 26:18, as well as by the Targum to Ps. 135:14, in all the above passages the Hebrew context deals with the people being God's "treasure," a figure of speech, which the Targum translates nonliterally as "beloved." In contrast to 1 Chr. 29:3, Eccl. 2:8 where the term is used nonfiguratively it is rendered literally by a variety of Aramaic terms. Tg. Ps.-Jon. and the Syr. are completely identical to Onq. in the present verse, whereas the other Pal. Tgs. (Neof., CTgF, and the Frg. Tg. [P and V to an extent]) have the literal *sgl* in addition to the interpretive one in the form of a partial simile—"you shall be to My name a *beloved* people, *like a treasured possession* from all of the nations . . . ." The LXX, however, renders it somewhat literal—*λαὸς περιούσιος*—"a peculiar people," as does the Vg. *peculium de cunctis populis*—"you shall be My peculiar possession above all people," for these translations cf. S.R. Driver, *The Book of Exodus.* Cambridge Bible for Schools and Colleges. Cambridge (Cambridge University Press), 1918, p. 17ϕf.

[6]The Hebrew has: "and he placed before them." The Targum renders the Hebrew root *sym*—"place" interpretively by the root *sdr*—"set in an orderly manner," just as in Exod. 21:1. In the present verse the Targum is identical to the *MRŠBY Yitrô* XIX:7, p. 140—"'and he placed before them' (Exod. 19:7). He *set them in order* before them." The Tgs. Ps.-Jon., Neof., CTgF, and the Frg. Tg. (P, V) also employ the root *sdr* here.

[7]See below Chap. 20, n. 10.

[8]The Hebrew has: "sanctify," which is here interpretively rendered "prepare" (as well as in vs. 14 below) and is in agreement with the Mekhilta (*ibid.* III, p. 213) to vs. 14: "'And He sanctified the people' (Exod. 19:14). He *prepared* them and washed their garments and purified them." Here the root *zmn* "prepare" could also mean "summon."

[9]See Gen. Chap. 11, n. 6.

[10]The Targum inserts the prepositional prefix to the infinitive which is implied in the Hebrew. Tg. Ps.-Jon. does likewise, while the Syr., the Frg. Tg. (P, V), and the CTgF add the negative, having "not to ascend."

[11]The Hebrew "touching" is a figure of speech, here interpretively rendered by the Targum to mean "approaching"—coming close enough to touch.

[12]Lit. "at the bottom part of."

[13]The Hebrew "and God answered him by a voice" is anthropomorphic and is accordingly circumvented in the Targum by a paraphrase employing the particle *qdm*. All the Pal. Tgs. (Ps.-Jon., Neof., CTgF, and the Frg. Tg. [P, V]) are here identical to the Targum.

perish. 22. And even the priests, who approached *to minister*[14] *before*[15] the Lord should sanctify themselves, lest the Lord shall *kill <some> of them.*"[d] 23. Then Moses said to the Lord, "The people cannot come up to Mount Sinai, for you have warned us saying, 'Border off the mountain and sanctify it.'" 24. So the Lord said to him, "Proceed to go down; then you and Aaron come up, while the priests and the people should not break through to go up to the Lord, lest he shall *kill <some> of them.*"[d] 25. Whereupon Moses went down to the people and spoke to them.

CHAPTER 20

1. Then the Lord spoke all these words as follows, 2. "I am the Lord your God who brought you out of Egypt, out of the place of slavery. 3. You should have no other *god*[1] beside Me. 4. Do not make for yourself an image or any likeness <of anything> that is in the heavens above or <of anything> that is on earth below, or <of anything> that is in the waters below the earth. 5. Do not bow down to them nor worship them, for I the Lord your God am a jealous God, avenging the sins of the fathers upon the *rebellious*[2] children, upon the third *generation*[3] and upon the fourth *generation*[3] of those who hate Me, when the children follow their *fathers*[a] *in sinning.*[4] 6. But performing kindness to thousands of *generations*[3] of those who loved Me, and observe My commandments. 7. Do not *swear*[5] in vain with the name of the Lord your God, for

Apparatus, Chapter 19 (Cont.)

[d] n has: "prevail against them," which approximates the Hebrew.

Apparatus, Chapter 20

[a] D has: "fathers' faults."

Notes, Chapter 19 (Cont.)

[14]An insertion, which expands the preceding "who approached" by supplying the purpose "to minister." The same insertion occurs in Tg. Ps.-Jon., while Tgs. Neof. and the Frg. Tg. (P, V) have the slightly different "who stand and minister, "the Tg. Neof. m. has "who approach (literal of the Hebrew) and minister."

[15]See Gen. Chap. 4, n. 1.

Notes, Chapter 20

[1]The Hebrew has the plural which has overtones of monolatry and is accordingly rendered into the singular by the Targum, as well as by Tg. Ps.-Jon. (according to D. Rieder, *Targum Jonathan Ben Uziel of the Pentateuch.* Jerusalem, 1974, p 112, who lists it as occurring only in ms. form and in the Basel Pentateuch edition of 1607), Tg. Neof., the Frg. Tg. (P), and CTgF.

the Lord will not acquit the one *who swears*[5] *falsely with His name.*[6] 8. Remember the Sabbath day by sanctifying it. 9. Six days you shall labor and perform all your work. 10. But the seventh day is a Sabbath to the Lord your God; <on it> you shall not perform any work—you, your son, your daughter, your servant, your maid, your

Notes, Chapter 20 (Cont.)

[2]This insertion, also in Tgs. Ps.-Jon., Neof., and the Frg. Tg. (P), is in agreement with the theological viewpoint set forward by the Rabbis in the following Rabbinic texts:

1. *b. Ber.* 7a "The Master said above: 'The righteous man who prospers is a righteous man son of a righteous man; the righteous man who is in adversity is a righteous man son of a wicked man.' But this is not so! For, here, one verse says: 'Visiting the iniquity of the fathers upon the children' (Exod. 34:7 = Exod. 20:5 = Deut. 5:9), and another verse says: 'Neither shall the children be put to death for the fathers' (Deut. 24:16). And a contradiction was pointed out between these two verses, and the answer was given that there is no contradiction. The one verse deals with children who continue in the same course as their fathers, and the other verse with *children who do not continue in the course of their fathers!*"
2. *b. Sanh.* 27b "Are not children then to be put to death for the sins committed by their parents? Is it not written, 'Visiting the iniquities of the fathers upon the children' (Exod. 34:7 = Exod. 20:5 = Deut. 5:9)? There the reference is to *children who follow their parents' footsteps* (lit. who hold in their hands the deed of their parents)."
3. *Mekhilta* (*ibid.* VI, p. 226) "'Visiting the iniquity of the fathers upon the children' (Exod. 20:5). When there is no skip, but not when there is a skip. How is this? The wicked son of a wicked father, who in turn also was the son of a wicked father. R. Nathan says: A destroyer the son of a destroyer, who in turn was the son of a destroyer."

The insertion also anticipates the addition at the end of this verse—"when the children follow their fathers in sinning."

[3]The Targum, as do Tgs. Ps.-Jon., Neof., and the Frg. Tg. (P), inserts "generation(s)" after "third" and "fourth" in the present verse and "thousands" in the following verse; the Syr. has this insertion only after "fourth" to refer to the preceding "third" as well, as after "thousands," while the LXX has it (γενεᾶς) only after "fourth" as does the Vg. *generationem.* The term, which is implied in the Hebrew also occurs in the Midrash and Talmud where these two verses are expounded, as follows:

1. *Mekhilta* (*ibid.*, p. 227)—"One might think that just as the measure of punishment extends over four *generations,* so also the measure of rewarding the good extends only over four *generations.* But Scripture says: 'Unto thousands' (Exod. 20:6). But: 'Unto thousands' I might understand to mean the minimum of 'thousands,' that is two thousand, but it also says: 'to a thousand *generations'* (Deut. 7:9)—*generations* unsearched and uncounted."
2. *b. Sot.* 31a "'To the thousands of them that love Me' (Exod. 20:6). It was taught: R. Simeon b. Eleazar said: He who acts [in obedience of the Torah] out of love [of the Almighty] is greater than one who acts out of fear. For the merit of the latter lasts one thousand *generations,* whereas the former merit lasts two. Here it is written, 'to the thousands of them that love Me . . . ,' whereas in reference to fear it is written 'and to them who keep His commandments [He shows mercy] for a thousand generations' (Deut. 7:9)."

[4]See n. 2 above.

[5]The Hebrew has: "do not take . . . who takes" which the Targum interpretively renders "to swear," as do the Tgs. Ps.-Jon., Neof. m., and the Frg. Tg. (P), as well as the Syr. and the Rabbis, for whose relevant texts see the following note.

[6]The Hebrew has: "who takes His name in vain." The Targum here renders the second occurrence of Hebrew *laššāw'* in this verse to mean "falsely," while the first one is rendered *lĕmaggānā'*—"in vain." A comparison with the other Aramaic Versions shows Tg. Ps.-Jon. having "in vain" throughout, while the Syr. has "falsely" in both instances. Tg. Neof. parallels Tg. Ps.-Jon. (with the exception of translating the Hebrew *ns'* literally) while Tg. Neof. m. has "swearing falsely" throughout. The Frg. Tg. (P) contains both renderings side by side and is hereby cited in part:

beast, or your alien who is in your *city.*[7] 11. For in six days the Lord made heaven and earth, the sea and everything that is in it; then He rested on the seventh day; therefore the Lord blessed the seventh day and sanctified it. 12. Honor your father and your mother so that your days may be prolonged in the land which the Lord your God is giving you. 13. Do not kill *any person,*[8] do not commitadultery; do not *steal,*[b] do not render false testimony against your fellow man; 14. Do not envy the house of your fellow man; do not envy the wife of your fellow man, nor his servant nor his maid, nor his ox nor his *donkey,*[c] nor anything that belongs to your fellow man." 15. When the entire people perceived the thunder and the fires, as well as the sound of the horn and the *mountain that smoked,*[d] and <as> the people saw <all this>, they trembled and stood at a distance. 16. Whereupon they said to Moses, "You speak with us and we shall listen, but *let it not be speaking*[e] *with us from before the Lord*[9] lest we shall die."

Apparatus, Chapter 20 (Cont.)

[b] l adds: "any person" in agreement with the Mekhilta (*Yitro Mesektā' dĕbĕḥôdeš* VIII, p. 232)—"'You shall not steal' (Exod. 20:15) ... this is a warning against stealing persons ... Hence what does the passage 'You shall not steal' speak of? Of one who steals persons..."

[c] h has: "friend," the spelling difference involving only the third letter which is *h* in the case of "friend," and *m* in the case of "donkey."

[d] b, g, k, and l have: "smoking mountain."

[e] n has: "let not a word be speaking."

[f] G, V, and c have "towards," which is closer to the Hebrew.

[g] n has: "slaughter."

[h] b and g omit, having the accusative instead: "your sheep and your cattle."

Notes, Chapter 20 (Cont.)

"...You shall not swear by the name of the Lord your God in vain, nor shall you take a false oath in My name; for the Lord your God ... will eventually exact punishment from whomever falsifies in My name ... and anyone who takes a false oath in My name, it is manifest before Me that on account of his sin I will destroy it ... and anyone who ... does not take a false oath..." The Sam. Tg., the LXX, and the Vg. are entirely literal here. From the above comparison, it is evident that more than one tradition existed as to the meaning of the term *laššāw'*which resulted in either an interpretive or literal rendering of this Hebrew word. This difference of traditions concerning *laššāw'* is also reflected in Rabbinic literature where its meaning is distinctly discussed. The relevant texts involved are hereby partially cited:

1. *Sifra Qĕdôšîm* II:6, p. 88b "'You shall not take the name of the Lord your God in vain' (Exod. 20:7). What is taught by the text, 'you shall not swear by My name falsely' (Lev. 19:12)? Scripture says: 'You shall not take the name of the Lord your God in vain,' from which you might think that one is culpable only if he employs the Ineffable Name. How do we know that substitute divine names too are included?—because it says: 'by My name,' which indicates 'whatever name I have.'" This Midrash, then, interprets *laššāw'*as "falsely," and connects our verse with Lev. 19:12, which explicitly has *laššāw'*to mean "falsely."

2. *b. Šebu.* 20b "'You shall not take the name of the Lord your God in vain' (Exod. 20:7). When R. Dimi came he said in the name of R. Johanan: (If one swears) 'I will eat' or I will not eat' (that is considered) a false (oath), and the warning (comes) from here, 'Do not swear falsely by My name' (Lev. 19:12), (whereas if he swears) 'I ate' or 'I did not eat' (that is considered) in vain, and its warning (comes) from here, 'Do not take the name of the Lord your God in vain' (Exod. 20:7)..."

The Talmud then cites the following Baraithā *"šāw'* (vain) and *šéqer* (false) are one and the same" in order to refute the above distinction, then responds that the above equation holds true only with respect to "flogging" and "sacrifice" which each type of oath incurs, but not that they are equal in meaning.

17. Then Moses said to the people, "Do not be afraid, *for the Glory of the Lord was revealed to you*[10] only in order to test you, and in order that *His reverence*[11] *should face you,*[12] so that you will not sin." 18. So the people stood at a distance, while Moses approached the *side of*[f] the dense cloud where there was the *Glory of the Lord.*[13] 19. And the Lord said to Moses, "Thus you shall say to the Israelites, 'You have seen that I have spoken with you from heaven. 20. Do not make *before Me*[14] *deities*[15] of silver, nor should you make deities of gold for yourselves. 21. You should make an earthen altar to Me and *sacrifice*[g] upon it your burnt-offerings and your *sanctified sacrifices*[16] *of*[h] your sheep and *of*[h] your cattle, wherever I shall *rest My Divine*

Notes, Chapter 20 (Cont.)

3. *Pesiqtā' Rabbātî Yoḏh Haddibrôt Paršāh Tinyānûtā'* XXII, p. 112 b—"Another comment: 'You shall not take the name of the Lord your God in vain' (Exod. 20:7). R. Simon said: If Scripture is speaking here of a false oath, has it not already been said elsewhere—'You shall not swear by My name falsely' (Lev. 19:12)? What then is intended by the apparent repetition, 'You shall not take the name of the Lord ... in vain'? That taking an oath even when affirming something which is true is taking God's name in vain." According to this Rabbinic tradition, the Exodus verse does not deal with swearing falsely.

[7]See Gen. Chap. 22, n. 13.

[8]An insertion not present in any of the other Ancient Versions. This insertion supplying a direct object—"any person"—may be associated with its presence in a related verse in Leviticus (20:10) as cited in the following Midrash:

Mekhilta (*ibid.* VIII, p. 232) "'You shall not commit murder' (Exod. 20:13). Why is this said? Because it says: 'Whosoever sheds *any person's* blood ...' (Gen. 9:6). We have just heard the penalty for it, but we have not heard the warning against it; therefore it says here: 'You shall not murder.'"

A. Cohn ("Onkelos und die Halacha." *Magazin* 1 (1874): 110) explains this paraphrase as referring to someone who committed suicide, pointing out that without the addition of "any person," the Biblical prohibition "do not kill" would only refer to killing someone else, the addition "any person" includes even oneself—hence suicide. The following Talmud also deduces the prohibition of suicide but from Gen. 9:5 instead: "'And surely your blood of your lives will I require'—R. Eleazar remarked that it meant I will require your blood if shed by the hands of yourselves." The difference between the deduction of the Targum (from Exod. 20:13) and the Talmud (from Gen. 9:5) is explained by Cohn to refer to the warning (*'azhārāh*) and the penalty (*'ōneš*), respectively.

[9]The Hebrew "let not God speak with us" is anthropomorphic and accordingly circumvented by two standard devices employed by the Targum: (1) the preposition *qdm* and (2) the transformation of the Hebrew active into a passive verb.

[10]The Hebrew "God came" is an anthropomorphism and is circumvented by the Targum by the use of the phrase "the Yeqārā' of the Lord" for which see Introduction VII D. 2, and changing the active Hebrew "came" to the passive "was revealed."

[11]i.e., reverence for Him.

[12]Lit. "should be on your faces."

[13]See Gen. Chap. 18, n. 11.

[14]The Hebrew "with Me" is difficult and accordingly interpretively rendered "before Me" using the preposition *qdm,* perhaps in referring back to the beginning of vs. 3 above—"You shall have no other gods *before Me.*" The other Ancient Versions also adjust their translation—Tg. Neof. and the Frg. Tg. (V) likewise have "before Me," while the LXX and the Syr. have "for yourselves," and the Vg. omits a translation entirely.

[15]See Gen. Chap. 31, n. 20.

[16]See above Chap. 10, n. 11.

Presence,[17] *there I shall send My blessings to you*[18] and bless you. 22. But if you make a stone altar for Me, do not construct them <by> hewing them; *do not raise*[i] your sword upon it and desecrate it. 23. Neither ascend My altar by way of steps so that your nakedness not be exposed on it.'

CHAPTER 21

1. Now these are laws which you should *set in order*[1] before them. 2. If you buy an *Israelite*[2] servant, he shall serve six years; then in the *seventh*[a] {year} he should depart *as*[b] a free person, without payment. 3. If he came in *alone*[3] he is to leave *alone;*[3] if he is a married person, his wife is to depart with him. 4. If his master gave him a wife and she gave birth to sons or daughters for him, the wife and her children are to belong to her master, whereas he is to depart *alone.*[3] 5. However, if the servant shall fervently declare, 'I love my master, my wife, and my children; I do not wish to depart *a*[c] free person.' 6. Then his master should bring him *before*[d] the *judges,*[e4] and he should bring him near a doorway *which is*[f] near the doorpost; and his master should pierce his ear with an awl, *and he is to be his working slave*[5] forever. 7. And if a man should sell his daughter

Apparatus, Chapter 20 (Cont.)

[i] a has: "so that you do not raise," while i, D, b, and g have: "lest you raise your sword."

Apparatus, Chapter 21

[a] n adds: "year," implied in the Hebrew.

[b] a omits, the Hebrew has it.

[c] d and g have: "as a"; the Hebrew omits it.

[d] c has: "to," as does the Hebrew.

[e] d has the singular.

[f] Sperber's text has: "or" as does the Hebrew, while the LXX omits it, and the Vg. has the conjunction "and" instead. Cf. A. Berliner, *Targum Onkelos: Einleitung zum Targum Onkelos.* Berlin, 1884, p. 231, who points to b. Qid. 22a that *'ô* is here to be understood as *'im* as in Exod. 21:36 meaning "when," and here meaning "to the door when it belongs to the doorpost" (i.e., is attached to it).

[g] Reading *lw* together with 6 Hebrew mss., the LXX[B(L)], the Vg., Sperber's text, and l, as against b and d, which have *l'* in agreement with the *ketiḇ* of MT.

Notes, Chapter 20 (Cont.)

[17]The Hebrew has "cause My name to be mentioned" which the Targum paraphrases "rest My Divine Presence" in agreement with Rabbi Ḥalafta of K'far Ḥananiah's exposition of this verse, m.'Abot III:6 "When ten sit and study Torah, *the Divine Presence rests* among them . . . How do I know this is true even of one person?—because it says, 'in every place where I cause My name to be mentioned I will come to you and bless you' (Exod. 20:24). Cf. also Tanḥ(A) *Wayyēṣē'* X; *Nāśō'* XXVI. The Mekhilta (*ibid.* XI, p. 243) "where I reveal Myself to you in the Temple" is similar to the Targum. Cf. also Deut. 12:5 and the Targum's similar paraphrase on God's name.

[18]The Hebrew "I will come to you" called for a paraphrase to avoid direct intercourse between God and man. Furthermore, God "coming," an anthropomorphic act, which was circumvented earlier in vs. 17 by the translation "was revealed," is here paraphrased—"there I shall send My blessings to you"—in context

as a maid, she is not to depart according to the departure of servants. 8. If she becomes displeasing in the sight of her master who had *kept her*[6] *for himself,*[g] then he should redeem her; he may not sell her to *another man*[7] by (his) domination over her. 9. But if he should keep her for his son, he is to treat her according to the customs of the

Notes, Chapter 20 (Cont.)

with what follows—"and bless you." Likewise R. Aqiba's statement in b. Ḥul. 49a— "(from Num. 6:27) we learn about a blessing for Israel by the priests, but by God we do not learn about. However, when it says 'and I will bless them' (Num. 6:27) we have the priests blessing Israel and God consenting to them."

Notes, Chapter 21

[1]The Hebrew has "place," which is here interpretively rendered "set in order" i.e., arrange, in agreement with the Aggadic interpretation of this phrase in the Mekhilta (*Mesek̲ta Nĕzîkîm-Mišpāṭîm* I, p. 246): ". . . Therefore it says: 'And these are the ordinances which you shall place before them' (Exod. 21:1). *Arrange them in proper order* before them like a table." Cf. also above Chap. 19, n. 6.

[2]See above Chap. 1, n. 9. The Hebrew *'éb̲ed 'ib̲rî* is here rendered "an Israelite," in agreement with the Mekhilta (*ibid.*, p. 247) which states so explicitly, as well as with the Talmud (b. B. Meṣ. 71a) which excludes the proselyte.

[3]The Hebrew has literally: "with his back" which is a figurative expression meaning—with his back, but with nothing else, i.e., alone, and is accordingly rendered by that translation in the Targum. A similar explanation was given in the Talmud by Rabbi Eliezer b. Jacob in a discussion with the Rabbis as to the meaning of the Hebrew word—*gappô*: b.Qidd.20a—"Our Rabbis taught: 'If he come in by himself (*bĕ-gappô*), he shall go out by himself (*bĕ-gappô*)'(Exod. 21:3)—he comes in with his (whole) body (*bĕ-gûp̲ô*) and goes out with his (whole) body (*bĕ-gûp̲ô*). Rabbi Eliezer b. Jacob said: Having come in *alone*, he goes out *alone*." Tgs. Ps.-Jon., Neof., CTgA, and the Syr. as well as the LXX (*μόνος*), are similar to R. Eliezer's interpretation.

[4]The Hebrew "God" (*Elohim*) is here interpretively rendered to mean "judge(s)" in agreement with the Mekhilta (*ibid.*, II, p. 252)—"'Then his master shall bring him unto God' (Exod. 21:6). To the court (judge(s))." Cf. also y. Qidd. 1:2, p. 59c. Tgs. Neof. and Ps.-Jon. as well as the Syr. agree with Onqelos, while CTgA has "to the entrance of the court"—the place where the judges sit. The LXX has "to the judgment seat of God" (*πρὸς τὸ κριτήριον τοῦ θεοῦ*).

[5]The Hebrew has: "and he should serve him." The Targum translation of this clause, as well as of its synoptic parallel in Deut. 15:17, emphasizing his servile status is similar to the original curse which Noah placed on his grandson Canaan—"may he be a slave of slaves unto his brethren" (Gen. 9:25) and the following exposition of this verse in the Midrash Tanḥ (B) Noah XXI, p. 50—"'a slave of slaves may he be to his brethren' (Gen. 9:25). Said Resh Lakish: Thus from Ham emerge eternal slaves . . . as it is written there (Deut. 15:17) 'and he will be a slave to you forever.'" Although the present verse does not deal with a Canaanite slave but with a Hebrew slave who is an Israelite, nevertheless the expression—*'éb̲ed pălaḥ* "a working (or field) slave" is common to both; it also occurs in the Tg. I to Esther 2:3, for which see my critical edition of this text based on the ms. Paris Heb. 110 of the Bibliotheque Nationale—*The First Targum to Esther*. New York (Sepher-Hermon Press, Inc.) 1983, p. 14. Tg. Ps.-Jon., CTgA, and the Syr. render similarly.

[6]This translation agrees with the opinion of R. Aqiba expressed in the following Mekhilta (*ibid.* III, p. 257)—"R. Aqiba says: He may sell (her), but if he wants to keep her for his wife he may do so."

[7]The Hebrew has: "a foreign people," which the Tg. Neof. renders—"a gentile man" (*gbr br 'mmyn*), an interpretation reflected in the following Mekhilta (*ibid.* III, p. 257): "'To sell her unto a foreign people, he shall have no power' (Exod. 21:8). This is a warning to the court not to allow the father to sell her to a gentile." Tg. Onq., here paralleled by Tg. Ps.-Jon., however, does not appear to follow this Rabbinic tradition. In fact, by rendering "to another man," he does not differentiate between a Jew or non-Jew, an interpretation which, in fact, appears to be opposed to that of the *MRŠBY* (*Mišpāṭîm* XXI:8, p. 166)" . . . I would assume he may not sell her to others . . . Scripture therefore states: 'to a (foreign) people he may

daughters *of Israel.*[8] 10. If he were to take for himself another one, he should not deny her *food,*[9] her clothing, or her conjugal rights. 11. If, however, he does not render *these*[h] three <things> to her, then she is to depart free, without payment. 12. Whosoever strikes a *person*[i] *thereby killing him,*[j] *shall surely be put to death.*[10] 13. If he did not stake him out, but was delivered into his hand *from before*[11] the Lord, then I will designate a place for you whereto he should flee. 14. If, however, a man schemes against his fellowman to kill him by design, you shall take him *from*[k] My altar *to put<him> to death.*[12] 15. And he who strikes his father or his mother shall surely be put to death. 16. And he who steals a *person*[l] *of the Israelites*[13] and sells him, when he be found in his possession, shall surely be put to death. 17. And he who curses his father or his mother shall surely be put to death. 18. Now if men quarrel, and one of the men struck his fellow man with a stone or with a fist, and he did not die but fell into idleness. 19. If <eventually> he would rise and walk about outside upon his <own> *strength,*[14] then the one who struck <him> shall be acquitted; he must only compensate <him> for his idleness, as well as pay the doctor's fee. 20. And if a man should strike his servant or his maid with a rod who died as a result of his action, he shall surely be *punished.*[15] 21. But if he will *survive*[16] for a day or two days, he shall not be *punished*[15] since he is his <own> property. 22. Now if men, who were quarreling, strike a pregnant woman and she suffers a miscarriage but it does not result in *death*[17] <to her>, a fine shall surely be imposed according to the amount set for her by the woman's husband, and it shall be rendered *on the order of*[18] *the judges.*[19] 23. *But if a death did result*[17] <to her>, then a life shall be offered for a life. 24. An eye for any eye, a tooth for a tooth, a hand for a hand, a foot for a foot. 25. A burn for a burn, a wound for a wound, a bruise for a bruise. 26. And if a man were to strike the eye of his servant or the eye of his maid and destroy it, he shall liberate him as a free person for his eye. 27. But if he knocked out the tooth of his servant or the tooth of his maid, he should liberate him as a free person

Apparatus, Chapter 21 (Cont.)

[h] k has: "any of these."
[i] E has: "man."
[j] n has the literal: "and he dies."
[k] M and b add: "before."
[l] b, d, and g have: "man."

Notes, Chapter 21 (Cont.)

not sell her' (Exod. 21:8)." According to this tradition, the ban is only against selling her to gentiles but not against selling her to another Israelite. The commentaries on Onqelos, nevertheless, attempt to show that the translation in the Targum is in accord with Rabbinic exposition of this verse by pointing to b. Qidd. 18a-b, where, according to both R. Aqiba's and R. Eliezer's opinion, he (the father or the master) may not sell her again to anyone, gentile or Israelite. Consequently, B.Z.J. Berkowitz (*Simlat Ger* in *Leḥem Abirim, op. cit.*, p. 26f.), as well as S. Wertheimer (*Or Ha-Targum*. Jerusalem, 1935, p. 56), points out that the Tg. could not render the Hebrew literally—"another people" as the prohibition to sell her extended to an Israelite as well. B. Schmerler (*Ahavat Yehonatan*. Pieterkob, 1908, p. 134) cites Prov. 5:10 and Eccl. 6:2 as examples where the Hebrew *nok̠rî* refers simply to "a stranger" not necessarily a gentile, hence "another" here is to be understood as a literal rendering.

[8]This addition in the Targum, also present in Tg. Ps.-Jon. and Tg. Neof. m. is reflected in both Mekhiltas, which follow.

1. *Mekhilta* (*ibid.*, p. 258)—"'He shall deal with her after the manner of the daughters' (Exod. 21:9)... so also when espousing any free Israelite woman...."

for his tooth. 28. Now if an ox were to gore a man or a woman to death, the ox shall surely be stoned and its flesh may not be eaten, whereas the ox's owner shall be acquitted. 29. But if the ox had been a gorer since yesterday *and earlier,*[20] and its owner was warned but he did not guard it, and it, then, proceeded to kill a man or a woman, the ox shall be stoned, and the owner, too, *shall be put to death.*[21] 30. If <demand of> *payment*[22] was placed upon him, then he may offer redemption for his life, according

Notes, Chapter 21 (Cont.)

2. *MRŠBY* (*ibid.*, p. 167)—"'He shall deal with her after the manner of the daughters' (Exod. 21:9). Just as with the daughters of Israel one is obligated (to provide them) with their sustenance, so, too, this one, one is obligated (to provide her) with her sustenance."

[9]This interpretive rendering is in agreement with the following Mekhilta (*ibid.*, III, p. 258)—"The term *š'rh* (Exod. 21:10) means 'her food,'" the Midrash using the root *zwn*, as does the Targum.

[10]See Gen. Chap. 26, n. 6.

[11]See Gen. Chap. 4, n. 1.

[12]The Hebrew has: "to die" which is here interpretively rendered "to put to death" as well as in virtually all the Ancient Versions (except for the Vg. which is literal). This interpretation is also reflected in the Mekhilta (*ibid.*, IV, p. 263)—"'You shall take him from My altar, etc.' (Exod. 21:14). This tells us that we interrupt him in his service, and he is led out *to be executed.*" Cf. also Rabba bar bar Ḥanah in the name of R. Joḥanan's statement in b.Yoma 85a.

[13]This addition in the Targum, also present in Tg. Ps.-Jon. and in the LXX, is no doubt related to Deut. 24:7 where it appears in the Hebrew text. In fact, the LXX extends the relationship even further, by including here—"and prevails over him," occurring in the Deuteronomy passage.

[14]The Hebrew *mš'ntw* is here rendered identically to the way it is interpreted in the following Mekhilta (*ibid.*, VI, p. 270): "*'l mš'ntw* means upon his (own) strength," the Midrash employing *bwryw*, the same term used in the Targum.

[15]The Hebrew has lit. "avenged" which is a figure of speech and accordingly rendered into its intended meaning by the use of the root *dyn* "punish," the same root employed by Tg. Ps.-Jon. who adds "by sword" i.e., decapitation; Tg. Neof. uses the root *pr'* with the same meaning, while CTgA and the Frg. Tg. (P) have *qns* with the identical meaning; the Syr. (*dyn*) parallels Tgs. Onq. and Ps.-Jon. here. The Mekhilta (*ibid.*, VII, p. 273) contains R. Aqiba's opinion which is similar to that of the Targum.

[16]The Hebrew lit. "stand" is idiomatic and accordingly rendered interpretively by the root *qym* "to survive," which is similar to *q'm*, the Aramaic equivalent of Hebrew "stand" (*'md*).

[17]The Hebrew has: "misfortune" or "accident," which is here as well as in the Tg. Ps.-Jon. interpretively rendered to mean "death." This is in total agreement with the Mekhilta (*ibid.* VIII, p. 276)—"'But if a misfortune occur' (Exod. 21:23). 'Misfortune' here means only death."

[18]An insertion, also present in Tg. Ps.-Jon., Tg. Neof., CTgA and the Syr.—"as the judges determine," but implied in the Hebrew.

[19]This translation of Hebrew *pĕlilîm*, paralleled in Tgs. Ps.-Jon., Neof., CTgA, and the Syr. as well as in the Vg., is reflected in the Mekhilta (*ibid*) "'And he should pay according to *pĕlilîm*' (Exod. 21:22). And *pĕlilîm* only means *judges*, as in the passage: 'Even our enemies themselves being judges (*pĕlilîm*)' (Deut. 32:31)."

[20]See Gen. Chap 31, n. 3.

[21]The Targum is here in agreement with R. Aqiba's opinion expressed in the following Mekhilta (*ibid.* X, p. 285)—"R. Aqiba said 'the ox shall be stoned and the owner, too, shall be put to death' (Exod. 21:29); it compares the execution of the owner to the execution of the ox, just like the execution of the owner is through twenty-three (judges) so also the execution of the ox is through twenty-three (judges)."

[22]The Hebrew "ransom" (*kōp̱er*) is here interpretively rendered to mean "money," as well as in Tgs. Ps.-Jon., Neof. and the Syr., in agreement with the opinion of the Rabbis in their debate in the Talmud—b.B.Qam.40a—"the Rabbis consider *kōp̱er* to mean payment in money, whereas R. Ishmael b. Beraqa considers *kōp̱er* to mean propitiation."

to what was placed upon him. 31. Whether the ox gores *an Israelite*[23] male or *an Israelite*[23] female, according to this judgment shall it be done to it. 32. If the ox should gore a servant or a maid, he shall give to his master money <totaling> 30 *selas,*[24] whereas the ox is to be stoned. 33. Now if a man were to open a pit, or if a man were to dig a pit and not cover it, and an ox or a donkey were to fall into it, 34. The owner of the pit is to render compensation; he shall recompense money to its owner, and the dead <one> shall belong to him. 35. Now if the ox of a man were to gore the ox of his fellowman and it would die, then they should sell the live ox and divide its *money,*[m] and also divide *the value of*[25] the dead one. 36. If, however, it became known that the ox was a gorer since yesterday *and earlier*[20] and its owner did not guard it, he shall surely pay an ox for an ox and the dead <one> shall belong to him. 37. If a man should steal an ox or a lamb and slaughter it or sell it, he shall pay five oxen for the ox and four sheep for the lamb.

CHAPTER 22

1. If the thief should be discovered in <the act of> breaking in and is struck so that he dies, there is no bloodguilt case against him. 2. If *the eye of witnesses falls*[1] upon him there is a bloodguilt case against him; he shall surely render compensation; if he does not have <the means>, he should be sold for his theft. 3. If the theft was indeed

Apparatus, Chapter 21 (Cont.)

[m] n has: "worth."

Apparatus, Chapter 22

[a] b, d, g, and l have: "and sheaves or standing corn, or a field would be consumed," as does the Hebrew.

Notes, Chapter 21 (Cont.)

[23]This insertion also present in Tg. Ps.-Jon. and in a slightly longer form in Tg. Neof.—"a male Israelite son or a female Israelite daughter" may be a reflection of the following Rabbinic expositions of this clause:

1. *Mekhilta* (*ibid.* XI, p. 286f) "'Whether it gored a son or a daughter' (Exod. 21:31) ... I still would only know about Israelites. How about proselytes? It says: 'According to this judgment shall it be done unto him' (*ibid.*)."

2. *b. B. Qam.* 44a "'Whether it gored a son or a daughter' (Exod. 21:31) ... there is liability for killing *man or woman* and there is liability for killing son or daughter ... Moreover, the case of *man and woman since they are under obligations to observe the commandments* (of the Law). . . ."

[24]See Gen. Chap. 20, n. 11.

[25]This insertion, implied in the Hebrew, is also contained in Tg. Ps.-Jon. while the Frg. Tg. (P, V) and Tg. Neof. insert "the profit of." It occurs frequently in the halakhic discussions of the case presented in this verse for which cf. Mekhilta *ibid.*, pp. 12, 290; b. B. Qam.34a-b; *MRŠBY ibid.*, p. 188. It is in full agreement with the following Mishna—B. Qam. 1:4 according to which the owner of a one-time goring ox pays half the damage from (the animal) itself.

discovered in his possession, from ox to donkey to lamb, *they*[2] being alive, he shall make recompense two *for one.*[3] 4. If a man causes a field or a vineyard to *be damaged*[4] by letting his livestock go and *consume*[4] another's estate, he must make compensation from the best of his field or from the best of his vineyard. 5. If a fire should occur and find <its way to some> thorns, *and consume sheaves or standing corn or a field,*[a] he who started the fire shall surely make recompense. 6. If a man give money or goods to his fellowman for safekeeping and they be stolen from the man's house; if the thief be discovered, he should make recompense two for one. 7. If the thief could not be found, then the owner of the house should be brought before *the judges*[5] <to swear> that he

Notes, Chapter 22

[1]The Hebrew "if the sun has risen upon him" is a figure of speech meaning that the matter is as clear as the sun, which is here accordingly rendered "if the eye of witnesses falls upon him." Rashi on this verse explains this Targum as follows: "that if witnesses surprise him before the owner of the house appears, and when the owner of the house is going towards him they warn him not to kill him (the thief) then he is punishable if he kills him; for since there are people watching him the thief *surely* has no thought of taking human life and will not kill the owner of the property." Cf. also Mekhilta (*Mesek̲tā' Nĕzîkîm Mišpātîm* XIII, p. 293) and b. Sanh. 73a as well as y. Sanh. VIII:8, p. 26c, where this figure of speech is recognized as such but differently explained. The Targum here follows neither the explanation of R. Ishmael nor that of R. Eliezer b. Jacob as set forth in y. Ket. IV:4, p. 28c.

[2]An explanatory insertion supplying a subject implied in the concise Hebrew text.

[3]An addition, also present in Tg. Ps.-Jon. and the Syr., as well as in the Sam. Heb. and the Sam. Tg., to further clarify the concise Hebrew text.

[4]The Hebrew *yab̲'er* is here rendered in accordance with the halakhic interpretation of this word meaning "damage" as set forth in the following Mishna—m. B. Qam. 1:1 "The principal categories of damage are four: The ox, the pit, the spoilator (*mab̲'ēh*) and the fire." In the discussion of this Mishna, the Talmud (b. B. Qam.3b) asks: "What is meant by *mab̲'ēh*? . . .and Samuel said it denotes Tooth (trespassing cattle doing damage)." Earlier (*ibid.* 3a) the discussion revolved around the Biblical source for this contention—"The Master enunciated: 'and it shall *consume*' (Exod. 22:4) denotes Tooth." Cf. likewise Mekhilta (*ibid.* XIV, p. 296) as well as y. B. Qam. I:1, p. 1a. This interpretation applying to the term *yab̲'ēr* at the beginning of the verse as well as to *ub̲'iēr* "consume" further on, is also followed by Tg. Ps.-Jon., the Syr., the LXX, and the Vg. In contrast, Tg. Neof. (and the CTgA to a great extent) translates this passage "If a man sets fire to a field or a vineyard, and leaves the fire to spread, this causing fire in the field of another. . . ." According to this view, the terms *yab̲'ēr* and *ub̲'iēr* are derived from the root *b'r* which, according to the following verse and 35:3, means "to kindle a fire." This interpretation, however, is anti-Halakhic as the Mishna (m. B. Qam. I:1) enumerates "fire" separately. For a discussion of this reading in Tg. Neof. *vis-a-vis* the Halakha, cf. M. Kasher, *Torah Shelema* 18 (1958):182-185; A. Díez Macho, "The Recently Discovered Palestinian Targum: Its Antiquity and the Relationship with the Other Targums." *VT Supplement* 7 (1959): 222-245, esp. pp. 225f; J. Heinemann, "Targum *šĕmôt* 22:4 *wĕ-ha-hălākāh ha-qĕdûmāh.*" *Tarbiz* 38 (1969):294-296; and G. Schelbert, "Exodus 22:4 in palästinischen Targum." *VT* 8 (1958):253-263.

[5]The Hebrew *Elohim* is here, as in Exod. 21:6 above, rendered "judges," as well as in the Tg. Ps.-Jon., CTgA, and the Syr. and the following Rabbinic exposition:

Mekhilta (*ibid.* XIX, p. 317)—"R. Aqiba said the verse deals with judges."

b.Sanh. 3b—"Whence do we deduce that three are needed (for the composition of a court)? From what the Rabbis taught: It is written 'The master of the house shall come near to the *judge*' (Exod. 22:7) here you have one; and again: 'the cause of both parties shall come before the *judge*' (Exod. 22:8), here you have two; and again: 'whom the *judge* shall condemn' (*ibid.*) so you have three . . ." R. Jonathan, however, argues that the verse employed the popular term ('*Elohim*' for a recognized judge), even as the current saying goes: "Whoever has a trial let him go to the *dayyān* (an authoritative judge)." See also above Chap. 21, n. 4.

did not lay a hand *upon what his fellowman delivered to him.*[6] 8. In all matters of guilt concerning an ox, a donkey, a lamb, a garment, <or> any loss whereof one says, 'This is it,' the case of both shall be brought *before*[b] *the judges;*[5] he whom *the judges*[5] declare guilty, shall make recompense two *for one*[3] to his fellowman. 9. If a man were to give to his fellowman a donkey, or an ox, or a sheep, or any livestock to guard, and it died or is injured, or is carried off while no one saw <it>, 10. An oath before the Lord shall be <imposed> between both of them that the one did not lay a hand *on what his fellowman delivered to him.*[6] Then the owner should *accept*[7] *the oath from him*[8] and he should not have to pay. 11. If, however, it had indeed been stolen from him, he shall surely make recompense to its owner. 12. If it was indeed torn, he is to bring *witnesses*[c] <to that effect>, for what was torn he does not have to make recompense. 13. Now if a man borrows <an animal> from his fellowman and it is injured or dies, if the owner was not with it, he shall surely make recompense. 14. If its owner was with it, he does not have to make recompense; if it was hired, it <the loss> *is*[d] covered by the hiring fee. 15. If a man should seduce a virgin who is not engaged, and he should lie with her, he shall surely *keep*[9] her as his wife. 16. If her father was adamantly unwilling to give her to him, he is to weigh out for him the money as bride-price for virgins. 17. Do not permit a sorceress to live. 18. Whoever lies with a beast shall surely be put to death. 19. Whoever sacrifices *to the abominations of the nations*[10] *shall be put to death,*[11] except <who sacrifices> to *the name of*[12] the Lord, exclusively. 20. Now, an alien you shall not wrong nor *oppress,*[e] for you were sojourners in the land of Egypt. 21. Do not

Apparatus, Chapter 22 (Cont.)

[b] a has: "up to," the literal version of the Hebrew.
[c] l has the singular, as does the Hebrew.
[d] k has: "would be."
[e] b, d, g, add: "him," as does the Hebrew.
[f] c has the literal: "hear."
[g] b has the plural.
[h] n has: "ripe fruits," employing *mlyyk* from the same root as the Hebrew.
[i] E has: "by a wild animal."

Notes, Chapter 22 (Cont.)

[6]The Hebrew has: "on his fellowman's property." The Hebrew term *mĕléket,* construct of *mĕlā'kāh,* usually has the meaning "work of" for which cf. Exod. 35:21, 24, 33, 35; 36:1, 3, 4; Lev. 13:48; Num. 28:18; 2 Chr. 8:16. In the context of the present verse its connotation is entirely different, referring to the "merchandise" (Tg. Ps.-Jon.), or "acquisitions" (Tg. Neof., CTgA), or "goods" (Syr. and Vg.) or "deposit" (LXX) of his fellowman. Accordingly, the Targum paraphrases "what his fellowman delivered to him" in order to clearly define just precisely what this term connotes here.

[7]See Gen. Chap. 4, n. 8.

[8]An insertion implied in the Hebrew, in agreement with the Mekhilta (*ibid.* XVI, p. 304), b. *Šebu.* 45a and b. B. Qam. 106a, according to all of which all those who are required to take an oath do not have to pay.

[9]The Hebrew has "pay a dowry" which is here rendered interpretively by the Targum "keep" while virtually all the other Ancient Versions (LXX, Vg., Sam. Tg., the Frg. Tg. (V), Tg. Ps.-Jon., Tg. Neof., CTgA) translate literally; only the Syriac deviates by rendering "take." The word *mhr,* which basically means "exchange" especially the price for a bride, occurs only three other times—all in noun forms (Gen. 34:12; in the following verse; and 1 Sam. 18:25), where it is consistently rendered literally by the Targum, who employs the same root as the Hebrew. Its occurrence in the present verse is its only verbal occurrence, which, in conjunction with the closing phrase—"as a wife," was felt by the Targum to convey something more than just a literal meaning, hence the use of the root *qym*, a versatile root in Aramaic used by the Targum in connection with marriage in Exod. 21:8, 9 and Deut. 28:54, 56 below.

afflict any widow or orphan. 22. For if you indeed afflict him, then, as he will surely cry out to me, I will surely *listen*[13] to his outcry. 23. Then My anger will become strong and I will kill you by sword and your wives will become widows and your children orphans. 24. If you were to lend money to My people—to the poor one among you, do not act as a pressing creditor towards him nor place an interest upon him. 25. If you are taking the garment of your fellowman as a pledge, you should return it to him by sundown. 26. For it is his only garment, it is his covering for his skin; with what <else> should he sleep? Now it will be when he will cry out to me, that I will *listen*[13] *to his outcry;*[f] for I am compassionate. 27. Do not slight *a judge,*[g5] nor curse the leader of your people. 28. Do not delay your *first fruits*[h14] and the priest's share of your produce; *separate*[15] for Me the firstborn of your sons. 29. Accordingly you shall do to your cattle <and> to your sheep; seven days it may remain with its mother; on the eighth day *separate*[15] it for me. 30. And you shall be sacred people to Me; so you may not eat flesh *torn from a live animal;*[i16] you shall cast it to the dog(s).

Notes, Chapter 22 (Cont.)

[10]The Hebrew has: "to (any) god(s)." The translation in the Targum, also present in Tg. Ps.-Jon., presupposes a Hebrew text that reads "other gods," which, in its actual occurrences Deut. 7:4; 11:16; 13:7, 14; 17:3; 18:20; 29:35 is rendered "the abominations of the nations" by the Targum. In fact the LXX^{AL} does read "other gods," as does the Sam. Heb., the Sam. Tg., and Tg. Neof. Cf. Introduction VII A.3.

[11]The Hebrew has: "shall be utterly destroyed," employing the term *ḥrm*—"anathema." This verb is rendered definitely in Tg. Neof. "shall be exterminated," while the Syr. translates more generally—"shall perish" as does the Targum here—"shall be put to death," while Tg. Ps.-Jon. is more specific—"shall be put to death by the sword." The Vg. parallels the Targum *morte moriatur,* while the LXX elaborates with *θανάτω 'εξολοθρευθήσεται*—"shall be destroyed by death." Rabbinic tradition likewise interprets this verse to refer to the act of idolatry, for which cf. *MRŠBY* (*Mišpāṭîm* XXII, p. 210); Mekhilta (*ibid.* XVII, p. 310); b. 'Abod. Zar. 51a; b. Sanh. 60b, 61a; y. Sanh. VII:11, p. 25b. Cf. also Lev. 27:29.

[12]This insertion, also present in Tg. Ps.-Jon., is associated with the following Midrash which comments on the present verse: Sifre *Éqeḇ* XLIII, p. 98—"Others say: If Israel would not have combined *God's name* with that of idols they would have been destroyed from the world. Whereupon R. Simeon b. Gamaliel said: But surely he who combines *God's name* with that of idols is condemned to destruction, as it says: 'Whoever sacrifices to any god(s) shall be utterly destroyed, except to the Lord alone.'" Cf. further R. Simon b. Yoḥai's statement in b. Sanh. 63a. Furthermore, it serves as a buffer between man and God as does the particle *qdm*. Cf. Lev. Chap. 16, n. 4.

[13]Lit. "accept," for which see Gen. Chap. 16, n. 1.

[14]In translating the Hebrew *ml'h* as "first fruits," the Targum is in agreement with the following Mekhilta (*ibid.* XIX, p. 318)—"*ml'tk* (Exod. 22:28), these are the first fruits which are taken from the fullness."

[15]The Hebrew has: "give," which is here rendered by the technical term "separate," employed in Rabbinic literature for "first fruits" (***bikkûrîm***) and the "priest's share of the crop" (*terûmāh*) here referred to in vs. 28a and the "firstborn of man" (*beḵôr*) in vs. 28b, as well as the "firstborn of animals" mentioned in vs. 29. Hence the following Midrash—Exod. Rab. XXXI:8 "For this reason does it say 'You shall not delay to offer the fullness of your harvest, and of the outflow of your presses' (Exod. 22:28) to teach that you must not *separate* the tithes outside their prescribed order; you must not *separate* tithe and then *terumah,* nor the second tithe before the first tithe. Furthermore, Num. 18:8-32 enumerates various gifts due to the Levites, which are rendered in the Targum as contributions that are to be "separated" when offered to God, cf. vs. 26-29, 32 there. Cf. Yalq. Shim. #351, p. 606f., where "the fullness of your harvest" is equated with "first fruits," and "the outflow of your presses" with *terûmāh.*

[16]The Hebrew has: "torn by beasts in the field." The present reading in Vat. 448 "torn from a live animal," which is also the version of Sperber's main text, would, according to S.D. Luzzatto (*Ohev Ger,*

CHAPTER 23

1. Do not *listen to*[1] a *false*[2] report, nor put in your hand with the wicked man to be a *false*[3] witness. 2. Do not follow the multitude *to commit evil,*[4] *nor refrain from teaching <when you are being asked> what is your opinion*[a] *on a dispute,*[5] *the final decision is to follow the majority opinion.*[6] 3. *And do not show compassion*[7] for a poor man in his lawsuit. 4. If you should meet your enemy's ox or (his) donkey wandering about, you shall surely return it to him. 5. If you should see your enemy's donkey crouching under its burden and you would refrain from *lifting it for him*[b8] you must indeed abandon *what is <planned> in your heart for it and with him, remove <it>.*[9] 6. Do not pervert the judgment of your poor man in his lawsuit. 7. Keep your distance from *a false matter*[c] and do not put to death an innocent one, nor *one who had already been dismissed by you from the lawsuit,*[10] for I will not acquit the guilty one. 8. And do not *accept*[11] a bribe, for a bribe blinds *the eyes of*[d] the wise and corrupts the words of

Apparatus, Chapter 23

[a] Ra has: "being sought of you."

[b] U, b, v, and d₂ have: "abandoning it" which as a literal translation makes no sense, unlike later in this verse where the same root *šbq* is used in the Targum to render the same Hebrew root *'zb* but with the significant addition "what is in your heart," in order to make sense of the Hebrew root *'zb* here meaning "to help."

[c] n has: "vain matters." Cf. Exod. 20:7 where "false" in the Hebrew is rendered "vain" in the Targum (although a different Aramaic term is used there).

[d] b, c, and g omit as does MT, though it is present in 12 Hebrew mss., the Sam. Heb., the LXX, and the Syr., as well as in a similar verse—Deut. 16:19.

[e] G and M have the plural, which is an interpretive rendering.

Notes, Chapter 22 (Cont.)

op. cit., p. 53) refer to the prohibition of *'ēḇer min haḥaî* "eating the flesh torn off a live animal," which is, in his opinion, not what is involved here. He therefore adopts the reading "torn by a wild beast," which is listed in the Apparatus to this Chapter as being the version of E (l and n). According to this reading, the prohibition involved is *tĕrēp̄āh,* and the Targum would here be in agreement with the Mekhilta (*Mišpāṭîm Meseḵta deKaspā'* XX, p. 321): "...and so also here in interpreting: 'Therefore any flesh that is torn of beasts in the field' (Exod. 22:30), you say, Scripture, speaking of the usual case, mentions the place where animals are likely to be torn."

Notes, Chapter 23

[1]The Hebrew has: "raise" which is here interpretively rendered to mean "listen to" and is in agreement with the Mekhilta (*Mišpāṭîm Meseḵta deKaspā'* XX, p. 321—"'You shall not raise a false report' (Exod. 23:1). Behold, this is a warning to one who *listens to* the slanderous tongue."

[2]See above Chap. 20, n. 6.

[3]The Hebrew has: "unrighteous"—using the root *ḥms,* which in the following Midrash is depicted as an individual who testifies falsely:

Mekhilta (*ibid.*, p. 322) "...'nor put your hand with the wicked etc.' (Exod. 23:1) ... Suppose one is told by his teacher: You know that even if a man should give me all the money in the world I would not prevaricate. But so-and-so does owe me a *mannah* and I have only one witness. Come now and join him in testifying in my favor so that I may recover what is due me. It is against just such conduct that it is said: '...nor put your hand'... etc.—Such a one would be *an unrighteous witness."* Cf. Deut. 19:16 and the Tg. Neb. to Isa. 59:6 where *ḥms* is similarly rendered.

[4]The Hebrew has "for evil," which the Targum renders by the *aphel* of *byš* in an interpretive manner.

[5]The Hebrew has: "and do not give (perverse) testimony in a dispute." The translation of this part of the verse in the Targum is almost totally divergent from the Hebrew text. In this vein one may cite the

the upright. 9. And do not oppress the alien, for you understand the life of the alien, since you were sojourners in the land of Egypt. 10. Now six years you shall sow your land and gather in its produce. 11. But during the seventh <year> let it lie fallow and abandon it, so that the poor ones may eat <of it> and the *wild beast*[e] consume their

Notes, Chapter 23 (Cont.)

following Rabbinic opinion on the subject: t. Meg. IV:41 (also present in b. Qidd. 49a) "R. Judah said: If one translates a verse literally, he is a liar." Rashi in the Talmudic version of this statement cites the present verse as an example—the person would say, in Rashi's words: "I will omit the additions of our Targum (Onqelos) but will translate this verse literally into Aramaic (Exod. 23:2)—'do not give (perverse) testimony in a dispute,' he is a liar." Whether this was the reason for the Targum's widely divergent translation is open to speculation. However, the particular translation itself—"nor refrain from teaching what is your opinion on a dispute"—may be related to the following Rabbinic exposition of this verse: t. Sanh. III:8—"Another explanation for 'do not give (perverse) testimony in a dispute by inclining ...' (Exod. 23:2). Scripture adds one more to them 'to incline after the majority to err—i.e., do not say at the time of the decision: It is sufficient that I see (it) like my teacher; but *rather say what is on your mind.*" The last clause is similar to the Targum's "nor refrain from teaching what is your opinion."

[6]The Hebrew has: "to incline after the majority to err." If the phrase "to incline" is routed with the preceding clause as many understood it, that would leave the clause—"follow the majority to err" to stand on its own. This might cause a misunderstanding as the following Midrash illustates:

Lev. Rab. IV:6, p. 92—"Rabbi Elaʿaša said: "A gentile asked R. Joshua b. Qorḥāh: "It is written in your Law 'follow the majority to err' (Exod. 23:2). Now we are more numerous than you, why then do you not become like us with regards to idolatry?'"

[7]The Hebrew "and do not favor (lit. adorn)" is figurative, and accordingly rendered interpretively.

[8]The Hebrew "from helping him" employs the root *ʿzb* here with the less common meaning of "to help" (the common meaning is "to abandon"). This situation misled the Targum to translate here interpretively by using the Eastern Aramaic *šql*—"to lift up" (that is precisely what the Syr. uses here). In fact, as can be seen from a number of manuscripts in the apparatus (see note *b* there), he even erroneously employed the root *šbq* "abandon," used regularly for *ʿzb* when the latter has that meaning in the Hebrew. The Targum continued with this misconception by rendering *mšbq tšbwq* for *ʿzb tʿzwb* at the end of this verse, which in turn led him to insert "what is planned in your heart for it," in order to make sense out of that part of the verse. Saadiah Gaon in his translation and commentary takes the first *ʿzb* in this verse to denote "abandon," while the second *ʿzb* he renders "help," accordingly, the meaning is "you should cease from *abandoning* him; rather *help* him." The Syr. uses the root *šql*—"lift up" throughout; accordingly the meaning would be "should you refrain from (helping) him lift it up, you shall surely (help) him lift it up." The Tg. Ps.-Jon. has "from *approaching* him" (using the root *qrb*) for the first *ʿzb,* while Tg. Neof. has "from (helping) him unloosen it" (using *prq*), whereas for the last two *ʿzb* occurrences, both these Pal. Tgs. like Tg. Onq. employ the root *šbq* adding "what is in your heart" (Tg. Neof.) or "the hatred in your heart" (Tg. Ps.-Jon.).

[9]See preceding note.

[10]The Hebrew has: "a righteous one." This paraphrase in the Targum is in complete agreement with the second case enumerated in the following Midrash:

Mekhilta (*ibid.,* p. 237)—"'And the innocent and righteous you shall not put to death' (Exod. 23:7).

1. Suppose one emerges from court declared guilty, but after a while they find evidence of his innocence. I might think that he should still be considered guilty. But it says 'the innocent you shall not put to death.' Has he come out from My court the same as he came out from your court? It is to teach you this that Scripture says: 'For I will not justify the wicked' (*ibid*)."
2. 'And the righteous you shall not put to death' (*ibid.*). Suppose *one emerges from court acquitted,* and after a while they find evidence of his guilt. I might think that they shall bring him back for a new trial. But it says: 'and the righteous you shall not put to death.'" Cf. also b. Sanh. 33b.

The Tg. Ps.-Jon. in his translation of Hebrew "the innocent" translates it according to the second case, and "the righteous" he renders by the first case.

[11]See Gen. Chap. 4, n. 8.

remainder, so you shall act towards your vineyard and (your) olive grove. 12. Six days you should perform your work but on the seventh day you shall rest, so that your ox and (your) donkey may rest, as well as the son of your maid, and the alien may rest. 13. Now beware of everything I have said to you; and do not mention the name of *the abominations of the nations,*[12] nor shall <it> be heard on your mouth. 14. Three times a year you shall celebrate a festival to me. 15. Observe the Festival of Unleavened Bread; seven days you shall eat unleavened bread as I commanded you, at the time of the month of Abib, for in it you departed from Egypt, so you shall not appear before Me empty-handed. 16. And the Festival of the Harvest of the firstfruits of your labor, of that which you sow in the field; and the Festival of Ingathering at the end of the year when you gather in <the results of> your labor from the field. 17. Three times a year all your males should appear before the Master of *the Universe,*[13] the Lord. 18. Do not offer the blood of My *Passover sacrifice*[14] with anything leavened; neither shall the fat of *the*[15] sacrifice be left overnight *away from the altar*[16] till morning. 19. The earliest of the firstfruit of your land you should bring to the *Temple*[17] of the Lord your God; *do not consume meat with milk.*[18] 20. Here I am about to send an angel ahead of you to guard you on the road, and to bring you to the place that I have prepared. 21. Beware of him and *listen*[19] *to his Memra,*[20] *do not refuse to listen to him,*[21] for he will not forgive your sins, because *his Memra is in My Name.*[22] 22. For if you will indeed *listen*[19] *to his Memra*[20] and do all that I say, then I will oppose those who oppose you

Notes, Chapter 23 (Cont.)

[12]See Introduction VII A.3.

[13]The Targum expands the Hebrew "Master" into "Master of the Universe," an epithet of God commonly used in Rabbinic literature, for which cf. b. Ber. 9b—*ribbônô šel 'ôlām*—"Lord of the Universe" and b. Yoma 87b *ribbôn hā'ôlāmîm.*

[14]The Hebrew has "sacrifice" which is here identified as the "Passover sacrifice" in agreement with the following Mekhilta (*ibid.,* p. 334)—"'You shall not offer the blood of My sacrifice with leavened bread' (Exod. 23:18). You shall not slaughter the *paschal lamb,* while the leavened bread is still there." Cf. also y. Pes. V:4, p. 32b "Whence do we know that one who slaughters the paschal lamb with leavened bread around, that he transgresses a negative commandment, it says 'do not offer the blood of my sacrifice with leavened bread' (Exod. 23:18)." The Tg. Ps.-Jon. also makes this identification.

[15]The Hebrew has "My" which is here rendered simply "the (sacrifice)." This translation is undoubtedly related to the Rabbinic interpretation of the Biblical word *ḥaggî* as referring to the *ḥagîgāh*—the festive offering of the visitors of the Temple on the three Pilgrimage Festivals, for which cf. b. Pes. 71a—"R. Kahana said: How do we know that the *'ēmûrîm* of the *ḥagîgāh* of the fifteenth are disqualified through being kept overnight? Because it is said: 'neither shall the fat of My feast (*ḥaggî*) remain all night until morning."

[16]This addition alludes to the law outlined in the Midrash concerning the overnight whereabouts of the sacrifice fat: Mekhilta (*ibid.,* p. 334f) "'Neither shall the fat of My sacrifice remain all night until morning' (Exod. 23:18). This passage comes to teach that the pieces of fat become unfit for use by being kept overnight on the pavement of the Temple floor . . . One might think that the limbs should become unfit for use even by being kept overnight upon the pile of wood on the altar. But Scripture says: 'On its firewood upon the altar all night unto the morning' (Lev. 6:2), declaring that they may be kept upon the pile of wood on the altar." Tg. Ps.-Jon. also contains this addition.

[17]The Hebrew "house" is identified as the Temple, in agreement with the following Rabbinic texts which make this identification:

1. *m. Bik.* I:9 "When do we learn that a man is answerable for them (the "firstfruits") until they are brought to the *Temple Mount?* Because it is written 'the first of the fruits of your land you shall bring into the house of the Lord your God' (Exod. 23:19), which teaches that a man is answerable

and oppress those who oppress you. 23. When My angel will go ahead of you and bring you to the Amorites, and the Hittites, and the Perizzites, and the Canaanites, and the Hivites, and the Jebusites, I will annihilate them. 24. Do not bow down *to their abominations*[12] nor worship them, nor do as they do, but utterly destroy them and

Notes, Chapter 23 (Cont.)

for them until they are brought to the *Temple Mount.*"

2. *t. Šeqal.* III:24 "Why did they say that (the law of) the firstfruits was not observed before the time of the Temple, because it says 'the first of the fruits of your land you shall bring into the house of the Lord' (Exod. 23:19). As long as you have a Temple you have (the law of) the firstfruits; if you have no Temple, you have no (law of the) firstfruits.

3. *m. Šeqal.* VIII:8 "(The laws of) the shekels and of the firstfruits have force only during the time of the existence of the Temple."

4. *y. Peah* V:5, p. 19a "Said R. Isaac: 'that you should bring the poor that are afflicted to (your) house' (Isa. 58:7). Said R. Abin: If you did this, I will consider it for you as if you had brought the firstfruits to the Temple, since it says here (Isa. 58:7) 'you will bring' and it says further on (Exod. 23:19) 'you should bring the firstfruits into the house of the Lord your God.'"

[18]The Hebrew: "do not boil a kid in its mother's milk" is here translated in accordance with the Halakha prohibiting the consumption of meat with milk. The following are the relevant Rabbinic sources:

b. Ḥul. 115b "The school of R. Ishmael taught: 'You shall not boil a kid in its mother's milk' is stated three times (Exod. 23:19; 34:26; Deut. 14:21); one is a prohibition against eating it, one is a prohibition against deriving benefit from it, and one a prohibition against cooking it." Cf. also *MRŠBY* (*Kî Tissā'* XXXIV:26, p. 224); and t. Mak. IV(III):7. Tgs. Neof. and Ps.-Jon. as well as the Frg. Tg. (P) elaborate here as follows:

"... My people, O House of Israel (Frg. Tg.) [Children of Israel (Neof. and Ps.-Jon.)] You shall not boil nor eat meat and milk with both of them (Frg. Tg.) mixed together."

Targum Onqelos, who renders "do not consume meat with milk" unqualifyingly, appears to be in agreement with the Mishna in Ḥul. (VIII:1) which states "*every* (type of) meat is forbidden to cook with milk," and although R. Aqiba explains this Mishna to exclude the meat of fowl and wild beast, he still considers these two types forbidden, if not by the Torah, then by the Rabbis. Thus, according to Berliner (*Targum Onkelos: Einleitung* ..., *op. cit.*, p. 234f.) the Targum could very well be in agreement with R. Aqiba's opinion by stating the matter unqualifyingly, without making any distinction as to what type of meat is meant by Scripture. As far as stating only the eating prohibition (here, as well as in Exod. 34:26 and Deut. 14:21) as opposed to the ruling in b. Ḥul. 115b cited above, according to which boiling and deriving benefit is forbidden as well, and m. Ḥul. VIII:1, and 4, which also forbids boiling and deriving benefit from such a mixture. Berliner (*op. cit., loc. cit.*) points out that perhaps the Targum desired to employ an act of ("eating") which is forbidden in all cases, whereas the acts of "boiling" and "deriving benefit" are permitted in certain cases as with fowl and wild beast or ritually unclean animals (b. Ḥul. 113a). Alternately, he suggests that in mentioning only the ban on the act of "eating," Onqelos wanted to accentuate the tradition which was well-known to all Jewish communities, whereas the ban against cooking and deriving benefit was not as widespread among Jews. S. Singer (*Onkelos und das Verhältniss seines Targums zur Halacha.* Berlin, 1881, p. 58) offers, in my opinion, a simple solution to this problem by reasoning that one normally cooks something which is otherwise permitted to be eaten or to be used. Thus it was not necessary to state the other two prohibitions.

[19]See Gen. 16, n. 1.

[20]See Introduction VII D. 1.

[21]The Hebrew has "do not defy him" which is interpretively rendered, specifying what defying involves.

[22]The Hebrew has "for My Name is in him." The Targum reverses the sense of the Hebrew—instead of God's name being in the angel, the latter's Memra is in God's name. This reversal avoids any misconception as to God's superiority over the angels, which the Hebrew could conceivably convey. Tg. Ps.-Jon. likewise contains this rendering, while Tg. Neof. has "My sacred name will be invoked upon him" and Neof.m—"the name of My Memra is upon him."

thoroughly smash their monuments. 25. Rather you should worship *before*[f23] the Lord your God; then He will bless your food and your *drink*[g24] and I will remove grievous sicknesses from your midst. 26. There will not be a childless or barren woman in your land; I will complete the number of your days. 27. I will send My terror ahead of you and I will *smash*[h] every nation against whom you will come to *fight,*[i25] and I will deliver all your enemies to you as *runaways.*[26] 28. Then I will send the hornet ahead of you and it will drive out ahead of you the Hivites, the Canaanites, and the Hittites. 29. I will not drive *them*[j] out ahead of you in one year, lest the land become desolate and the *wild beast*[k] will outnumber you. 30. Little by little I will drive *them*[j] out ahead of you, until you will *increase*[l27] and will take possession of the land. 31. Then I will establish your border(s) from the Red Sea to the Sea of the Philistines, and from the wilderness to the *Euphrates;*[m] for I will *deliver*[n] the inhabitants of the land into your power, and *you*[o] will drive them out before you. 32. Do not establish a covenant with them *or with their abominations.*[12] 33. They shall not live in your land, lest they will cause you to sin towards Me, for you will worship *their abominations*[12] since they will be a snare to you."

CHAPTER 24

1. Now to Moses He said, "Come up *before*[a1] the Lord, you and Aaron, Nadab and Abihu and seventy of the elders of Israel and bow down from a distance. 2. Then Moses alone should approach to the Lord, but they should not approach; whereas the people should come up with him." 3. So Moses came and related to the people all the words of the Lord and all the laws. Then the people replied *in one voice*[b] and said, "{According to} all the words which the Lord has said we shall do." 4. Then Moses wrote down all the words of the Lord and arose early in the morning and built an altar at the foot of the mountain, as well as twelve *monuments*[c] for the twelve tribes of Israel. 5. And he sent the *firstborn*[2] of the Israelites and they offered burnt offerings,

Apparatus, Chapter 23 (Cont.)

[f] v and c omit, having the direct accusative *yt* instead.
[g] R, U, c and v have the plural, as the Hebrew has the plural—"waters."
[h] J, b, d_2, g and Ra have: "throw into panic," as does the Hebrew, while l has: "kill."
[i] v_b, i, b, and g have: "to wage war."
[j] n has the singular third person pronoun here, as does the Hebrew.
[k] b, d, g, and M have the plural. Cf. note e above.
[l] E, b, and d_2 have: "multiply."
[m] g adds: "river."
[n] l, as do 16 Hebrew mss., adds: "all."
[o] n has the first person singular, as do the Sam. Heb., the LXX, and the Vg.

Apparatus, Chapter 24

[a] a has: "before the Memra of."
[b] n has: "as one" which is interpretive.
[c] E and v have the singular, as does the Hebrew.
[d] i omits "here," while b, d, v, B, and D omit "this," as does the Hebrew.

sacrificed *sanctified offerings*[3] {in the form of} bulls *before*[1] the Lord. 6. Then Moses took half the blood and placed it in the bowls, and half the blood he sprinkled on the altar. 7. And he took the book of the covenant and recited <it> *before*[1] the people, whereupon they said, "Everything the Lord has said we will do and *accept*."[4] 8. Whereupon Moses took the blood and sprinkled it *on the altar to atone for the people*,[5] and he said, "*Here, this*[d] is the blood of the covenant which the Lord has

Notes, Chapter 23 (Cont.)

[23]See Gen. Chap. 4, n. 1.

[24]The Hebrew has "waters" which is figurative and accordingly rendered into its intended meaning. Tg. Ps.-Jon. is identical to Onq. here, while the LXX has *καὶ τὸν οἶνόν σου καὶ τὸ ὕδωρ σου*—"and your *wine* and your water."

[25]This is an insertion implied in the concise Hebrew text, also present in Tg. Ps.-Jon.

[26]Lit. those who turn their backs.

[27]See Gen. Chap. 1, n. 9.

Notes, Chapter 24

[1]See Gen. Chap. 4, n. 1.

[2]The Hebrew has: "young men" which is translated literally by Tg. Neof., the Syr., the LXX and the Vg. The Targum's rendering—"firstborn," also in Tg. Ps.-Jon., is reflected in the following Rabbinic texts:

1. *MRŠBY* (*Mišpāṭîm* XXIII:5, p. 220) "'And he sent the young men of the Israelites' (Exod. 24:5)— these are the firstborn."
2. *Num. Rab.* IV:8 "... Likewise at the time that Moses made offerings at Sinai, the firstborn were the ones who made offerings (too), as it says: 'and he sent the young men of Israel' (Exod. 24:5). Who were 'the young men'— the young ones among the firstborn. 'And they offered up burnt offerings'—this teaches you, that no one except the firstborn made offerings." Thus the Mishna (m. Zeb. XIV:4) "Before the Sanctuary was erected, the worship service was performed by the firstborn." Cf. also b. Zeb. 112b.

Cf. also b. Zeb. 115b. There also is the extant tradition that a reading of *za'ăṭûṭe*—"the elect of" once existed in place of the Hebrew *na'ărē*—"the young men of" for which cf. b. Meg. 9a and Sop. VI:4.

[3]See above Chap. 10, n. 11.

[4]See Gen. Chap. 16, n. 1. Interestingly, the LXX also circumvents the problem of seeing God by rendering—*καὶ εἶδον τὸν τόπον οὗ εἱστήκει ὁ θεὸς τοῦ Ἰσραήλ*—"they saw the place where the God of Israel stood."

[5]The Hebrew has "on the people," which is interpretively rendered by the Targum, as well as by Tg. Ps.-Jon., according to which Moses did not actually sprinkle the blood "on the people" but "on the altar on behalf of the people." This interpretation is reflected in only one other source—the following Midrash:

Mekhilta to Deuteronomy in *Midrash Tannaim on the Book of Deuteronomy*, ed. D. H. Hoffmann (Berlin, 1908-09; recent Israeli rep., place and date of publication not given, p. 57; also in M. Kasher's *Torah Shelema* XIX, p. 256) "'and Moses took the blood and sprinkled it on the people' (Exod. 24:8)—on the altar on behalf of the people. You say—on the altar on behalf of the people, or is it—on the people, literally? Therefore it says: 'a continual burnt offering throughout your generations' (Exod. 29:42), 'a continual burnt offering which was ordained on Mt. Sinai' (Num. 28:6), it compares the burnt offerings of Mt. Sinai to the burnt offerings of (future) generations, just as the burnt offerings of (future) generations require libations so do the burnt offerings of Mt. Sinai require libations. R. Aqiba says: It compared the burnt offerings of Mt. Sinai to the burnt offerings of (future) generations just as the burnt offerings of Mt. Sinai, (all of it was) on the altar, so also the burnt offerings of (future) generations, (all of it was) on the altar." It is in R. Aqiba's statement that the proof is sought concerning the sprinkling of the blood to be on the altar rather than on the people, as all of the libations were made

established with you in accordance with all these words." 9. Then Moses and Aaron, Nadab and Abihu, as well as the seventy of the elders of Israel went up, 10. and they perceived *the Glory of*[6] the God of Israel and beneath *the throne of His Glory*[7] <was something> like the work of *a precious stone*[8] *and in appearance like the sky*[9] for purity. 11. Yet *the leaders of*[10] the Israelites *were not injured*[11] even though they perceived *the Glory of*[6] the Lord; *and they rejoiced in their sacrifices which were accepted*[e] *as though they were eating and drinking.*[12] 12. Then the Lord said to Moses, "Come up *before*[1] me to the mountain and remain there, and I will give you the tablets of *stone*[f] and the Law and the commandment(s) which I have written for their instruction." 13. So Moses and Joshua his attendant proceeded to ascend the mountain *upon which the Glory of the Lord was revealed.*[13] 14. Now to the elders he said, "Wait here for us till we return to you, and here Aaron and Hur are with you; whoever has a legal matter, let him approach them." 15. When Moses ascended the mountain, a cloud covered the mountain. 16. Now the Glory of the Lord settled on Mount Sinai and the

Apparatus, Chapter 24 (Cont.)

[e] S and v add "with pleasure."
[f] v and k have the plural.
[g] U, b, and d_2 add: "the sight of."

Notes, Chapter 24 (Cont.)

on the altar with the burnt offerings on Mt. Sinai. See further the remarks of A. Díez Macho on this problem in his *Neophyti I*: Exodus. Madrid-Barcelona (Consejo Superior De Investigaciones Cientificas), 1970, p. 479, n. 3.

[6]See Introduction VII D.2 for this insertion as man cannot see God, for which cf. Exod. 33:18 and 20.

[7]The Hebrew has: "His feet." The Targum circumvents this anthropomorphism by rendering "throne of His Glory," which Maimonides points out (cf. *Maimonides' Guide for the Perplexed,* translated by M. Friedländer. New York [Pardes Publishing House, Inc.] 1904, p. 37) shows how the Targum "keeps free from the corporeality of God, and everything that leads thereto, even in the remotest degree," since he does not translate "under His throne" which could suggest the idea that God is supported by a material object, and consequently lead to a misconception involving the corporeality of God; he rather refers the throne to God's Glory. The selection of throne as a translation for foot may be related to Isa. 66:1—"the heaven is My throne, the earth My footstool." As B.Z.J. Berkowitz (*Ḥalifot Semalot, op. cit.,* p. 71) points out, just as in the Isaiah passage throne and footstool are in parallelism, likewise in the present verse "earth" which in Isaiah is symbolized by "footstool" is then contrasted by "heaven" at the end of this verse. Of the Pal. Tgs., only Tg. Ps.-Jon. mentions "throne," yet even this Targum as well as the Frg. Tg. (P and V) and Tg. Neof., circumvents the Hebrew anthropomorphism "His feet" by inserting "footstool" hence producing "the footstool of his feet" (after which Tg. Ps.-Jon. adds "spread out under His throne").

[8]The Hebrew has: "a pavement of sapphire" which all the Pal. Tgs. render literally, as do the Syr., the LXX, the Vg., and the Sam. Tg. Tg. Onq.'s nonliteral rendering—"a precious stone" is explained by N. Adler (*Netina La-Ger, op. cit.,* on this verse) as an attempt to tone down any form of materialization, concreteness, or tangeability implied in the image transmitted by "a pavement of sapphire," as in Exod. 28:18; 39:11, the Targum renders Hebrew "sapphire" as *šabzíz.* Onqelos' rendering here is paralleled in the Tg. Neb. to Ezek. 1:26; and 10:1 where Hebrew "sapphire stone" is rendered "precious stone." Adler's view is disputed by S.B. Schefftel (*Bi'ure Onqelos, op. cit.,* p. 104) who points to Isa. 54:11 where "sapphires" is rendered "precious stones" by the Tg. Neb. although there

cloud covered it {for} six days; then He summoned Moses on the seventh day from the midst of the cloud. 17. And the perception of the Glory of the Lord was *like*[g] a consuming fire on the top of the mountain in the sight of the Israelites. 18. Then Moses entered into the midst of the cloud and ascended the mountain; and Moses was on the mountain {for} forty days and forty nights.

Notes, Chapter 24 (Cont.)

no materialization of God is involved. He, therefore, offers the opinion that in Hebrew the word "sapphire" generally denotes "precious stones" of all kinds and not specifically that particular gem, except for Exod. 28:18; 39:11 where it refers specifically to it.

[9]The Hebrew has: "like the essence of the sky." Here the word "essence" = Hebrew *'ĕṣem*, is used idiomatically, as it is in the common expression "on that very day" (for which cf. Gen. 7:13; 17:23, 26; Exod. 12:17, 41, 51; Lev. 23:21, 28, 29, 30; Deut. 32:48; Josh. 5:11; Ezek. 24:2; 40:1), accordingly the Targum paraphrases. Furthermore, the translation in the Targum somewhat tones down the Hebrew simile and parallels the thought of the following Midrash—*MRŠBY, ibid.*, p. 221: "'like the essence of,' the sky for purity' (Exod. 24:10). I would think precisely like it, it therefore says: 'like the essence of,' this teaches that the ear was made to hear only what it can hear (perceive)."

[10]The Hebrew has *'ăṣîlē*, an obscure term, which the Tg. Neof. and Frg. Tg. (P) render "the youths," while Tg. Ps.-Jon. identifies them as "Nadab and Abihu, the beautiful youths," in contrast to the Syr. which has "elders," the LXX, "the chosen ones" and the Vg., "the ones of." Only the LXX reading is reflected in Rabbinic literature as can be seen from the following story in the Talmud which details the origin of the first Greek translation of the Torah: "It is related of King Ptolemy who brought 72 elders and placed them in 72 (separate) rooms . . . he went to each one of them and said to him: Translate for me the Torah of Moses your master. God then prompted each one of them and they all conceived the same idea and wrote for him . . . 'And he sent *the elect* of the Israelites' (Exod. 24:5); 'And against *the elect* of the Israelites He did not put forth His hand' (Exod. 24:11) . . . ."

The Talmud renders both *na'ărê* (vs. 5) and *'aṣîlê* (vs. 11) by *za'ăṭûṭê* "the elect," for which cf. n. 2 above, while Meturgeman (s.v. *z'ṭṭ*) cites a Jerusalem Targum that has *za'ăṭûṭê* in the present verse. Cf. further M. Goshen-Gottstein, *Fragments of Lost Targumim* (in Hebrew) Part I. Ramat Gan (Bar Ilan University Press), 1983, p. 64, #208, and S. Talmon, "The Three Scrolls of the Law that were Found in the Temple Court" (in Hebrew). *Studies in the Bible: Presented to Professor M. H. Segal*, ed. J.M. Grintz, and J. Liver. Jerusalem (Kiryath Sepher Ltd.), 1964, pp. 56f. and 262f.

[11]The Hebrew has the anthropomorphic "He did not put forth His hand," which the Targum circumvents by "were not injured"—the *result* of the *act*—"did not put forth." The Frg. Tg. (P) and Tg. Neof., oddly enough, are literal here, while Tg. Ps.-Jon. paraphrases—"He did not send His plague."

[12]The Hebrew has: "and they ate and drank." The Targum here elaborates on their rejoicing in their sacrifices because they were (willingly) accepted by God, an addition also present in the Frg. Tg. (P) and Tgs. Neof. and Ps.-Jon. This addition does not appear to have any parallels in Rabbinic sources. B.Z.J. Berkowitz (*Simlat Ger, op. cit.*, p. 52) offers the following interesting explanation—the statement in the preceding verse "they saw the God of Israel" refers to God's Glory (as the Targum renders it) descending from heaven in the form of a fire and consuming all of the sacrifices that they offered (which were, according to vs. 5 above, burnt offerings and peace offerings), in the same manner as with Elijah (1 Kgs. 18:39) when a fire descended from God and consumed the burnt sacrifice, as well as other things. This was a sign to them that God had accepted their sacrifices, as a result of which they began to rejoice by eating and drinking, only here, as a result of having perceived the Glory of God, they were in a sense like angels concerning whom it is stated in the Tg. Neof. (to Gen. 18:18) "it seemed as if they were eating and drinking," hence the Targum renders "as though they were eating and drinking." Löwenstein (*Nefesh Ha-Ger, op. cit.*, p. 69) however observes that the sign from heaven that their sacrifices were accepted was the very fact that they did not die as a punishment for looking at God.

[13]See above Chap. 3, n. 4.

CHAPTER 25

1. Then the Lord said to Moses as follows, 2. "Speak *with*[a] the Israelites that they *set apart*[1] an offering for Me; you should accept the offering for Me from every man whose heart is willing. 3. This is the {type of} offering you should accept from them: gold, (and) silver, and copper. 4. Blue, (and) purple, (and) scarlet yarn, (and) fine linen, and goats' hair. 5. And red rams' skins, as well as scarlet skins, and acacia wood. 6. Oil for lighting, aromatics for the anointing oil and for the aromatic incense. 7. Beryl stones and setting stones for *insertion into*[2] the ephod and (into) the breastplate. 8. Then let them make *before*[3] Me a sanctuary *and I will let My presence rest*[4] among them. 9. According to all that I show you, the design of the sanctuary and the design of all its vessels, so you should do. 10. Now they should make an ark of acacia wood, its length two and a half cubits, and one and a half cubits its width, and one and a half cubits its height. 11. Then you should overlay it <with> pure gold; inside and outside should you overlay it, and make *upon*[b] it a golden molding all around. 12. Then cast for it four golden rings and place <them> on its four joints, two rings on one of its sides and two rings on the other side. 13. And you should make poles of acacia wood and overlay them <with> gold. 14. Then you should insert the poles into the rings on the sides of the ark, to carry the ark through them. 15. The poles should be in the rings of the ark; they are not to be removed from it. 16. Then you should deposit in the ark the Testimony which I will give you. 17. And you should make a cover of pure gold; its length is <to be> two and a half cubits, and its width a cubit and a half. 18. Then you should make two cherubs of gold; you should make them *extended*[5] from the two sides of the cover. 19. Make one cherub from one side and one cherub from the other side; <extending> from the cover you should make the cherubs, from its two sides. 20. Now the cherubs should have their wings spread upwards, overshadowing the cover with their wings, while their faces should be opposite each other in the direction of the cover; <thus> should be the faces of the cherubs. 21. Then place the cover on top of the ark, and into the ark deposit the Testimony which I shall give to you. 22. *And I will appoint My Memra*[6] {to be} there for you, and I will discuss with you from above the cover from between the two cherubs which are on top of the Ark of Testimony, all that I shall command you for the Israelites. 23. Then make a table of acacia wood, two cubits {in} its length, a cubit {in} its width, and one and a half cubits {in} its height. 24. And overlay it <with> pure gold and make *for it*[c] a golden molding all around. 25. And make for it a rim, a handbreadth *in height*[7] all around, and make a golden molding for its rim all around. 26. Then make for it four golden rings, and place the rings on the

Apparatus, Chapter 25

[a] b has: "to."

[b] i_a and l have: "for," as do 6 Hebrew mss., the Sam. Heb., the LXX, and the Syr.

[c] s omits.

four joints of its four legs. 27. Opposite the rim should the rings be, *as a place*[8] for the poles to carry the table. 28. Then make poles of acacia wood and overlay them <with> gold, so that they could carry the table with them. 29. And you should make its trays, and its dishes, and its libation bowls, and its jugs with which libations are poured; of pure gold you should make them. 30. Then place the display bread on the table {to be} before Me constantly. 31. And you should make a lampstand of pure gold; you should make its base, (and) its shaft, its cups, its calyxes, and its lilies *extended*[5] from the lampstand; they should be {extensions} of it. 32. Now six branches are to extend from its sides, three branches of the lampstand from its one side, and three branches of the lampstand from its other side. 33. Three cups should be embroidered on one branch with a calyx and a lily and three cups should be embroidered on another branch with a calyx and a lily, accordingly for each of the six branches that extended from the lampstand. 34. Now on the lampstand <were to be> embroidered four cups with a calyx and a lily. 35. And a calyx beneath two branches <extending> from it, and a calyx beneath two branches <extending> from it, and a calyx beneath two branches <extending> from it; for the six branches that extended from the lampstand. 36. Their calyxes and their branches should <extend> from it, all of it beaten <from> one piece of pure gold. 37. Then make seven lamps and light the lamps that they illuminate its face. 38. And its tongs and its pans <are to be> of pure gold. 39. Make it and all these vessels from a talent of pure gold. 40. Observe and make <them> according to their design, which you were shown on the mountain.

Notes, Chapter 25

[1]The Hebrew "take" is here rendered by the tenchical term "separate" employed in Rabbinic literature for the act of giving *tĕrûmāh*, as in Exod. 22:28, 29 where it is also used to translate Hebrew "give" with regards to the various shares of the crop due to the priest, for which cf. there n. 12. The Syr. and Tg. Neof. are identical here, while Tg. Ps.-Jon. is literal.

[2]An addition implied in the Hebrew, but no doubt borrowed from Exod. 28:11; 39:13 where it renders the explicit Hebrew *mûsabboṯ* ("inserted"). Tgs. Neof. and Ps.-Jon. render identically, but use the root *qb'*, in contrast to *šq'* of the Targum.

[3]See Gen. Chap. 4, n. 1.

[4]The Hebrew "and I will rest" is somewhat anthropomorphic attributing a human act to God. The translation transfers this act to the Presence of God (the Glory of the Presence of God in Tg. Neof.) = *Shekhinta*, for which see Introduction VII D.3.

[5]The Hebrew "beaten" denotes the idea of being made from one piece. The Targum employs the passive participle form of the root *ngd*—"stretch," "draw out," "extend"—to depict the cherubim as extending directly from the cover itself, thus forming one piece with it. Tgs. Ps.-Jon. and Neof. use the same root.

[6]The Hebrew "I will meet you" is anthropomorphic and accordingly circumvented by the Targum which employs the Memra, as do Tgs. Neof. and Ps.-Jon.

[7]This insertion is also in the Tg. Ps.-Jon., the Syr., and in the Vg. (*altam*). Rashi here summarizes the debate which exists in b. Men. 96b and b. Sukk. 5a concerning the location of this rim: "some say it was on top, all the way around the table like the vertical ledge that is on the edges of the table of noblemen, while others say it was fixed beneath the table from leg to leg on the four sides of the table and that the table top rested upon the ledge." The Targum by his insertion of "in height" appears to be in agreement with the opinion that the rim encircled the table on the top.

[8]The Hebrew has "enclosures" lit. houses which is figurative and accordingly rendered into its intended meaning. Tgs. Neof., Ps.-Jon. and the Sam. Tg. render likewise, as does the Syr.

CHAPTER 26

1. Now the sanctuary you are to make of ten curtains of finely twisted linen, and blue and purple and scarlet yarn <with> a design of cherubs; you should make them {like} the work of an artisan. 2. The length of a curtain is to be twenty-eight cubits and its width four cubits, {the measurement} of each curtain, one dimension for all the curtains. 3. Five of the curtains should be coupled to each other, and five <other> curtains should be coupled to each other. 4. Then you should make loops of blue wool on the edge of one curtain *from*[a] the side of the place of coupling, and accordingly you should do at the edge of the curtain at the other side of the place of the coupling. 5. Fifty loops you should make on one curtain, and fifty loops you should make on the other side of the place of the coupling of the curtain; the loops should be directed to face each other. 6. Then you should make fifty golden hooks and couple the curtains one to the other with the hooks, and the sanctuary will become a unit. 7. And you should make curtains of goats' hair to stretch over the tent; you should make them eleven curtains {altogether}. 8. The length of a curtain is <to be> thirty cubits and the width of a curtain four cubits; one dimension for <each of> the eleven curtains. 9. Then couple five curtains separately and six curtains separately and fold over the sixth curtain towards the front of the tent. 10. And you should make fifty loops on the edge of the curtain on one side of the place of coupling and fifty loops on the edge of the curtain on the other side of the place of coupling. 11. Then you should make fifty copper hooks and insert the hooks into the loops, then couple the tent and it will become a unit. 12. Now as for the overlapping excess of the tent curtains, half of the extra curtain should hang over the rear of the sanctuary. 13. A cubit from this <side> and a cubit from that <side> left over in the length of the curtain of the tent should hang over the sides of the sanctuary from either side to cover it. 14. Then you should make a covering for the tent of red rams' skins and a covering of scarlet skins above <it>. 15. Then you should make the planks for the sanctuary of acacia wood, upright {in position}. 16. Ten cubits the length of the plank, and one and a half cubits the width of each plank. 17. <There should be> two hinges for each plank in parallel connection to each other; accordingly, you should do with all the planks of the sanctuary. 18. And you should make the planks for the sanctuary {totaling} twenty planks in the direction of the south side. 19. Then make forty silver sockets {to go} beneath twenty planks—two sockets beneath one plank per two hinges, and two sockets beneath another plank per two hinges. 20. And for the other side of the sanctuary in the direction of the north <side>—twenty planks. 21. And forty of its sockets <should be> of silver, two sockets beneath one and two sockets beneath another plank. 22. And for the rear <side> of the sanctuary to the west, make six planks. 23. And two planks you should make for the corners of the sanctuary at their <far> end. 24. Now they are to be directed towards

Apparatus, Chapter 26

[a] v has: "on."
[b] b and g have: "its," as does the Hebrew.
[c] I has: "you" as do 6 Hebrew mss., the LXX and the Syr.
[d] a omits.
[e] J, U, a, b, and Ra have: "an embroiderer" as does the Hebrew with its *nomen agentis.*

each other below and into a unity they should be directed towards each other at *their*[b] top into one ring; accordingly it should be for both of them—they should form the two corners. 25. So there will be eight planks with their silver sockets {totaling} sixteen sockets; two sockets for one plank and two sockets for another plank. 26. Then you should make bars of acacia wood, five for the planks of one side of the sanctuary. 27. And five bars for the planks of the other side of the sanctuary, and five bars for the planks of the side of the sanctuary at their rear end to the west. 28. Now the center bar at the middle of the planks is to extend from end to end. 29. And you should overlay the planks <with> gold and make their rings of gold *as a location*[1] for the bars; and you should overlay the bars <with> gold. 30. Then you should raise up the sanctuary according to its manner which you were shown on the mountain. 31. Then you should make a curtain of blue and purple and scarlet yarn and twisted linen, *he*[c] should make it the work of an artisan <with> *a design of*[d] cherubs. 32. And you should place it on four posts of acacia wood, overlaid <with> gold; their hooks <should be of> gold, upon four silver sockets. 33. Then you should place the curtain beneath the hooks, and bring in there within the curtain the Ark of the Testimony, so that the curtain will separate for you between the Holy and (between) the Holy of Holies. 34. And you should place the cover upon the Ark of the Testimony in the Holy of Holies. 35. And you should place the table outside the curtain and the lampstand opposite the table on the south side of the sanctuary, whereas the table you should place on the north side. 36. Then you should make a cover for the entrance of the sanctuary of blue and purple and scarlet yarn, and twisted linen, the work of *embroidery.*[e] 37. And you should make for the cover five posts of acacia wood and overlay them <with> gold; their hooks <should be of> gold, and cast for them five sockets of copper.

CHAPTER 27

1. Then you should make an altar of acacia wood the length is <to be> five cubits and the width five cubits—the altar is to be square and its height three cubits. 2. And you should make for it horns on its four corners; its horns should be {sculptured} from it; and you should overlay it <with> copper. 3. And you should make its pots for gathering its ashes, and its shovels, and its basins, and its flesh hooks, and its fire pans; all of its vessels you should make of copper. 4. And you should make a grating of meshwork of copper; then you should make on the meshwork four copper rings, upon

Notes, Chapter 26

[1]See above Chap. 25, n. 8.

its four corners. 5. Then you should place it beneath the *gallery*[1] of the altar, below it, so that the meshwork should be halfway up the altar. 6. And you should make poles for the altar, poles of acacia wood, and overlay them <with> copper. 7. Then *he should insert its poles*[a] into the rings, so that the poles should be on the two sides of the altar when carrying it. 8. You should make it hollow of boards, as *I have shown you*[2] on the mountain; accordingly you should do. 9. Then you should make the courtyard of the sanctuary towards the south side, hangings for the courtyard of fine twisted linen, one hundred cubits in length on one side. 10. And its posts, <should total> twenty and their sockets, twenty, <made of> copper, while the hooks for the posts and their sockets <are to be of> silver. 11. So likewise for the north side in length, hangings, one hundred <cubits in> length, and its posts, twenty <cubits>, and its sockets twenty <cubits made> of copper, the hooks for the posts and their sockets <are to be of> silver. 12. Now the width of the courtyard on the west side—the hangings fifty cubits, their posts ten <cubits> with their sockets ten <cubits>. 13. And the width of the courtyard on the front side, eastward—fifty cubits. 14. And fifteen cubits of hangings for one side, their posts <totaling> three and their sockets <totaling> three. 15. And for the other side fifteen cubits of hangings, their posts <totaling> three, and their sockets <totaling> three. 16. And for the entrance of the courtyard a cover of twenty cubits {made} of blue, and purple, scarlet yarn, and fine twisted linen, the work of *embroidery;*[b] their posts <totaling> four, and their sockets <totaling> four. 17. All the posts of the courtyard around <it should be> gilded with silver, {and} their hooks <should be of> silver but their sockets of copper. 18. The length of the courtyard is <to be> one hundred cubits, the width *fifty all around*[3] and the height five cubits of fine twisted linen, and their sockets of copper. 19. All the vessels of the sanctuary for all its service, and all its pins, as well as all the pins of the courtyard <are to be> of copper. 20. Now you should command the Israelites that they bring to you pure olive oil pressed for lighting, to kindle the *lights*[4] <that they may burn> continually. 21. In the Tent of Meeting outside the curtain which is over the Testimony, Aaron and his sons are to arrange it from evening to morning before the Lord, <as> an everlasting ordinance for *the generations*[5] of the Israelites.

Apparatus, Chapter 27

[a] b, d, l, k, and n have: "and the poles should be inserted," as does the Hebrew.

[b] J, E, and b have: "an embroiderer" as does the Hebrew with its *nomen agentis.*

Apparatus, Chapter 28

[a] b, d, g, and a have the singular, as does the Hebrew.
[b] b, d, and g have the singular, as does the Hebrew.
[c] b, d, g, and l have the singular, as does the Hebrew.
[d] J, G, k, and l have: "on" which is interpretive.
[e] F adds: "you should engrave."
[f] E has the plural, while b and d have: "with seals."

Notes, Chapter 27

[1]The Hebrew *krkb* is here rendered by the identical term used in the following Talmud (b. Zeb. 62a)—"R. Jose b. Juda said *krkb* (Exod. 27:5) refers to the gallery (*swbb*)."

[2]The Hebrew has: "you were shown." Tg. Ps.-Jon. as well as the Syr. and the Sam. Tg. (A) here equal the Targum in rendering "I have shown" as the Hebrew has it in 25:9.

CHAPTER 28

1. Now, you should bring into association with you Aaron and his sons from among the Israelites to serve *before*[1] Me—Aaron, Nadab, and Abihu, Eleazar, and Ithamar, the sons of Aaron. 2. Then you should make sacred garments for your brother Aaron for dignity and for praise. 3. Now, {as for} you, you should tell all the wise of heart whom I have filled with a spirit of wisdom that they should make Aaron's garments in order to sanctify him in order to serve *before*[1] Me. 4. And these are the garments that they should make: A breastplate, an Ephod, a robe, *checkered tunics,*[a] *turbans*[b] and sashes;[c] and they should make the sacred garments for your brother Aaron and for his sons in order to serve *before*[1] Me. 5. Then they should take the gold, and the blue and purple and scarlet yarn, and the fine linen. 6. Now they should make the Ephod of gold, blue and purple, scarlet yarn and fine twisted linen, the work of an artisan. 7. It should have two shoulder-pieces coupled; *at*[d] its two sides it should be coupled. 8. Now the adorned turban which is upon it, made like it, should be <made> from it—of gold, blue, purple, and scarlet yarn, and twisted fine linen. 9. Then you should take the two beryl stones and engrave on them the names of the Israelites. 10. Six of the names on one stone, and the names of the remaining *six*[e] on the other stone, in order of their birth. 11. The work of an artisan *in precious stone,*[2] *the script is <to be> distinct,*[3] *like*[4] the engraving of a *signet*[f] you should engrave the two stones

Notes, Chapter 27 (Cont.)

[3]Lit. "fifty by fifty."

[4]The Hebrew has the singular, which is here rendered by the plural as it is in the Tgs. Ps.-Jon. and Neof. as well as the Syr. and the Sam. Tg. Adler (*Netina La-Ger, op. cit.*, on this verse) explains it to refer to Exod. 25:37. This position is disputed by M. Löwenstein (*Nefesh Ha-Ger, op. cit.*, p. 75) who says that Exod. 25:37 refers to Moses while here the verse pertains to Aaron. B.Z.J. Berkowitz (*Simlat Ger, op. cit.*, p. 54f.) points out that we have here simply an idiomatic singular in the Hebrew which the Targum normally renders into the plural. There is, however, a Rabbinic tradition that it referred to a particular single light —*MHG* (Exod., p. 612): "That the Western Light should burn continually."

[5]Lit. their generations, whereas the Sam. Heb., the LXX and the Syr. have: "your (pl.) generations."

Notes, Chapter 28

[1]See Gen. Chap. 4, n. 1.

[2]The Hebrew "stone" is defined in the Targum (also in Tg. Ps.-Jon., who has "pearl") as "a precious stone" in reference to vs. 9 above, where these two stones are described as beryl stones.

[3]This insertion in the Targum is explained by Y. Koraḥ (*Marpe Lashon*, in Pentateuch edition *Sefer Keter Torah: Ha-Ta'ağ Ha-Gadol*. Jerusalem 1960: Exodus, p. 230f.) as follows: It could have stated "the engraving is (to be) distinct like the engraving of a signet" but the Targum tried to avoid the repetitive "engraving . . . engraving," so he chose the word "script" as in Exod. 39:30 "the script (like) the engravings of a signet." Now in vs. 36 below the Hebrew reads "and you should engrave upon it (like) the engravings of a signet ring," which the Targum renders—"you should engrave upon it a distinct script" omitting "like the engraving of a signet ring," since here the subject is the plate which did not contain "engraved" script but rather "protruded" script like that of golden dinars. This explanation Koraḥ cites in the name of Ya'er (for whose identity see Gen. Chap. 10, n. 1). He himself, however, points out that the Targum omitted the above due to the awkward phrasing which would result from it, i.e., "and you should engrave upon it a distinct script like the engraving." Proof of it is seen in Exod. 39:6 where the subject is the beryl stones, as in the present verse, and yet the Targum omits "like the engraving of a signet ring" even though here the script was truly "engraved."

[4]The Targum adds the *kaph* of comparison to clarify the simile implied in the Hebrew.

with the names of the Israelites; inserted and set in gold you should make them. 12. Then you should set the two stones onto the shoulder-pieces of the Ephod, as memorial stones for the Israelites, and Aaron should bear the names on his two shoulders before the Lord as a memorial. 13. Now you should make gold casings. 14. <Make> two chains of pure gold like a cord; you should make them plaited work; and you should place the plaited chains unto the settings. 15. Then you should make a breastpiece of judgment, the work of an artisan; like the work of the Ephod you should make it—of gold, blue, and purple, and scarlet yarn, and fine twisted linen you should make it. 16. It should be square, doubled in fold, a span {in} its length and a a span {in} its width. 17. Then you should complete it with *a stone setting*[g] of four rows of precious stone(s); the first row: Carnelian, topaz, smaragd—row one. 18. And the second row: Turquoise, sapphire, and emerald. 19. And the third row: Jacinth, agate, and amethyst. 20. And the fourth row: Chrysolite, beryl, and jasper; they should be in gold casings in their setting. 21. Now the stones shall be according to the names of the Israelites—twelve, corresponding to their names, *the script is to be distinct,*[3] *like* [4] the engraving of a seal, each should be with his name according to the twelve tribes. 22. Then you should make for the breastpiece cord-like chains <in> plaited work of pure gold. 23. And you should make for the breastpiece two gold rings and place the two rings unto the two sides of the breastpiece. 24. Then you should place the two gold chains unto the two rings on the sides of the breastpiece. 25. And the two chains that are on its two sides you should place unto the two settings and place <them> unto the two shoulder-pieces opposite its front. 26. Then you should make two gold rings and place them unto the two sides of the breastpiece on its edge, on the side of the Ephod from within. 27. And you should make two gold rings and place them unto the two shoulder-pieces of the Ephod beneath <it>, opposite its front, facing the place of its coupling, above the sash of the Ephod. 28. Then they should join the breastpiece with its ring to the Ephod's ring through a thread of blue wool to be on the sash of the Ephod, so that the breastpiece does not become dislocated from the top of the Ephod. 29. Now Aaron should bear the names of the Israelites in the breastpiece of judgment over his heart upon entering the sanctuary for a memorial before the Lord, continually. 30. Then you should place in the breastpiece of judgment the Urim and the Thummin and they should be over the heart of Aaron *before*[1] the Lord; and Aaron should bear the <instruments> of judgment for the Israelites over his heart *before*[1] the Lord, continually. 31. Then you should make a robe for the Ephod entirely of blue wool. 32. Not *its opening*[h] should be *folded*[5] towards its inside; a twisted band should surround its opening completely; it should be the work of a fine weaver; it should be to him like the opening of a coat of mail, so that it would not tear. 33. Then you should make pomegranates <of> blue, purple, and scarlet yarn on its hems, completely surrounding its hem(s), and gold bells between them round about. 34. A gold bell and a

Apparatus, Chapter 28 (Cont.)

[g] a has the plural which is interpretive.
[h] A and E have: "the tip of its opening," as does the Hebrew.
[i] l has the interpretive "by."
[j] a has: "their."
[k] c has: "on Aaron's forehead," but omits the following word—"continually."
[l] J, L, a, and b have: "an embroiderer," as does the Hebrew with the *nomen agentis.*

pomegranate, a gold bell and a pomegranate, on the hems of the robe round about. 35. Now it should be on Aaron while officiating, so that its sound is heard when he enters the sanctuary before the Lord and when he departs, that he may not die. 36. Then you should make the front plate of pure gold and engrave on it *in distinct script*[3]: 'Sacred to the Lord.' 37. And you should place it *on*[i] a thread of blue wool, and it should be upon the turban; opposite the front of the turban should it be {located}. 38. Now it should be on Aaron's forehead, and Aaron should bear the iniquities <resulting from> the sacred things which the Israelites would be consecrating through all of their sacred donations; now it should be *on his forehead*[k] continually to be accepted for them *before*[1] the Lord. 39. Then you should weave a tunic in checkered form, and make a headband of fine linen, and a sash you should make the work of *embroidery.*[l] 40. Now for Aaron's sons you should make tunics, and {also} make for them sashes and turbans, for dignity and for praise. 41. Then place them on your brother Aaron and on his sons accompanying him, and anoint them *and offer their sacrifices*[6] and sanctify them that they may officiate *before*[1] Me. 42. And you should make for them undergarments of fine linen to cover the naked flesh; they should be from the hips to the thighs. 43. Now they should be on Aaron and on his sons when they enter the Tent of Meeting or when they approach the altar to officiate in the sanctuary, so that they do not incur guilt and die; {this should be} an everlasting ordinance for him and for his sons after him.

Notes, Chapter 28 (Cont.)

[5]This insertion, according to Rashi, meant that it was turned in towards the inside—the turn-in serving as its seam. It was weaver's work (woven as such with the robe) and not with a needle.

[6]The Hebrew has "ordain them" lit. fill their hand(s), which is a technical term for *install* or *institute* to a priestly office, according to S.R. Driver (*Exodus op. cit.*, p. 311)—originally, meaning to fill the priest's hands with the first sacrifices—a meaning here given to this phrase in the Targum—"and offer their sacrifices." The Tg. Ps.-Jon. is identical here, while Tg. Neof. is even more instructive here, having—"and you shall complete the offering of their hands." Y. Koraḥ offers the following helpful explanation: Every Hebrew expression of "filling the hand" is rendered "offering a sacrifice" in the Targum, even where idolatry is involved, and even where no sacrifice or offering is involved. He points out that the Hebrew expression "filling" means "completion" and is so rendered in the Targum to Gen. 29:27—"fill, i.e., complete, this seven year period," while the expression "hand" symbolizes "the power of one's will." Accordingly, "the offering of a sacrifice" is here equated with "the completion of one's will," since the basic reason for offering a sacrifice with man is to offer the animal to God in exchange for atonement for one's life whether that was for commission of a sin, in which case he may have been condemned to death, or for a contribution out of love and respect for God. Thus, Koraḥ suggests that on this basis the act of offering a sacrifice is called "fulfilling one's will"—one's personal will is fulfilled as if he had actually offered his own fat and blood upon the altar. He then cites three examples to illustrate this theory—2 Chr. 29:31 (to support the present verse with actual sacrifice to God); 2 Chr. 13:9 (where sacrifice to idolatry is involved) and Exod. 32:39 (where the expression is used not with reference to sacrifice at all). Cf. further Exod. 29:9, 29, 33, 35; Lev. 8:33; 16:32; 21:10; Num. 3:3; Ezek. 43:26; 1 Chr. 29:5, especially the instructive example of Exod. 29:22 concerning "the ram of installation."

CHAPTER 29

1. Now this is the thing you should do to them to consecrate them to officiate *before*[1] Me: Take a bull, a young bull, and two rams without blemish. 2. Also unleavened bread, as well as unleavened cakes mixed in oil, and unleavened wafers spread with oil; make them of choice wheat flour. 3. Then you should place them into a basket and offer them in the basket, as well as the bull and the two rams. 4. Now Aaron and his sons you should present at the entrance of the Tent of Meeting and wash them with water. 5. Then you should wash the garments and dress Aaron in the tunic and the robe of the Ephod, and the Ephod and the breastpiece, and *dress*[2] him with the sash of the Ephod. 6. And you should place the turban on his head and put the sacred crown upon the turban. 7. Then you should take the anointing oil and pour <it> on his head thereby anointing him. 8. And present his sons and dress them in tunics. 9. Then gird Aaron and his sons with *sashes*[3] and *dress*[2] them in turbans so that they should have the priesthood as an everlasting ordinance; *and you should offer the sacrifice of Aaron and the sacrifice of his sons.*[4] 10. Now you should present the bull in front of the Tent of Meeting, and Aaron, as well as his sons, should lay their hands on the head of the bull. 11. And you should slaughter the bull before the Lord, at the entrance of the Tent of Meeting. 12. Then you should take of the bull's blood and put it on the horn of the altar with your finger, while the *remainder*[5] of the blood you should pour out at the base of the altar. 13. Now you should take all the fat that covers the inner part(s), as well as the lobe that is above the liver, and the two kidneys with the fat that is on them, and *offer*[6] <them> on the altar. 14. And the flesh of the bull, as well as its hide and its excrement, you should burn with fire outside the camp; it is a sin offering. 15. Then you should take the one ram, and Aaron, as well as his sons, should lay their hands on the head of the ram. 16. And you should slaughter the ram, then take its blood and sprinkle (it) against the altar, completely around it. 17. Now the ram you should divide into pieces, and rinse its inside and its legs, and place <them> with its limbs and its heads. 18. And *offer*[6] the entire ram on the altar; it is a burnt offering *before*[1] the Lord to be accepted willingly; it is *an offering*[7] *before*[1] the Lord. 19. Then you should take the second ram, and Aaron as well as his sons, should lay their hands on the head of the ram. 20. And you should slaughter the ram and take of its blood and place <it> on the tip of Aaron's right ear and on the lobe of his sons' right ear(s), as well as on the thumb(s) of their right hand(s), and on the big toe of their right feet; then you should sprinkle the blood against the altar, completely around it. 21. Then you should take of the blood from the altar and of the anointing oil, and sprinkle it on Aaron and on his garments, and on his sons and on the sons' garments, so that he will become sanctified, as well as his garments, and his sons, and his sons' garments with him. 22. And you should take from the ram, the fat and the tail <fat>, as well as the fat that covers the inner parts, and the lobe that is above the liver, and the two kidneys and the fat that is on them, as well as the right thigh, for it is a ram of *the offerings.*[4] 23. And one flat loaf of bread and one cake <type> of bread <smeared in> oil, as well as one wafer from the basket of the unleavened bread which is before the Lord. 24. Now you should place all {of these} in the hands of Aaron and in his sons' hands, and wave them <as> a wave offering before the Lord. 25. Then you should take them off their hands and offer them on the altar with the burnt offering to be accepted willingly before the Lord; it is an

offering *before*[1] the Lord. 26. Now you should take the breast of Aaron's ram of *the offerings*[4] and wave it <as> a wave offering before the Lord, and it should be your portion. 27. And you should sanctify the breast of the wave offering and the thigh of the heave offering, which were waved and heaved from the ram of *the offerings*[4]—from that which was Aaron's and from that which was his sons. 28. And it should be <due> to Aaron and to his sons from the Israelites by an everlasting ordinance, for it is a heave offering, and a heave offering it should be from the Israelites, *from the sanctified sacrifices;*[8] it is their heave offering to the Lord. 29. Now the garments of the sanctuary which belong to Aaron, should belong to his sons after him to be anointed in them *and to present in them their offerings.*[4] 30. Seven days should the priest who succeeds him from his sons wear them, when he enters the Tent of Meeting to officiate in the sanctuary. 31. Now the ram *of the offerings*[4] you should take and boil its flesh in a sacred place. 32. Then Aaron and his sons should eat the flesh of the ram, and the bread that is in the basket at the entrance of the Tent of Meeting. 33. And they should eat those by which atonement was made *to present their offerings*[4] to sanctify them, but an alien may not eat <*them*>,[9] for these are sacred. 34. Now if any of the flesh of *the offerings*[4] or of the bread was left over by morning, then you should burn by fire that which was left over; it is not to be eaten for it is sacred. 35. And you should do to Aaron and to his sons according to all that I commanded you; for seven days *you should present their offerings.*[4] 36. Now a bull for a sin offering; you should *prepare*[10] each day for atonement, and you should purify the altar by offering atonement on it,

Notes, Chapter 29

[1]See Gen. Chap. 4, n. 1.

[2]The Hebrew has "gird" *wĕ'āp̱adĕtā*, which in conjunction with the following object *ḥēšeḇ hā'ēp̱ōd* creates a cognate accusative sequence, which cannot be recreated in Aramaic. An identical verbal form does not exist in Aramaic. The only possible root-*zrz* ("gird")—the very same root used in the Targum for Hebrew *ḥgr* in vs. 9 below, is here foregone in favor of the more common root *tqn* with the specialized meaning "to dress," a root which the Syr. also uses, while the Tgs. Ps.-Jon. and Neof. render "gird" but employ the root *ṭks.*

[3]The Hebrew has the idiomatic singular, for which see Gen. Chap. 21, n. 7.

[4]See above Chap. 28, n. 6.

[5]Lit. all.

[6]The Hebrew has: "burn," lit. cause the sacrifice to go up in smoke, which is the technical meaning of Hebrew *qṭr* in the *hiphil.* The Targum consistently renders this term by the *aphel* of *nsq*—"offer up," lit. to cause to rise.

[7]The Hebrew has "an offering by fire" (*'iššeh* < *'ēš* "fire"). Rashi points out that it denotes the burning of the parts which had been placed on the fire. In fact the Talmud (b. Zeb. 46b) relates fire and sacrifice directly to each other in the following Mishna: "The sacrifice is slaughtered for the sake of six things . . . for the sake of fire offerings . . ." on which the Gemara elaborates: "'An offering made by fire' [intimates that] it must be for the sake of *an offering made by fire,* excluding the charring of the meat (which means the intention to make roast pieces of flesh) which is not valid." Cf. likewise Sifra *Wayyiqrā'* IV:6, p. 7b. Tgs. Neof. and Ps.-Jon. as well as the Syr. also have "offering" here.

[8]The Hebrew has: "their sacrifices of peace offerings" which the Targum interpretively renders "the sacrifices of their sacred things" or ("their sanctified sacrifices"). For the equation of "peace offering" = sanctified sacrifice see above Chap. 10, n. 11.

[9]The LXX^{AF}, as well as the Vg., actually adds "of them" (*'απ αυτῶν*), while the LXX^{B} adds "of it" (*-τοῦ*).

[10]Lit. make.

and you should anoint it to consecrate it. 37. For seven days you should make atonement for the altar and consecrate it; then the altar will become most sacred; whosoever will *approach*[11] the altar shall become consecrated. 38. Now this is what you should *offer*[10] on the altar: Two year-old lambs each day, continually. 39. One lamb you should *offer*[10] in the morning, and the other lamb you should *offer*[10] at twilight. 40. And a tenth <of a measure> of fine flour that is mixed with a quarter of a hin of beaten oil, and a libation of a quarter of a hin of wine for one lamb. 41. And the other lamb you should *offer*[10] at twilight according to the morning offering and its oblation should you *offer*[10] it, to be accepted willingly *<as>an offering*[a][7] *before*[1] the Lord. 42. A continual burnt offering for your <future> generations at the entrance of the Tent of Meeting before the Lord, *where I will appoint My Memra*[12] to be there for you, to speak with you there. 43. *And I will appoint My Memra*[12] to be there for the Israelites and will be sanctified through My Glory. 44. Then I will sanctify the Tent of Meeting and the altar and will sanctify Aaron and his sons to officiate *before*[1] Me. 45. And I will rest *My Presence*[13] among the Israelites and be God to them. 46. Then they will realize that I am the Lord their God who brought them out of the land of Egypt to rest *My Presence*[13] among them; I am the Lord their God.

CHAPTER 30

1. Then you should make an altar *to burn upon it*[1] aromatic incenses; make it of acacia wood. 2. Its length is <to be> a cubit, its width a cubit; it is to be square, and its height is <to be> two cubits, {while} its horns should be <sculptured> from it. 3. Now you should overlay it <with> pure gold—its top and its sides completely around <it>, as well as its horns; and you should make for it a golden molding completely around <it>. 4. And two golden rings you should make for it {to be} beneath its molding for its two corners; you should make it at its two <opposite> sides, and *it*[a] should be as a place for the poles with which to carry it. 5. Now you should make the poles of acacia wood and overlay them with gold. 6. And you should place it in front of the curtain which is before the Ark of Testimony, in front of the cover that is over the Testimony, where *I shall appoint My Memra*[2] for you {to be} there. 7. Then Aaron should let

Apparatus, Chapter 29

[a] a omits. The Hebrew has: "an offering by fire."

Apparatus, Chapter 30

[a] i has: "they," as do the Sam. Heb., the LXX, the Syr., and the Vg.

[b] s has: "dresses," as does the Hebrew.

[c] D has the singular, as does the Hebrew.

[d] i_a, c, and n have the plural, as does the Hebrew.

[e] n has the interpretive: "one time."

[f] b, c, k, and l have: "of," as does the Hebrew.

[g] b, d, and M have: "of," as does the Hebrew.

[h] b has: "to," as does the Hebrew.

perfumed spices rise upon it every morning; he should let the incense rise when he *prepares*[b] the lights. 8. And when he kindles the lights, he should let the perfumed incense rise at twilight, continually before the Lord, for all your {future} generations. 9. Do not offer upon it alien perfumed incense or a burnt offering or a meal offering, nor should you pour any *libations*[c] on it. 10. Now Aaron shall achieve atonement on its *horn*[d] once a year with the blood of the atoning sin offering; *once*[e] a year he should achieve atonement on it for your {future} generations; it is most sacred to the Lord." 11. [Then the Lord spoke with Moses as follows,] 12. "When you take the census of the Israelites according to their count, then each person should give a ransom for his life *before*[3] the Lord as you count them, so that there should not occur any *fatality*[4] among them as you count them. 13. This is what all those who pass through the counting procedures should give—half a *Sela,*[5] of the *Selas*[5] of the sanctuary, twenty *Ma'ah*[5] per *Sela,*[5] half a *Sela,*[5] a heave offering *before*[3] the Lord. 14. All those who pass through the counting procedures, from the age of twenty years and above should give the heave offering *before*[f] the Lord. 15. The rich should not give more than, neither should the poor give less than, a half Sela, in donating the heave offering *before*[g] the Lord to atone for your lives. 16. Then you should take the atonement money from the Israelites and present it for the service of the Tent of Meeting, and it should be as a memorial for the Israelites before the Lord to atone for your lives." 17. [Then the Lord spoke *with*[h] Moses as follows,] 18. "Now you should make a laver of copper and its stand of copper, for *sanctification;*[6] then place it between the Tent of Meeting and (between) the altar, and put water there. 19. Then Aaron and his sons are

Notes, Chapter 29 (Cont.)

[11]See above Chap. 19, n. 11.
[12]See above Chap. 25, n. 6.
[13]See above Chap. 24, n. 4.

Notes, Chapter 30

[1]An insertion implied in the Hebrew. Nevertheless, Adler (*Netina La-Ger, op. cit.*, on this verse) correctly points out that the Targum understood the Hebrew *miqṭar* here to have been a *miqtal* type noun which, B. Schmerler (*Ahavat Yehonatan, op. cit.*, p. 206) points out, is in construct with its following genitive and separate from the preceding noun—"altar" in the absolute form. This leaves *miqṭar qĕṭōret* ("aromatic incenses") syntactically meaningless. Accordingly, the Targum adds the infinitive and supplies the indirect object.

[2]See above Chap. 25, n. 6.

[3]See Gen. Chap. 4, n. 1.

[4]See above Chap. 9, n. 4.

[5]See Gen. Chap. 20, n. 11 for the *šéqel* = *séla'* equivalence, and Lev. Chap. 27, n. 8 for the *gērāh* = *mā'āh* equation.

[6]The Hebrew has "for washing." Naḥmanides on this verse points out that the Targum renders any washing concerned with sacred matters by the term "sanctify" (*qdš*) as in the present case, while ordinary "washing" pertaining to cleanliness is rendered by the root *sḥy* as in Gen. 18:4. This interpretive rendering is in agreement with the following Rabbinic statement—b. Zeb. 21b: "R. Jose, son of R Ḥanina, said: You may not wash in a laver which does not contain sufficient (water) for the *sanctification* of four priests, for it says: 'That Moses and Aaron and his sons *wash* their hands and their feet from it' (Exod. 30:19)." Cf. further, I. Pick-Berlin, *Mine Targuma.* Wilna, 1836, p. 11, and Y. Koraḥ, *Marpe Lashon, op. cit.*, p. 254.

to *sanctify*[6] their hands and their feet from it. 20. When they enter the Tent of Meeting they should *sanctify*[i][6] themselves with water, that they may not die, or when they approach the altar to officiate, to offer a *sacrifice*[7] *before*[3] the Lord. 21. Then they should *sanctify*[6] their hands and their feet that they may not die, and it should be to them an everlasting ordinance, for him and his *sons*[8] for their {future} generations." 22. [Then the Lord spoke *with*[h] Moses as follows,] 23. "Now you should take choice spices—five hundred <in> weight of pure myrrh, and aromatic cinnamon half of it *the weight of*[9] two hundred and fifty, and aromatic cane, two hundred and fifty *in weight.*[9] 24. And cassia, five hundred <in weight> in *Selas*[5] of the sanctuary, as well as a hin *full*[10] of olive oil. 25. Then you should make it into a sacred anointing oil, thoroughly aromatic blend, the work of a perfumer; it should be the sacred anointing oil. 26. And you should anoint with it the Tent of Meeting and the Ark of Testimony. 27. And the table with all its vessels, and lampstand and its vessels, as well as the altar for aromatic *incenses.*[11] 28. And the altar for *burnt offerings*[11] with all its vessels, and the laver with its stand. 29. Then you should consecrate them that they may be most sacred; whosoever *approaches*[12] them will be consecrated. 30. Now you should anoint Aaron and his sons and consecrate them to officiate *before*[3] Me. 31. Now to the Israelites you should say as follows, 'This should be the sacred anointing oil *before*[j] Me for your {future} generations. 32. It should not be poured on the flesh of {any} man's body, and you should not reproduce anything in its likeness; it is sacred, and sacred it should be <held> by you. 33. Whoever compounds aromatics like it, and whoever places it on a layman shall be cut off from his people.'" 34. Then the Lord said to Moses, "Take aromatic spices, gum resin (and) onycha (and) galbanum aromatics, and pure frankincense, *each should be equal in weight.*[13] 35. And make it into a fragrant blend of aromatic incense, the work of a perfumer, mixed and pure, for the sanctuary. 36. Then you should grind some of *it*[k] *into fine powder*[14] and place some of it in front of the Testimony at the Tent of Meeting where *I will appoint My Memra*[2] for you; it should be most sacred to you. 37. Now the aromatic incense which you will make, do not reproduce it in its likeness for yourselves; it should be sacred to *you*[l] *before*[3] the Lord. 38. Whoever reproduces any like it to smell of it, will be cut off from his people."

Apparatus, Chapter 30 (Cont.)

[i] I actually has the *ithpa'al* of *qdš* here: "they should be sanctified" or "they should sanctify themselves."
[j] G has the literal: "to."
[k] I adds "thoroughly" as does the Hebrew.
[l] the singular, whereas C has the plural as do the Sam. Heb., the LXX, and Tgs. Ps.-Jon. and Neof., for which cf. vs. 31 above.

Apparatus, Chapter 31

[a] b has: "to," as does the Hebrew.
[b] G, v, and I add: "of prophecy," while h adds: "of wisdom."
[c] I adds: "all" as do the Cairo Geniza fragments, the Sam. Heb., the LXX, the Syr., and a host of Hebrew mss. as the Hebrew contains it in Exod. 30:27.
[d] i has: "spoke with."

Notes, Chapter 30 (Cont.)

[7]See above Chap. 29, n. 7.
[8]See Gen. Chap. 3, n. 8.
[9]An insertion, also in the Tgs. Ps.-Jon. and Neof. and the LXX (σίκλους) and the Vg. (*siclos*), implied in the Hebrew which stated it explicitly in the following verse to cover the present verse as well.

CHAPTER 31

1. [Then the Lord spoke *with*[a] Moses as follows,] 2. "See I have *consecrated*[1] by name Bezalel, son of Uri, son of Hur, from the tribe of Judah. 3. And I have perfected him with a *spirit*[b] *from before*[2] the Lord, for wisdom and for intelligence, as well as for knowledge in all {kinds of} craft. 4. To instruct artisans to work with gold, {and with} silver, and (with) copper. 5. And in the art of setting of precious stones and carving of wood, to work in all {kinds of} craft. 6. Moreover, I have assigned to him Oholihab, son of Aḥisamakh, from the tribe of Dan; and into the heart of all those who are wise in heart, I have placed wisdom that they may make everything that I have commanded you. 7. The Tent of Meeting, and the Ark of the Testimony, as well as the cover which is on it, and all the vessels of the sanctuary. 8. The table *with*[c] its vessels, and the pure lampstand with its vessels, as well as the altar of aromatic incense. 9. The altar for the burnt offerings with its vessels and the laver with its base. 10. The officiating garments and the garments for the sanctuary for Aaron the priest, as well as his sons' officiating garments. 11. The anointing oil and the aromatic incense for the sanctuary according to everything that I commanded you, you should do." 12. The the Lord *said to*[d] Moses as follows, 13. "Now you should speak with the Israelites saying, 'Nevertheless, you

Notes, Chapter 30 (Cont.)

[10]An insertion, also in Tgs. Neof. and Ps.-Jon., explained by B. Schefftel (*Bi'ure Onqelos, op. cit.*, p. 114) as serving the same function for the liquid measure—hin—here pertaining to oil, as the addition of "weight" in the preceding verse did as a dry measure. "Full" occurs in the text with regards to the *Omer* (Exod. 16:33), with a *fist* (Exod. 9:8), and with *palm* (Num. 7:14). Cf. Löwenstein, (*Nefesh Ha-Ger, op. cit.*, p. 77) who connects the Targum's insertion here with R. Eliezer b. Zadok's opinion in b. Men. 87b according to whom there were markings in the hin measure indicating thus far for a bullock, thus far for a ram, and thus far for a lamb. The Targum here inserts "full" intentionally to emphasize that for olive oil there was no such limit but a *full* hin was its measure.

[11]Plural for Hebrew singular, for which see Gen. Chap. 21, n. 7.

[12]See above Chap. 19, n. 11.

[13]The Hebrew has lit. "part for part shall it be" which the Targum renders interpretively to mean "equal in weight," as do Tgs. Neof., Ps.-Jon., and the Syr., as well as the Vg. (*ponderis*). The expression *mtql bmtql* in the Targum is in agreement with Rabina's identical one in the following Rabbinic statement—b. Ker. 5a: "What is the meaning of 'of each shall there be a like weight' (Exod. 30:34)? Said Rabina: That one should not weigh first with the weight (*mšql bmšql*) and use afterwards the weighed amount as a weight for the others."

[14]Lit. "and beat it into powder." The Targum here converts the infinitive Hebrew *hādēq* into a finite verb thus creating a sort of verbal hendiadys. Tgs. Neof. and Ps.-Jon. render similarly.

Notes, Chapter 31

[1]The Hebrew has: "called," which the Targum here renders interpretively "consecrated." Tg. Neof. m. contains both this rendering, as well as the literal, "called." M. Löwenstein (*Nefesh Ha-Ger, op. cit.*, p. 78f) explains the Targum's translation of Hebrew *qārā'tî* here in the sense of "establishing and raising someone to a position of dignity/greatness," in the case of Bezalel it was to build the Sanctuary and its vessels. He points to Gen. 12:2 where the Hebrew "and I will make your name great" is rendered by the Targum "and I will raise your name to greatness."

[2]See Gen. Chap. 4, n. 1.

should observe My Sabbath days, for it is a sign between *My Memra*[3] and (between) you for your {future} generations to realize that I am the Lord who has consecrated you. 14. Moreover, you should observe the Sabbath for it is sacred to you; whoever desecrates it will surely be put to death, for whoever does work on it, that person will be cut off from *among*[e] his people. 15. Six days work should be done, but on the seventh day there should be a sabbath of rest, sacred to the Lord; whoever does work on the Sabbath day will surely be put to death. 16. Now the Israelites should observe the Sabbath, *celebrating*[4] *the Sabbath*[f] for their {future} generations as an everlasting covenant. 17. It is a sign between *My Memra*[3] and (between) the Israelites forever, that in six days the Lord made heaven and earth, and on the seventh day He ceased <from work> and rested.'" 18. When He finished speaking with him on Mount Sinai, He gave to Moses the two tablets of the Testimony, stone tablets inscribed with the finger of the Lord.

CHAPTER 32

1. When the people realized that Moses was late in coming down from the mountain, the people gathered around Aaron and said to him, "Proceed to make us *deities*[1] who will go in front of us for this man Moses who brought us up out of the land of Egypt, we do not know what became of him." 2. So Aaron said to them, "Take off the gold earrings that are on the ears of your wives, your sons, and your daughters, and bring <them> to me." 3. Whereupon all the people took off the gold earrings that were on their ears and brought <them> to Aaron. 4. So Aaron took <them> and shaped it with a chisel and made it <into> a molten calf; whereupon they exclaimed, "These are your *gods,*[1] O Israel, who have brought you up out of the land of Egypt." 5. When Aaron saw <this>, he built an altar before it, and Aaron proclaimed, saying, "Tomorrow will be a feast *before*[2] the Lord." 6. Then they rose early the following day and offered up burnt offerings and presented *sacrifices;*[3] and the people *reclined*[4] to eat and (to) drink and they got up to indulge in revelry. 7. Then the Lord said to Moses, "Proceed to *descend,*[a] for your people whom I brought up out of the land of Egypt have become corrupt. 8. They have quickly turned aside from the path that I commanded them <to take>; they made for themselves a molten calf and bowed down

Apparatus, Chapter 31 (Cont.)

[e] i omits, as do a few Hebrew mss., the Syr., and Tg. Ps.-Jon.

[f] h omits, as does the LXX which pluralizes the preceding word "Sabbath" and adds a suffix αυτά—"them" to the "celebrating." The Vg. renders similarly.

Apparatus, Chapter 32

[a] l adds "from here," as do the Syr. and the LXX.

[b] Lit. "spoke;" E and s have: "schemed."

to it and sacrificed to it and said, 'These are your *gods,*[1] O Israel, who have brought you up out of the land of Egypt.'" 9. And the Lord said to Moses, "*It is revealed to Me*[5] <that> here this people is a stiff-necked people. 10. So now, *let go of your prayer*[6] *from before Me*[2] that My anger may become strong against them and I will destroy them and make you into a great nation." 11. Then Moses *prayed*[7] *before*[2] the Lord his God and said, "Why, O Lord, why would Your anger become strong against Your people whom You have brought up out of the land of Egypt with great power and a mighty hand? 12. Why should the Egyptians say as follows, 'With evil <intent> did He bring them out to kill them *between*[8] the mountains and to destroy them from the face of the earth?' Renege from the power of Your anger, and relent from the harm that You *promised*[b] to do to Your people. 13. Remember Abraham, Isaac, and Israel Your

Notes, Chapter 31 (Cont.)

[3]See Introduction VII D. 1.
[4]Lit. "doing."

Notes, Chapter 32

[1]See Gen. Chap. 31, n. 20.
[2]See Gen. Chap. 4, n. 1.
[3]See above Chap. 10, n. 11.
[4]See Gen. Chap. 37, n. 7.
[5]See Gen. Chap. 29, n. 8.
[6]The Hebrew has: "let me alone," which the Targum here and in Deut. 9:14 interpretively renders to refer to Moses' intercession with prayer on their behalf. This interpretation, also contained in the translation of Tgs. Neof. and Ps.-Jon., is reflected in the following Rabbinic statements on this verse:

1. Tanḥ (A) *Kí Tissā'* XXII "'and now leave Me alone, etc.' (Exod. 32:10). From here you learn that the Holy One, blessed be He, created an opening for Moses to seek (pray for) mercy for them."
2. *b. Ber.32a* "'and now leave Me alone, etc.' (Exod. 32:10). R. Abbahu said: Were it not explicitly written, it would be impossible to say such a thing. This teaches that Moses took hold of the Holy One, blessed be He, like a man who seizes his fellow man by his garment and said before Him: Sovereign of the Universe, I will not let go of You until you forgive and pardon them."

[7]The Hebrew *wayĕḥal(<ḥlh)* "implore" is here interpretively rendered "prayed," the Targum employing the standard root *ṣly,* as do the Syr., and Tg. Neof., as well as the LXX '**εδεήθη**. This interpretive rendering is widely reflected in Rabbinic tradition as the following sources show:

1. *b. Ber. 32a* "'and Moses implored the Lord his God' (Exod. 32:11). R. Eleazar said: This teaches that Moses *stood in prayer* before the Holy One, blessed be He." Cf. further there the identical opinion of R. Eliezer the Great.
2. *Sifre Wā'etḫanān* XXVI, p. 39f. "There are ten expressions for prayer ... it is (also) called *ḥîlwy* as it says: 'and Moses implored (*wayĕḥal*)'—Exod. 32:11.
3. *b. Ber. 30b* "What interval should be left between one prayer and another. R. Huna and R. Ḥisda gave different answers ... the other said long enough to fall into an interceding frame of mind ... quoting the text 'and Moses interceded (*wa-yĕḥal*)'—Exod. 32:11."
4. Tanḥ(B) *Wayyērā'* IX, p. 90 "... likewise you find with the Patriarchs of the world, when they *pray,* they *pray* with awe, as Moses said: 'and I fell down before the Lord' (Deut. 9:18, 25)—he was seeking compassion for Israel, as it says 'and Moses implored' (*wa-yĕḥal*), he girded his loins in *prayer.*" Cf. also Exod. Rab. XLIII:1.

[8]The Hebrew has: "in" which the Targum and the Syr. render by the preposition *byn,* expanded even further by Tg. Ps.-Jon. "between the mountains—Tabor, Hermon, Siryon, and Sinai."

servants to whom You have sworn *by Your Memra*[9] and spoken *with*[c] them, 'I will multiply your *children*[10] like the stars of the sky; and this entire land of which I have spoken, I will give to your children and they will possess <it> forever.'" 14. Whereupon the Lord relented from the harm He had *promised*[d] to do to His people. 15. So Moses turned and descended from the mountain with the two tablets of the Testimony in his hand, tablets inscribed on both their sides; they were inscribed on the one and on the other side. 16. Now the tablets were the work of the Lord, and the writing was the writing *of the Lord,*[e] *explicit*[f] on the tablets. 17. When Joshua heard the sound of the people as they were shouting, he said to Moses, "There is a sound of war in the camp." 18. But he said, "Neither the sound of *warriors who are victorious in battle,*[11] nor the sound of *weak ones who are defeated,*[11] but the sound of *those who indulge in revelry*[11] do I hear." 19. So when he approached the camp and saw the calf and the dancing, Moses' anger became powerful and he cast the tablets from his hands and shattered them *at the foot of*[12] the mountain. 20. Then he took the calf which they had made and burnt it in the fire and ground <it> until it became *powdery*[g] and scattered <it> upon the surface of the water and made the Israelites drink <it>. 21. Now Moses said to Aaron, "What did this people do to you that you have brought on it <such> a great sin?" 22. Whereupon Aaron said, "Let not my master's anger become strong; you know this people that it is evil. 23. Now they said to me, 'Make *gods*[1] for us who will go ahead of us, for this man Moses who brought us up from the land of Egypt, we do not know what became of him.' 24. So I said to them, 'Whoever has gold, take <it> off and give <it> to me; whereupon I cast it into the fire and this calf emerged." 25. Moses realized that the people *were worthless,*[13] that Aaron *had made them worthless*[13] *by causing them to assume a bad reputation*[h] *for their generation.*[14] 26. Then Moses stood at the gate of the *camp*[i] and proclaimed, "Let those who fear the Lord come to me"; whereupon all the Levites gathered to him. 27. And he said to them, "So says the Lord, God of Israel, 'Each man is to place his sword at his thigh; then go back and forth from gate to gate throughout the camp, and kill each *person*[j] his brother, and each man his fellow man, and each person his relative.'" 28. Whereupon the Levites did according to Moses' word; and about three thousand men of the people fell on that day. 29. Then Moses said "Let *your hands present today an offering*[k15] to the Lord, for each <has been> against his son and against his brother, that He may *bring*[l] blessings upon you today." 30. Now it was on the following day that Moses said to the people, " You have committed a great sin; but now I will go up *before*[2] the Lord; perhaps I can achieve atonement for your sin(s)." 31. So Moses returned to the Lord and said, " Please! This people has committed a great sin and made for themselves *deities*[1] of gold. 32. But now, perhaps you would only forgive their sin(s); but if not, erase me now from Your book that You have written." 33. Whereupon the Lord said to Moses, "Whoever

Apparatus, Chapter 32 (Cont.)

[c] I has: "to," as does the Hebrew.
[d] Lit. "spoke;" E has "schemed."
[e] n has: "from before the Lord."
[f] b has: "impressed."
[g] I adds: "as dust."
[h] c and I have: "by bringing out a bad reputation about them."
[i] I has: "tent."
[j] C and n have: "man," as does the Hebrew.
[k] E omits "your hands;" b and g have: "an offering today;" I has: "your offering today"; while n has: "your offerings today."
[l] n has: "to give," as does the Hebrew.

sinned *before*[2] Me will I erase from My book. 34. So now proceed to lead the people to the place I spoke of to you, here My angel will go ahead of you; however, on the day of My visitation, I will punish them <for> their sin(s)." 35. Then the Lord struck the people *for having enslaved themselves to*[16] the calf which Aaron had made.

Notes, Chapter 32 (Cont.)

[9]See Introduction VII D. 1

[10]See Gen. Chap. 3, n. 8.

[11]The Hebrew has: ". . . the tune of victory nor . . . the tune of defeat but . . . the sound of song . . . ." The Targum here expands the Hebrew "victory" into "warriors who are victorious in battle," "defeat" into "weak ones who are defeated," and "of song" into "of those who indulge in revelry." In the first of the tri-cola passage, the Targum understood the Hebrew *'ănôṯ* < *qal* of *'nh*—"respond," and here referring to the responsive cry to those who are victorious in battle, yet this word is only implicit in the Targum. The same holds true for the second colon, where *'ănoṯ* is also understood as a responsive cry, but here as that of those who suffered defeat in war; likewise here, this word is only implicit in the context of the paraphrase. The third colon in the Hebrew *'annôṯ* < *piel* of *'nh* "afflict," "distress" is here entirely ignored, in favor of a translation that relates to the end of vs. 6 above, involving the revelry in which the people indulged. There, the revelry is explained by the following Rabbinic sources as involving idolatry, among other offenses:

1. *Eliyahu Rabba* XIII (XIV), p. 61 "As R. Aqiba put it . . . *Revelry also leads to idolatry.* Scripture tells us that 'the people sat down to eat and to drink, and rose up to engage in revelry' (Exod. 32:6)."
2. *Exod. Rab.* XLI:12 "'and the people sat down to eat and to drink then arose to engage in revelry' (Exod. 32:6). The Holy One, blessed be He, said to Moses: 'They have arisen to engage in revelry with the idols, and you sit here? Go down!'"

The Pal. Tgs. explicitly mention idolatry in their rendering of the third colon in the present verse:

Tg. Ps.-Jon.—"the sound of those engaged in idolatry and their revelry before it (idol)."

Tg. Neof.—"the sound of those praising idolatry."

Frg. Tg. [*P, V*]—"the sound of those praising idolatry."

[12]The Hebrew has "beneath" which the Targum here renders interpretively to mean at the foot, i.e., the bottom of the mountain. Cf. above Exod. 19:17 and n. 12 there.

[13]The Hebrew has: "had broken loose (that Aaron) had let them loose." The Targum here translates the Hebrew *pr'* by the Aramaic *bṭl* "annul, make worthless," which is in agreement with the following Rabbinic exposition of this passage:

b. Šabb. 119b "R. Joshua b. Levi said: He who responds 'Amen, May His Name be blessed,' with all his might, his decreed sentence is torn up, and it is said: 'When retribution (*pr'wt*) was annulled (*biprō'a*) in Israel, for that the people offered themselves willingly. Bless the Lord! Why? When retribution was annulled' (Judg. 5:2). R. Ḥiyya b. Abba said in R. Joḥanan's name: Even if he has a taint of idolatry, he is forgiven, it is written here, 'when retribution was annulled' (*biprō'a pĕrā'ôṯ*—Judg. 5:2) while elsewhere it is written—'and Moses saw that the people had broken (*paru'a*), for Aaron had let them loose' (*pĕrā'ōh*)."

[14]The Hebrew has: "for they were a derision, lit. a whisper, to their enemies." The Targum here parallels the Pal. Tgs. who render: "they acquired for themselves a bad reputation for all generations" (so the Frg. Tg. and Tg. Neof., while Tg. Ps.-Jon. only differs by having "for their generation," which is precisely the reading of Tg. Onq.). The rendering of Hebrew "enemies" here *qāmêhem* lit. "those who rise up against them, "by *dārêhôn* "their generations" is explained by a commentator cited by M. Kasher in *Torah Shelema* XXI, p. 141, n. 213 as in Num. 32:14 "now here you have risen up (*qámtem*) in place of your fathers," where the root *qwm* is associated with "a generation."

[15]See above Chap. 18, n. 6.

[16]The Hebrew has: "for having made," which the Targum here interpretively renders "for having enslaved themselves." The Tg. Ps.-Jon. also deviates from the Hebrew, rendering—"for having engaged in revelry," as does the Syr.—"for having worshipped." Naḥmanides explains the Targum's nonliteral

CHAPTER 33

1. Then the Lord spoke with Moses, "Proceed to ascend from here you and the people which you brought up out of the land of Egypt, to the land which I swore to Abraham, to Isaac, and to Jacob saying, 'To your *descendents*[1] will I give it.' 2. Now I will send an angel ahead of you and drive out the Canaanites, (and) the Hittites, (and) the Perizzites, the Hivites, and the Jebusites. 3. To a land *producing*[2] milk and honey, but I will not *remove My presence from your midst,*[a3] even though you are a stiff-necked people, lest I destroy you on the way." 4. When the people heard this *distressing*[4] matter, they mourned and no one put his armament equipment on himself. 5. Then said the Lord to Moses, "Say to the Israelites, 'You are a stiff-necked people; if for one moment I were to *remove My Presence from your midst*[3] I would destroy you; so now *remove*[b] your armament equipment from yourself *and it will be revealed to Me*[5] what I will do with you.'" 6. Whereupon the Israelites removed the armament equipment at Mount Horeb. 7. Now Moses took the tent and pitched it outside the camp far from the camp and called it the *Tent of the Place of Instruction.*[6] Now, anyone *seeking instruction from before the Lord*[6] would go out to the *Tent of the Place of Instruction*[6] which is outside the camp. 8. So when Moses would go out to the tent, all the people would rise and stand, each one at the entrance of his tent, and gaze after Moses till *he would enter*[c] the sanctuary. 9. Now when Moses would enter the tent, the pillar of the cloud would descend and stand at the entrance of the tent and speak with Moses. 10. When all the people saw the pillar of the cloud standing at the entrance of the tent, all the people rose and bowed down, each at the entrance of his

Apparatus, Chapter 33

[a] b and n have: "in your midst" without the *m* prefix. See n. 3 below.

[b] h has the literal: "lower."

[c] l has the literal "his entering into."

Notes, Chapter 32 (Cont.)

rendering of Hebrew "made" to a rule of thumb that the Targum does not translate literally an action that is attributed to two parties. Accordingly, he could not render literally "for having made the calf" as the verse immediately thereafter attributes the making of the calf to Aaron. A similar situation occurs in Gen. 39:22 where the Targum likewise deviates from offering a literal translation. Consequently, the Targum renders the Hebrew *'āśû* "they made" into "enslaved themselves" (*'ištaʻbādû*), as the people were not the ones who made the calf but it was Aaron who made it. The people who are here mentioned as being the target for God's plague, were the ones who embraced, kissed, and were impassioned towards the calf. This punishment is detailed in the following Talmudic passage:
b. Yoma 66b ". . . whosoever embraced and kissed (the calf) died the death (at the hands of heaven)." Death by 'the hands of heaven' meant the plague. Cf. also Gen. 12:5 where Hebrew *'āśû*—"made" is likewise rendered by the *šaphel* of *'bd.*

Notes, Chapter 33

[1]See Gen. Chap. 3, n. 8.

[2]See above Chap. 3, n. 13.

[3]The Hebrew has: "go up into your midst." Related to the difficulty of this translation in the Targum, which appears to be directly the opposite of what the Hebrew states, there are problems with the

tent. 11. Now the Lord would speak with Moses *literally*[7] just as one would speak with his fellow man, and he would return to the camp, while his attendant, Joshua son of Nun, the youth, would not depart from the tent. 12. Then Moses said to the Lord, "See, You have said to me, 'Bring up this people,' but You have not made known to me

Notes, Chapter 33 (Cont.)

Hebrew text itself. Löwenstein (*Nefesh Ha-Ger, op. cit.*, p. 83) poses the question succinctly—Is not God in heaven and you are on earth? Therefore, how could the Hebrew state: "I will not *go up into* your midst"? Berkowitz (*Simlat Ger, op. cit.*, p. 65) elaborates further, pointing out that God's resting His presence (*šeḵināh*) among mankind is depicted in Scripture by the act of "descending," thus "the Lord *descended* upon Mt. Sinai" (Exod. 19:20); "and I will *descend* and speak with you there" (Num. 11;17). In contrast, God's removal of His Presence is depicted by the act of "ascending," as in Gen. 17:22—"then the Lord *ascended* from Abraham." This act of "ascending" is expressed by the Aramaic root *slq*, denoting "removal." Berkowitz, along with the majority of Onqelos commentaries, attempts to resolve this difficulty in the Hebrew text by correctly pointing out that the *beth* prefix of the Hebrew *b-qirbĕḵā* "in your midst" should be understood in the sense of a *mem* prefix meaning "from," as in Lev. 8:32 "and that which remains from the flesh (Hebrew *b-bāśār*) and from the bread (Hebrew *b-léḥém*)," and in Gen. 35:13 "and the Lord *ascended* from him; from the place (Hebrew *b-māqōm*) where He spoke to him." Accordingly, the Hebrew makes sense—"for I will not ascend *from* your midst" the following conjunction *kî* must then be translated "even though" in contrast to the first time this conjunction occurs in this verse where it means "for." The Targum, too, falls into place, and no longer translates against the sense of the Hebrew. The same adjustment on *b-qirbĕḵā* in vs. 5 will lend sense to the Hebrew and consequently to the translation of the Targum. An alternative explanation is offered by Y. Koraḥ (*Marpe Lashon, op. cit.*, p. 273f.). He reasons that the Hebrew "for I will not ascend into your midst" was intentionally phrased so as to leave room for the deduction— "into *your* midst" will I not ascend, but I will ascend into the midst of *an angel*. Otherwise the verse should have read "I will not ascend *with you*" (the very reading of the LXX and the Vg.). Accordingly, the Hebrew text could have two different connotations. One, favorable towards Israel, that God will not remove His Presence from them, in that it will be present in an angel whom He will send ahead (vs. 2 above). The other would be detrimental towards Israel, in that they themselves were not worthy enough to have God's Presence dwell among them. The Targum takes the former approach, as is seen from the context of succeeding verses (12, 14, 15, 16). Cf. further J. Eisenberg, *Yanḥenu:* Exodus. Warsaw, 1900-1901, p. 41; Schefftel, *Bi'ure Onqelos, op. cit.*, p. 118; S.D. Luzzatto, *Ohev Ger, op. cit.*, p. 55; and Adler, *Netina La-Ger, op. cit.*, to this verse; the later two citing a variant in Onqelos that reads *bênāḵ* without the *mem* prefix, for which cf. the Apparatus for this chapter note a. According to them this version in the Targum would offer better sense than with the *mem* prefix. Tgs. Ps.-Jon. and Neof. render similarly here.

[4]Lit. "evil."

[5]See Gen. Chap. 3., n. 1.

[6]The Hebrew has: "Tent of Meeting" (*'ōhel mō'ēd*) which is usually rendered literally, for which cf. Exod. 39:32; 40:2, 26, 30, 32, 34; Lev. 1:1; Num. 8:9, 15. Adler (*Netina La-Ger, op. cit.*, on this verse) differentiates between this edifice, which was located outside the camp as pointed out in the present verse, and the Tent of Meeting which was part of the Sanctuary. Löwenstein (*Nefesh Ha-Ger, op. cit.*, p. 84) concurs, further pointing out that the present edifice was set up expressly at this time only for the specific purpose of instruction in the Law of God, as this verse itself points out "now anyone seeking instruction from before the Lord." This same situation existed in earlier times as can be seen from Gen. 25:22, where Rebeccah "went to seek the Lord" rendered by the Targum "to seek instruction from before the Lord." Berkowitz (*Ḥalifot Semalot, op. cit.*, p. 75) comments on the odd combination here of the Aramaic *bêṯ maškan 'ûlpānā'*, why both *bêṯ* and *maškan*, as *bêṯ 'ûlpānā* occurs in Gen. 25:27 and *maškan zîmnā'* is the usual equivalent for Hebrew *'ōhel mō'ēd* as pointed out above? He concludes that inasmuch as it served both as Moses' tent and as a place for instruction it therefore was known by this compound name.

[7]The Targum through this translation circumvents the overtly anthropomorphic Hebrew "face to face."

whom You will send with me. Moreover, you have said to me, 'I have *consecrated*[8] you by name and you have also found compassion *before Me.*[9]' 13. So now, if now I have found compassion *before You,*[9] make known to me now *the way of Your goodness*[10] that I may know *Your love*[11] in order that I may find {further} *compassion*[12] *before You,*[9] *and reveal to You*[13] that this people is Your people." 14. Then He said, "*My Presence*[14] will go and I will lead you." 15. Whereupon he said to Him, "If *Your Presence*[14] will not walk amongst us, we will not go up from here. 16. For how will it be known here that I have found *compassion*[12] *before You,*[9] I and Your people? Unless when *Your Presence*[14] walks with us, *so that wonders will be performed for us—for me and for Your people—<who are> different*[15] from every people that is on the face of the earth." 17. Thereupon the Lord said to Moses, "Also this matter that you spoke <of> I will do; for you have found *compassion*[12] *before Me,*[9] and I have *consecrated*[8] you by name." 18. So he said, "Show me, now, Your Glory." 19. And He said, "I will make all My *goodness*[d] pass before you and will proclaim <Myself> with My name, the Lord, before you; and I will be gracious to whom I will be gracious and show compassion on whom I will show compassion." 20. Then He said, "You will not be able to see *the face of My Presence;*[e14] for no *man*[f] may see Me and live." 21. And the Lord said, "Here is a place *prepared*[16] *before Me;*[9] now you are to stand on the rock. 22. So when My Glory passes by, I will place you in a cleft of the rock *and will shield you with My Memra*[17] until I have passed by. 23. *Then I will remove the Word of My Glory,*[18] and you will perceive *that which is behind Me,*[19] *but what is in front of Me*[19] will not be seen."

Apparatus, Chapter 33 (Cont.)

[d] a and n have: "glory."
[e] n has: "glory" in accordance with its reading in the preceding note and vs. 18 above.
[f] a has: "person" as does the Hebrew.

Apparatus, Chapter 34

[a] E has: "man," which is literal.

Notes, Chapter 33 (Cont.)

[8]See above Chap. 31, n. 1.

[9]See Gen. Chap. 4, n. 1.

[10]The Hebrew "Your ways" is expanded in the Targum to "the way of Your goodness," as it is in Tg. Ps.-Jon. B. Schmerler, (*Ahavat Yehonatan, op. cit.*, p. 229) points out that the Hebrew is plural, as God manifests many ways and they are enumerated in Exod. 34:6-7 below, and said to be entirely of justice in Deut. 32:4. Here Moses is requesting to know one particular way—that of God's goodness, which is specifically mentioned in vs. 19 below.

[11]The Hebrew "(that I may know) You" is here circumlocuted in order to avoid direct contact between man and God, since man can only know God by studying His ways, as clearly articulated in the following Midrash:

Sifre *'Éqeb* XLIX, p. 114 "'to follow in all His ways' (Deut. 11:22). These are the ways of God: 'The Lord is a compassionate and gracious God' (Exod. 34:6) and it says: 'and it shall come to pass that whosoever shall call on the name of the Lord shall be delivered' (Joel 3:5). Now is it possible for men to call in the Name of God? However, God is called 'The Merciful One,' you too be called 'merciful one'. . . ."

[12]See Gen. Chap. 6, n. 8.

[13]See Gen. Chap. 29, n. 8.

CHAPTER 34

1. Then the Lord said to Moses, "Carve yourself two tablets of stone like the first ones, and I will inscribe on the tablets the words that were on the first tablets which you shattered. 2. Now you should be ready by morning and ascend Mt. Sinai in the morning and stand there *before*[1] Me on the top of the mountain. 3. And no *person*[a]

Notes, Chapter 33 (Cont.)

[14]The Hebrew "My face" is anthropomorphic, and accordingly translated by the use of ***Šĕkîntā'***, God's "Presence." Likewise in the following two verses where "Your face" occurs, although in vs. 20 below "My face" is rendered "the face of My Presence."

[15]The Hebrew has: "so that we be distinguished, I and Your people." The Targum here elaborates on the clause "that we be distinguished" by specifying that this distinction will come about because "wonders will be performed for us." Adler (*Netina La-Ger, op. cit.*, to this verse) may be correct in pointing out that what follows in the Targum—"for me and for Your people who are different"—appears to be a second translation for that Hebrew passage. Although it may merely be an elaboration on an elaboration, simply explaining that "we are different from every people" in that "wonders will be performed for us." The Aramaic term for "wonders"—***pĕrîšān*** as equivalent for Hebrew "we be distinguished"—***wĕniplînû*** < *pl'*, here employed by the Targum, as well as the Syr. and Tg. Ps.-Jon., is also used in the identical situation in Exod. 9:4 above. Tg. Neof. is similar here—"in that signs and wonders will be performed for us."

[16]An insertion, also present in Tgs. Ps.-Jon. and Neof., but implied in the Hebrew.

[17]The Hebrew "and I will cover you with My hand" is anthropomorphic, and accordingly circumvented by the paraphrase involving the *Memra* which will "shield" (for Hebrew "cover") Moses. Tg. Ps.-Jon. renders similarly here, while Tg. Neof. and the Frg. Tg. (P, V) oddly enough are literal here.

[18]The Hebrew "then I will remove My hand" is anthropomorphic and circumvented by rendering "hand" with "the Word of My Glory" (*yĕqārā'*). Tgs. Neof., Ps.-Jon., and the Frg. Tg. (P.V.) have: "and I shall remove the groups of angels who stand and minister before Me," which mentions angels as does the following Midrash:

Pesîqtā' Rabbāṯi X: Kî Tissā', p. 37b "... the Holy One, blessed be He, then acceded to his (Moses') prayer, saying: Since you press this matter, I will put you in a cleft of a rock, and even as I pass by, I shall defend (lit. "cover") you with My hand, so that the *angels of anger* will not strike you ... What did Moses do? He set himself in a cleft of the rock as the Glory of the Holy One, blessed be He, passed by, and when the *angels* came to strike Moses ... He defended him with His hand." Cf. also Mekhilta *Bō' Meseḵtā' dePisḥā'* XI, p. 38, and Num. Rab. XIV:19.

[19]The Hebrew "My back" is anthropomorphic and consequently paraphrased into "that which is behind Me," likewise "My face" is paraphrased "that which is in front of Me." The other Aramaic Versions paraphrase differently and are hereby summarized:

Tg. Neof. "...the word of the Glory of My Presence ... (but) the face of the Glory of My Presence."

Tg. Ps.-Jon. "...the knot of the Tefillin of the hand ... (but) the Glory of My Presence and the face of the Glory of My Presence...."

Frg. Tg. [*P*] "...the Word of the Lord ... but the Glory of My Presence...."

[*V*] "...the Word of the Glory of My Presence ... (it is impossible for you to see)."

Berkowitz (*Ḥalifot Semalot, op. cit.*, p. 75) poses the obvious question, why the Targum does not render "My face" here "(the face of) My Presence" as in vs. 14, 15, and 20 above? He reasons that since "My back" in this verse had to be rendered "that which is behind Me," the complementary clause "My face" had to be translated "that which is in front of Me."

Notes, Chapter 34

[1]See Gen. Chap. 4, n. 1.

should go up with you, nor should any *person*[b] be seen anywhere on the mountain; neither should sheep or cattle graze at the front of that mountain." 4. So he carved the two tablets of stone like the first ones, and Moses arose early in the morning and ascended Mt. Sinai as the Lord had commanded him, and took the two tablets of stone in his hand. 5. Now the Lord *revealed Himself*[2] in a cloud and stood there with him; and he proclaimed the name of the Lord. 6. *Then the Lord made His Presence pass*[3] in front of him, and he proclaimed, "O Lord! O Lord! Compassionate and gracious God, <who> *keeps anger at a distance*[4] and abounds *in doing true goodness.*[5] 7. Maintaining kindness to the thousandth *generation,*[6] forgiving *iniquities,*[7] rebellion, and *sins;*[7] *pardoning those who return to His Law; whereas those who do not repent He does not acquit;*[8] He visits the iniquities of the fathers upon *rebellious*[9] children and <upon> children's children, upon the third *generation*[6] and fourth *generation.*[6]" 8. Thereupon Moses hurriedly bowed low to the ground and paid homage. 9. And he said, "If now I have found *compassion*[10] before You, O Lord, let *the Presence of the Lord*[3] now walk among us; although this is a stiff-necked people, forgive our iniquities, and our sins, and make us Your possession." 10. Then the Lord said, "Here I am about to establish a covenant; before all your people I will perform <such> wonders which *have*[c] not been created for the entire world and all the nations; then *every nation*[d] among whom you are {living} will perceive how awesome is the work of the Lord which I perform for you. 11. Observe that which I command you today; here I am about to drive out before you the Amorites and Canaanites, (and) Hittites and Perizzites, (and) Hivites and Jebusites. 12. Beware lest you establish a covenant with the *inhabitant*[e] of the land into which you are about to *enter,*[f] lest they be a snare in your midst. 13. Rather you should tear down their altars, and smash their statues, as well as cut down their Asherah poles. 14. For you must not worship *the abominations of the nations*[11] because the Lord whose name is Jealous, is a jealous God. 15. Lest you establish a covenant with the *inhabitant*[g] of the land, for when they stray after their *abominations,*[11] and sacrifice to *their abominations,*[11] they will invite you and you will eat of *their sacrifices.*[12] 16. Then you will take {some} of *their*[h] daughters {as wives} for your sons(s); *they will cause their daughters*[h] *to stray*[i] after *their abominations*[11] then *cause your sons to stray*[j] and *their abominations.*[11] 17. You should not make molten

Apparatus, Chapter 34 (Cont.)

[b] I has: "man." See preceding note.
[c] v, b, g, and I have the plural: "have," as does the Hebrew.
[d] G has: "all nations."
[e] n has the plural, which is interpretive.
[f] I has: "settle," an interpretive reading.
[g] I has the plural. See note e above.
[h] E has: "its," as does the Hebrew.
[i] Sperber's text has the literal: "their daughters will stray."
[j] h has: "your sons will stray," as does the LXX.
[k] L and d actually have the conjunction *ka'ăšer*—"as," as do many Cairo Geniza mss., the Sam. Heb., the LXX, and the Syr., while MT has *'ăšer* only.
[l] b, d, and k omit; the Hebrew does not have it.
[m] g and I have: "and every male livestock you should consecrate, the firstborn of herd and of flock."

Notes, Chapter 34 (Cont.)

[2]See Gen. Chap. 11, n. 2.

[3]The Hebrew: "Then the Lord passed (in front of him)" presented a situation in direct conflict with Exod. 33:20, according to which no man is able to see God and live. Accordingly, the Shekhinah ("Divine Presence") of God is here used instead; it is also used in Tg. Ps.-Jon while Tg. Neof. and the

gods for yourself. 18. Observe the Feast of Unleavened Bread; seven days you should eat unleavened bread <*as*>[k] I commanded you during the month of Abib, for in the month of Abib you departed from Egypt. 19. The first {offspring} of every womb, *it*[l] is Mine, *and every livestock you should consecrate, the firstborn males*[13] *from the herd or flock.*[m] 20. Now the firstborn of the donkey you should redeem with a lamb, but if you do not redeem <it>, you should strike it mortally; every firstborn of your sons you

Notes, Chapter 34 (Cont.)

Frg. Tg. (P, V) use "the Glory of His Divine Presence."

[4]The Hebrew has: "slow to anger." The Targum here deviates in translating "keeps anger at a distance," a deviation that can be better understood in the light of what the Pal. Tgs. have here:

Tg. Ps.-Jon. "long suffering and brings compassion near."

Tg. Neof. and the Frg. Tg. [*V*] "keeps anger at a distance and brings compassion near."

It becomes obvious that Onqelos and the Pal. Tgs. at one point in their development contained an identical text here, which may well have been that of Tg. Neof. and the Frg. Tg. (V). This text, not only rendered the Hebrew "slow to anger" interpretively "keeps anger at a distance," no doubt because of the anthropomorphism involved, but also expanded it with the complementary "and brings compassion near." The Tg. Ps.-Jon. altered the first half of this translation, perhaps to conform more closely to the Hebrew, while retaining the expansion intact. Tg. Onq. dropped the expansion, while retaining the first half intact.

[5]The Targum adds: "in doing" to supply the predicate, implied in the Hebrew. For the translation of "true kindness," see Gen. Chap. 32, n. 6.

[6]See above Chap. 20, n. 3.

[7]See Gen. Chap. 4, ns. 4 and 9.

[8]The Hebrew "yet He does not remit all punishment" is somewhat difficult as it reads ***wĕnaqqēh** lō **yĕnaqqeh*** lit. "and He acquits, He does not acquit." The Targum, in rendering the first half, translates "acquits" by "pardons" appropriately adding "those who return to His Law"; then renders the second half literally "He does not acquit" again appropriately adding "those who do not repent." The Tg. Ps-Jon. is identical here but adds at the end—"on the day of the great judgment," an addition also present in Tg. Neof. and the Frg. Tg. (V), both of which have different preceding paraphrases. The Targum's paraphrase, which as stated above, was stimulated by the somewhat difficult Hebrew wording, is precisely reflected in the Talmud and the Midrash, as follows:

b. Yoma 86a and b. Šebu.39a "R. Eleazar said: It is impossible to say, 'He will not acquit' (Exod. 34:7) since it says: 'He will acquit' (*ibid.*); nor is it possible to say: 'He will acquit,' since it is said: 'He will not acquit'; how is that to be explained? 'He clears the guilt' of those who repent, and does not 'clear the guilt' of those who do not repent." Cf. also Sifre Zuta *Nāśō'* VI:26 (the Midrash cited in Kasher's *Torah Shelema* XXII, p. 68, # 75) in *Siphre D'Be Rab*, ed. H.S. Horovitz. Jerusalem (Wahrmann Books), 1966, p. 248, and t. Yom. V:9

[9]See above Chap. 20, n. 2.

[10]See Gen. Chap. 6, n. 8.

[11]See Introduction VII A.3.

[12]The Hebrew singular is here pluralized as in the LXX and in the Syr., Tg. Neof. and the Tg. Ps.-Jon. See also Gen. Chap. 21, n. 7.

[13]The Hebrew has: "that drop a male." The following attempt to explain the difficult Hebrew word *tizzāḵār* is made by Rashi: "...which it (the mother animal) brings forth as male... The *taw* of *tizzāḵār* expresses the feminine gender and refers to the animal in labor (i.e., the prefix is 3rd fem. sing. not 2nd. masc. sing.); the subject to *tizzāḵār* must be supplied—'the mother animal.'" The Targum likewise felt the difficulty of the Hebrew word and paraphrased "consecrate the males," as did the Tg. Ps.-Jon., while the Frg. Tg. (V) has: "all your firstborn males" and Tg. Neof.: "all your male livestock." Likewise, the other Ancients struggled with this difficult Hebrew word, as the Syr. has: "every firstling among your cattle," the LXX completely rearranges this verse: ***πᾶν διανοιγον μήτραν ’εμὸι τὰ αρσενικὰ πᾶν πρωτότοκον μόσχου, κάι πρωτότοκον προβάτου***—"The males of

should redeem; none should appear *before*[14] Me empty-handed. 21. Six days you should labor, but on the seventh day you should rest; at plowing time and harvest time you should rest. 22. Now the Feast of Weeks you should observe with the firstfruits of the wheat harvest, and the Feast of Ingathering *at the end*[15] *of* the year. 23. Three times a year all your males should appear *before*[14] *the Master of the Universe,*[16] the Lord, God of Israel. 24. When I will drive out the nations before you and widen your territory, no *person*[b] will envy your land when you go up to appear *before*[14] the Lord your God three times a year. 25. Do not offer the blood of My *Passover sacrifice*[17] with anything leavened; neither should you let the fat of the Passover festal offering remain overnight till *morning.*[n] 26. The earliest of the firstfruit of your land you should *bring*[o] *to the Temple*[18] of the Lord your God; *do not consume milk with meat.*[19]" 27. Then the Lord said to Moses, "Write down these words, for in accordance with these words I have established a covenant with you and with Israel. 28. Now he was there *before*[p] the Lord forty days and forty nights; bread he did not eat, and water he did not drink, and he wrote down on the tablets the terms of the covenant—the Ten Commandments. 29. Now when Moses descended from Mt. Sinai, and the two tablets of the Testimony were in Moses' hand(s) during his descent from the mountain, Moses did not realize that the radiance of the *glory*[20] of his face *increased*[21] since He had spoken with him. 30. When Aaron and all the Israelites saw Moses, and here the radiance of the *glory*[20] of his face *increased,*[21] they were apprehensive in approaching him. 31. Then Moses called to them, and Aaron as well as all the leaders *in*[q] the congregation returned to him, and Moses spoke *with*[r] them. 32. Afterwards, all the Israelites approached, and he commanded them concerning everything that the Lord spoke to him on Mt. Sinai. 33. When Moses finished speaking with them he placed a veil over his face. 34. And when Moses went in before the Lord to speak with Him, he would remove the veil until he departed. He would then depart and tell the Israelites what he was commanded. 35. The Israelites would notice *Moses' face*[s] *because*[t] the radiance of the *glory*[20] of Moses' face had *increased;*[21] then Moses would place the veil on his face until *he went in*[u] to speak with Him.

Apparatus, Chapter 34 (Cont.)

[n] D, G, i, and n add: "outside of the altar."
[o] a has: "bring in."
[p] b, d, c, and n have: "with," as does the Hebrew.
[q] n has the interpretive: "of."
[r] b and d have: "to," as does the Hebrew.
[s] M has: "the expression of Moses' face."
[t] k has the interpretive: "and here," as in vs. 30 above.
[u] l has: "his coming in," as does the Hebrew.

Apparatus, Chapter 35

[a] D has: "bring it," as does the Hebrew.
[b] d and l have: "of," as does the Hebrew.

Notes, Chapter 34 (Cont.)

everything that opens the womb are mine; every firstborn of oxen and every firstborn of sheep," as does the Vg—*omne, quod aperit vulvam generis masculini meum erit de cunctis animantibus, tam de bobus, quam de ovibus meum erit*—"all the male kind that opens the womb, shall be mine. Of all beasts both of oxen and of sheep, it shall be mine."

[14]The Hebrew has *pny* lit. "My face," which is here rendered as if there was an *l* prefix present *lpny*—"before Me," which circumvents the anthropomorphism. Similarly, in vss. 23, 24 below the

CHAPTER 35

1. Then Moses gathered the entire community of the Israelites and said to them, "These are the things that the Lord has commanded {you} to do. 2. Six days you should do work, but on the seventh day you should have sanctity, a Sabbath of rest *before*[1] the Lord; whoever does work on it should be put to death. 3. You should not light a fire throughout your places of residence on the Sabbath day." 4. Then Moses said to the entire community of the Israelites as follows, "This is the thing that the Lord commanded saying, 5. 'Set apart from among you an offering before the Lord; all those whose hearts are willing should *bring*[a] an offering *before*[b] the Lord—gold, silver, and copper. 6. Blue and purple and scarlet yarn, and fine linen, and goats' hair. 7. And red rams' skins, as well as scarlet skins, and acacia wood. 8. And oil for lighting and spices for the anointing oil, and for the aromatic incense. 9. And beryl stones and setting stones for insertion into the ephod and (into) the breastplate. 10. Now all those who are wise in heart among you should come and do all that the Lord has commanded. 11. The Sanctuary, its tent, and its cover, its hooks, and its planks, its bars, its posts, and its sockets. 12. The ark and its poles, the cover, and the curtain for the cover. 13. The table and its poles as well as all its vessels, and the display bread. 14. And the lampstand for lighting and its vessels and its lights, as well as the oil for lighting. 15. And the altar for aromatic incense and its poles, and the oil for anointing and the aromatic incense, as well as the cover for the entrance, for the entrance of the Sanctuary. 16. And the altar for burnt offerings and its copper grating of meshwork, its poles and all its vessels, the laver and its base. 17. The grating of meshwork for the

Notes, Chapter 34 (Cont.)

Hebrew *pny* "face of" is rendered as if it were *lpny* "before."

[15]The Hebrew "turn" (*tĕqûpāh*) lit. "circuit or completion (of the year)" is here rendered "end of" or "going out," the precise translation given in Exod. 23:16 above where the Hebrew actually is *ṣē'ṯ* "going out" in the synoptic passage.

[16]See above Chap. 23, n. 13.

[17]See above *ibid.*, n. 14.

[18]See above *ibid.*, n. 17.

[19]See above *ibid.*, n. 18.

[20]The Hebrew has "skin." The Tg. Ps.-Jon. here renders "the radiance of his facial features shone brightly from the radiance of the Glory of the Lord's Presence," according to which Moses' radiance derived from that of God's Glory. This state of affairs is supported by many Rabbinic traditions which state that Moses derived these "rays of splendour" from the Divine Presence, for which cf. Tanḥ(B) *Kî Tissā'* XX, p. 119; Tanḥ (A) *Kî Tissā'* XXXVII; Exod. Rab. XLVII:6; Deut. Rab. III:12. Consequently, the Targum rendered "skin" as "glory," since Moses' skin had by now, as a result of contact with the Glory of God's Divine Presence, turned into something more than just human skin and increased in radiance, hence the Targum's insertion "increased" also present in the Frg. Tg. (P, V) which reads "the radiance of his face increased."

[21]An insertion, for which see end of preceding note.

Notes, Chapter 35

[1]See Gen. Chap. 4, n. 1.

courtyard, its posts, and its sockets, and the cover for the entrance to the courtyard. 18. The pins for the sanctuary, and the pins for the courtyard and their ropes. 19. The officiating garments for officiating in the sanctuary, and the garments for the sanctuary for Aaron the priest, as well as his sons' garments for officiating.'" 20. Then the entire community of the Israelites departed from before Moses. 21. Now everyone whose heart was willing, and whose spirit *was perfected within him,*[c] brought the heave offering *before*[d] the Lord for the work of the Tent of Meeting and for all of its service, and for the garments of the sanctuary. 22. Then the men and the women, all those who were willing in heart, brought chains, bracelets, and rings, and feminine ornament(s), anything of gold; and everyone who would present a wave offering of gold before the Lord. 23. As well as everyone who had in his possession blue, purple, and scarlet yarn, and *fine linen,*[e] and goats' hair and red rams' skins and scarlet skins brought <them>. 24. Whoever presented a *wave offering*[f] of silver and copper, brought the heave offering *before*[d] the Lord, and everyone who had in his possession acacia wood for any work of the service brought <it>. 25. Now every woman, wise of heart, spun with her hands and brought what was spun in blue and purple and scarlet yarn, as well as in fine linen. 26. And all the women, who cleverly were *willing of heart,*[2] spun the goats' hair. 27. Whereas the leaders brought the beryl stones and setting stones for insertion into the Ephod and (into) the breastplate. 28. And aromatic spice as well as oil for lighting and for the anointing oil and for the aromatic incense. 29. Every man and woman who *was willing of heart*[2] to bring <anything> for all the work which the Lord has commanded to be done through Moses, <these> Israelites brought <as> a freewill offering to the Lord. 30. Then Moses said to the Israelites, "See, the Lord has *consecrated*[3] by name Bezalel, son of Uri, son of Hur, of the tribe of Judah. 31. And He perfected in him a *spirit*[g] from before the Lord for wisdom and for intelligence, as well as for knowledge in all <kinds of> craft. 32. To instruct artisans to work with gold, and with silver, and with copper. 33. And in the art of setting of precious stones and carving of wood, to all <kinds of> artistic craftsmanship. 34. And <the ability> to teach has He placed in his heart, to him, and to Oholiab, son of Aḥisamakh, of the tribe of Dan. 35. He perfected in them wisdom of heart to do any kind of work of the carver, designer, and embroiderer in blue, purple, and scarlet yarn and in fine linen, and of the weaver; <as> workers in all crafts and instructors of artisanships.

Apparatus, Chapter 35 (Cont.)

[c] G and a have: "perfected him," which is literally closer to the Hebrew.
[d] l has: "of," as does the Hebrew.
[e] c and n have: "fine twisted linen."
[f] l has: "heave offering" which is the consistently used equivalent for Hebrew *tĕrûmāh* by the Targum, while "wave offering" is used for Hebrew *tĕnûpāh* throughout.
[g] G and l add: "of prophecy," as they did in Exod. 31:3 above.

Apparatus, Chapter 36

[a] n has: "further brought," as does the Hebrew.
[b] n adds: "of the side," as do Tgs. Ps.-Jon. and Neof., as well as 48 Hebrew mss., and the Sam Heb.

CHAPTER 36

1. Then Bezalel and Oholiab and every person who was wise of heart, to whom the Lord gave wisdom and intelligence to know how to carry out all the work of the sanctuary service, did according to all that the Lord had commanded." 2. And Moses summoned Bezalel, and Oholiab, and every person wise of heart in whose heart the Lord had placed wisdom, everyone who was *willing of heart*[1] to approach the task and carry it out. 3. So they took from Moses every gift offering which the Israelites had brought for the work of the sanctuary service to *construct*[2] it; but they *continued to bring*[a] him the freewill offering every morning. 4. Then came all the wise ones who were doing all the work of the sanctuary, each from his <assigned> task <on> which they were working. 5. And they said to Moses, "The people are bringing more than enough for the work which the Lord had commanded to be done." 6. So Moses ordered that a *proclamation*[3] be circulated throughout the camp as follows, "Let no man or woman make any further effort towards a gift offering for the sanctuary"; so the people stopped bringing. 7. Now the effort was already more than enough for all the work to be done, and then more. 8. Then everyone, who was wise of heart in carrying out the work, made the Sanctuary of ten curtains of finely twisted linen, and blue and purple and scarlet yarn, in a design of cherubs; the work of an artisan did he make them. 9. The length of one curtain {was} twenty-eight cubits and the width four cubits, that measurement of each curtain; one dimension for all the curtains. 10. Then he coupled five of the curtains to each other, and five of the other curtains did he couple to each other. 11. Then he made loops of blue wool on the edge of one curtain from the side of the place of the coupling; likewise did he do at the edge of the other side of the place of coupling. 12. He made fifty loops on one curtain, and fifty loops he made on the other side of the place of the coupling of the curtain; the loops were directed to face each other. 13. Then he made fifty golden hooks and coupled the curtains one to the other with the hooks and the Sanctuary became a unit. 14. Then he made curtains of goats' hair to stretch over the Sanctuary; he made them eleven curtains {altogether}. 15. The length of each curtain {was} thirty cubits and four cubits the width of each curtain; one dimension for {each of} the eleven curtains. 16. Then he

Notes, Chapter 35 (Cont.)

[2]The Hebrew "whose heart lifted them" is idiomatic and accordingly paraphrased into its intended meaning. A variation of this idiom occurs in vs. 29 below "whose heart made them willing to contribute," which is similarly paraphrased. Tg. Ps.-Jon. is identical here, while Tg. Neof. has "whose hearts prompted them" in both cases, and Tg. Neof. m. has "whose hearts were big" in both cases. The Syr. paraphrase "who were determined in their hearts" in both instances.

[3]See above Chap. 31, n. 1.

Notes, Chapter 36

[1]See above Chap. 35, n. 2.

[2]Lit. "make."

[3]The Hebrew lit. "voice, sound" is here interpretively rendered by *krûz* a Greek LW < *κήρυξ*—"proclamation."

coupled five curtains separately, and six curtains separately. 17. And he made fifty loops on the edge of the curtain on one side of the coupling, and fifty loops on the edge of the curtain on the other side of the place of coupling. 18. Then he made fifty copper hooks to couple the tent, so that it became a unit. 19. And he made a covering for the tent of red rams' skins and a covering of scarlet skins above <it>. 20. Then he made planks for the Sanctuary of acacia wood, upright {in position}. 21. The length of each plank {was} ten cubits and the width of each plank one and a half cubits. 22. {There were} two hinges for each plank in parallel connection to each other; likewise he did with all the hinges of the Sanctuary. 23. Then he made the planks for the Sanctuary {totaling} twenty planks in the direction of the south side. 24. Then he made forty silver sockets <to go> beneath twenty planks—two sockets beneath one plank per two hinges, and two sockets beneath another plank per two hinges. 25. And for the other side of the Sanctuary in the direction of the north <side>, he made twenty planks. 26. And forty silver sockets; two sockets beneath one plank and two sockets beneath the other plank. 27. And for the rear <sides> of the sanctuary <to> the west, he made six planks. 28. And two planks he made for the corners of the Sanctuary at their <far> end. 29. Now they were directed towards each other below, and as one were they directed towards each other at their top into one ring; accordingly he did for both of them towards the two corners. 30. Then there were eight planks with their silver sockets <totaling> sixteen sockets; two sockets for one plank and two sockets for another plank. 31. Then he made bars of acacia wood, five {of them} for the planks of one side of the Sanctuary. 32. (And) five bars for the planks of the other side of the Sanctuary, and five bars for the *planks*[b] of the Sanctuary at their rear end <to> the west. 33. Now he made the center bar at the middle of the planks to extend from end to end. 34. And he overlaid the planks with gold and made their rings of gold as a location for the bars and overlaid the bars with gold. 35. Then he made a curtain of blue (and) purple, (and) scarlet yarn, and twisted linen; he made *it*[c] <like> the work of an artisan {with} a design of cherubs. 36. And he made for it four posts of acacia wood; their hooks <were made of> gold, and he cast for them four silver sockets. 37. Then he made a cover for the entrance of the tent of blue and purple and scarlet yarn, and twisted linen, the work of *embroidery.*[d] 38. And its posts {totaled} five as {did} its hooks, and he overlaid their tops and their sockets <with> gold, and five sockets <with> copper.

Apparatus, Chapter 36 (Cont.)

[c] n has: "them," as do 33 Hebrew mss.
[d] J, E, a and d have: "an embroiderer," as does the Hebrew with its *nomen agentis.*

Apparatus, Chapter 37

[a] a has: "with their."
[b] a adds "for him" here as well.
[c] n has the plural, as does the Sam. Heb.
[d] D has the plural, as does the Sam. Heb.
[e] I has: "sides."
[f] I has: "corners."

CHAPTER 37

1. Then Bezalel made the ark of acacia wood, two and a half cubits its length, and one and a half cubits its width, and one and a half cubits its height. 2. And he overlaid it <with> pure gold inside and outside, and he made a golden moulding around it. 3. He then cast for it four golden rings for its four joints, two rings on one side and two rings on the other side. 4. And he made poles of acacia wood and overlaid them <with> gold. 5. He then inserted the poles into the rings on the sides of the ark to carry the ark. 6. And he made a cover of pure gold, two and a half cubits <in> its length and one and a half cubits <in> its width. 7. He then made two cherubs of gold; he made them extended from the two sides of the cover. 8. One cherub from one side and one cherub from the other side <extending> from the cover did he make the cherubs, from the two sides. 9. Now the cherubs <appeared> *their*[a] wings spread upwards, overshadowing the cover with their wings, while their faces <were> opposite each other; in the direction of the cover were the faces of the cherubs. 10. Then he made a table of acacia wood, two cubits <in> its length, one cubit <in> its width, and one and a half cubits <in> its height. 11. And he overlaid it <with> pure gold and *made*[b] a golden moulding around <it>. 12. And he made for it a rim, a hand-breadth <in> its height around <it>, and he made a golden moulding for its rim around it. 13. Then he cast for it four golden rings, and placed the rings on the four joints of its four legs. 14. Opposite the rim were the rings (located), as a place for the poles to carry the table. 15. Then he made poles of acacia wood and overlaid them <with> gold to carry the table. 16. And he made the vessels which go with the table—its trays, (and) its dishes (and) its jugs, and its bowls with which libations are poured, of pure gold. 17. Then he made a lampstand of pure gold; he made the lampstand, extending its *base*[c] and its *shaft,*[d] its cups, its calyxes, and its lilies, all <extended> from it. 18. Now six branches extended from its sides, three branches of the lampstand from its <one> side and three branches of the lampstand from its other side. 19. Three cups were embroidered on one branch, <with> a calyx and a lily, and three cups were embroidered on another branch <with> a calyx and a lily; accordingly for the six branches that extended from the lampstand. 20. Now on the lampstand were embroidered four cups with a calyx and a lily. 21. And a calyx beneath two branches <extending> from it, and a calyx beneath two branches <extending> from it, and a calyx beneath two branches <extending> from it; for the six branches that extended from it. 22. Their calyxes and their branches <extended> from it, all of it beaten <from> one piece of pure gold. 23. Then he made its seven lamps, and its tongs and its pans of pure gold. 24. From a talent of pure gold did he make it and all its vessels. 25. Then he made an altar of acacia wood for aromatic incense a cubit <in> its length, a cubit <in> its width, <it was> square, and two cubits <in> its length; its horns were <sculptured> from it. 26. And he overlaid it <with> pure gold—its top, and its sides, completely around it, as well as its horns; and he made a golden moulding for it completely around <it>. 27. And he made two golden rings for it to be beneath its moulding for its two *corners,*[e] at its two <opposite> *sides,*[f] as a *place*[1] for the poles with

Notes, Chapter 37

[1]See above Chap. 25, n. 8.

which to carry it. 28. And he made the poles of acacia wood and overlaid them <with> gold. 29. Then he made the anointing oil for the sanctuary and aromatic incense pure, the work of a perfumer.

CHAPTER 38

1. Then he made the altar for burnt offering of acacia wood; five cubits {in} its length, and five cubits {in} its width, {it was} square, and three cubits {in} its height. 2. And he made its horns for its four corners; its horns were <sculptured> from it, and he overlaid it <with> copper. 3. And he made all the vessels for the altar—its pots for gathering ashes, (and) its shovels, (and) its basins, (and) its flesh hooks, and its fire pans—all of its vessels did he make of copper. 4. And he made a copper grating of meshwork for the altar, beneath its gallery, from below, halfway up <the altar>. 5. And he cast four rings for the four corners of the grating of meshwork, as *a place*[1] for the poles. 6. And he made the poles for the altar of acacia wood and overlaid them <with> copper. 7. And he inserted the poles into the rings on the sides of the altar with which to carry it; hollow of boards did he make it. 8. And he made a laver of copper and its stand of copper, *from the mirrors of the women who came to pray*[2] at the entrance of the Tent of Meeting. 9. Then he made the courtyard towards the south side; the hangings of the courtyard <were> of fine twisted linen, one hundred cubits <in length>. 10. Their posts < totaled> twenty, and their sockets, twenty, <made of> copper, while the hooks for the posts and their sockets <were of> silver. 11. And for the north side <allow> a hundred cubits; their posts <totaled> twenty, and their sockets twenty; the hooks for the posts and their sockets <were of> silver. 12. Now to the west side <there were> hangings fifty cubits, their posts <totaled> ten and their sockets ten; while the hooks for the posts and their sockets <were> of silver. 13. And to the front side, eastward, <there was> fifty cubits. 14. Fifteen cubits of hangings for the side, their posts <totaled> three, and their sockets three. 15. And for the other side from either end to the entrance of the courtyard <were> hangings <of> fifteen cubits; their posts <totaled> three, and their sockets three. 16. All the hangings of the courtyard completely around <it were> of fine twisted linen. 17. And the sockets for the post <were of> copper, the hooks for the posts and their sockets <were of> silver, and their tops were overlaid with silver, and they were gilded <with> silver—all the poles of the courtyard. 18. Now the cover for the entrance of the courtyard <was> the work of *embroidery,*[a] <made of> blue, (and) purple, (and) scarlet yarn, and fine twisted linen, twenty cubits <in> length, and five cubits <in> height, opposite the hangings of the courtyard. 19. And their posts <totaled> four, and their sockets four, their hooks

Apparatus, Chapter 38

[a] J, L, a, and b have: "an embroiderer," as does the Hebrew with its *nomen agentis.*

<were> of silver with their tops and their sockets overlaid with silver. 20. Now all the pins that surrounded the Sanctuary and the courtyard <were made> of copper. 21. These are the amounts of <the materials for> the Sanctuary, the Sanctuary of the Testimony, which were ordered according to the *order*[3] of Moses, the work of the Levites under the direction of Ithamar, son of Aaron, the priest. 22. Now Bezalel, son of Uri, son of Ḥur, of the tribe of Judah, had made all that the Lord had commanded Moses. 23. Moreover, with him was Oholiab, son of Aḥisamakh of the tribe of Dan, carver, designer, and embroiderer in blue, purple, (and) scarlet yarn and fine twisted linen. 24. All the gold that was used for the work in all the work of the sanctuary—the wave offering of gold <amounted to> 29 talents and 730 *Selas,*[4] according to the sanctuary *Selas.*[4] 25. Now the silver of those who were counted <in the census> of the community <amounted to> 100 *talents*[5] and 1,775 *Selas*[4] according to the sanctuary *Selas.*[4] 26. The weight was per capita, half a *Sela*[4] according to the *Selas*[4] of the sanctuary for all those who passed through the counting procedures from the age of twenty years and above, 603,550 {men}. 27. Now the 100 *talents*[5] of silver were for casting the sockets of the sanctuary and the sockets for the curtain, 100 sockets to the 100 *talents,*[5] a talent per socket. 28. And of the 1,775 {*Selas*} he made hooks for the posts and overlaid their tops and gilded them. 29. Now the copper for the wave offering <amounted to> 70 *talents*[5] and 2,400 *Selas.*[4] 30. And of it he made the sockets for the entrance of the Tent of Meeting and the copper altar with its copper grating and all the accessories of the altar. 31. As well as the sockets for the courtyard all around <it> and the sockets for the entrance of the courtyard, and all the pins of the Sanctuary and all the pins of the courtyard all around <it>.

Notes, Chapter 38

[1]See above Chap. 25, n. 8.

[2]The Hebrew has: "from the mirrors of the serving women who served." The word for "serve" *haṣṣōḇ'ōṯ . . . ṣoḇ'û* is uncertain. The Targum renders *haṣṣōḇ'ōṯ* "the women who came to pray" as does the Syr.; Tg. Neof. expands it some more—"the righteous women who prayed," while Tg. Neof.m. and the Frg. Tg. (P, V) have "the chaste women who stood . . ."

By far the most elaborate version of this Aggadic rendering is contained in Tg. Ps.-Jon. "from the copper mirrors of the chaste women, at the time when they came to pray at the entrance of the Tent of Meeting, they would be standing by their wave offering and offer praise and gratitude, while manifesting desire for their husbands. Subsequently they gave birth to righteous children at the time when ritually pure from the defilement of their menstrual flow." This Aggadah is also present in various forms in Rabbinic literature, primarily in the Midrash Tanḥ (A) *Piqqudēh* IX, and *Numb. Rab.* IX:14—". . . Because the laver was made from the mirrors of women, as its says 'and he made the laver of copper . . . from the mirrors of the serving women. . . .' (Exod. 38:8), those women who had said: 'God bear witness for us that we went out of Egypt chaste.' When Moses came to make the laver, God said to him: Make it from those mirrors, which were not fashioned for purposes of immorality, and their daughters shall be tried by them as to whether they are chaste like their mothers." According to the above-mentioned Midrash Tanḥuma, the women who are referred to here as *haṣṣōḇ'ōṯ* < *ṣb'*—"host," used to entice their husbands into having sexual relations with them by means of mirrors in spite of the heavy labor placed upon them by the Egyptians. This was considered meritoriously to their credit by God, who rewarded them with multiple births. Consequently, the "hosts" of Israelites who left Egypt as mentioned in Exod. 12:41, 51, are accredited to these women, whose copper mirrors are now being used for the laver, according to God's command to Moses.

[3]See Gen. Chap. 45, n. 13.

[4]See Gen. Chap. 20, n. 11.

[5]See Gen. Chap. 21, n. 7.

CHAPTER 39

1. And from the blue, and purple, and scarlet yarn they made the officiating garments to officiate at the Sanctuary; and they made the Sanctuary garments that were Aaron's, as the Lord had commanded Moses. 2. Then he made the Ephod of gold, blue, (and) purple, (and) scarlet yarn, and fine twisted linen. 3. And they hammered out sheets of gold and cut threads to be worked into the blue, (and) into the purple, (and) into the scarlet yarn, and into the fine twisted linen—the work of an artisan. 4. They made for it coupled shoulder pieces, united at two of its corners. 5. Now the adorned turban which was upon it, made like it, was made from it—of gold, blue, purple (and) scarlet yarn, and twisted fine linen, as the Lord had commanded Moses. 6. Then they made the beryl stones, inserted and set in gold, engraved *in distinct script*[a1] with the names of the Israelites. 7. And he placed them on the shoulder pieces of the Ephod <as> memorial stones for the Israelites, as the Lord had commanded Moses. 8. Then he made the breastpiece the work of an artisan, like the work of the Ephod—of gold, blue, (and) purple, (and) scarlet yarn, and fine twisted linen. 9. It was square; doubled in fold did they make the breastpiece, a span {in} its length, and a span {in} its width, double in fold. 10. Now they completed it with a setting of four rows of precious stone(s); the first row: Carnelian, topaz, smargad—row one. 11. And the second row: Turquoise, sapphire, and emerald. 12. And the third row: Jacinth, agate, and amethyst. 13. And the fourth row: Chrysolite, beryl, and jasper; {they were} inserted and set in gold in their completed state. 14. Now the stones were according to the names of the Israelites—twelve corresponding to their names, <in> *distinct script,*[1] twisted like the engraving of a seal, each with his name according to the twelve tribes. 15. Then they made for the breastpiece corded chains {in} plaited work of pure gold. 16. And they made two settings of gold and two gold rings, and placed the two gold rings into the two sides of the breastpiece. 17. Then they placed two gold chains on the two gold rings, on the two sides of the breastpiece. 18. And the two chains which were on its two sides, they placed into the two settings, then placed them on the shoulder pieces of the Ephod opposite its front. 19. Then they made two gold rings and placed them at the sides of the breastpiece on its edge, on the side of the Ephod from within. 20. And they made two rings of gold and placed them at the two sides of the Ephod beneath <it>, opposite its front, facing the place of its coupling, above the sash of the Ephod. 21. And they joined the breastpiece with its ring to the ring of the Ephod through a thread of blue wool to be on the sash of the Ephod, so that the breastpiece did not become dislocated from on top of the Ephod, as the Lord had commanded Moses. 22. Then he made a robe for the Ephod the work of a fine weaver, entirely of blue wool. 23. Now the opening of the robe *was folded*[2] over its center, like the opening of a coat of mail surrounding its opening completely, so that it would not tear. 24. And they made for

Apparatus, Chapter 39

[a] n adds: "like the engraving of a signet," for which see above Chap. 28, n. 3.

[b] J, L, a and b have: "an embroiderer," as does the Hebrew with its *nomen agentis.*

[c] i, b, d, and g add: "like the engraving of a signet," while d, h, and l add: "engraved." See further above Chap. 28, n. 3.

[d] n omits.

the hems of the robe pomegranates <of> blue, purple, and scarlet yarn, twisted. 25. Then they made bells of pure gold and placed the bells between the pomegranates, all around the hems of the robe between the pomegranates. 26. A bell and a pomegranate, a bell and a pomegranate on the hems of the robe all around for officiating, as the Lord had commanded Moses. 27. Then they made tunics of fine linen and the work of a fine weaver, for Aaron and (for) his sons. 28. And a turban of fine linen, and the *adornment*[3] for the turbans of fine linen, as well as the linen undergarments of fine twisted linen. 29. And the sashes of fine twisted linen, (and) blue, purple, and scarlet yarn, the work of *embroidery,*[b] as the Lord had commanded Moses. 30. Then they made the front plate for the sacred diadem entirely of gold and they wrote *on it*[c] *<in> distinct script*[1] "Sacred to the Lord." 31. And they *suspended*[4] it on a thread of blue wool to *fix*[5] it upon the turban above, as the Lord had commanded Moses. 32. Then the entire work for the *Sanctuary,*[d] the Tent of Meeting was completed, and the Israelites did according to all that the Lord had commanded Moses; so they did. 33. So they brought the Sanctuary to Moses, the tent and all its accessories, its hooks, its planks, its bars, and its posts, as well as its sockets. 34. And the covering of red rams' skins, as well as the covering of scarlet skins, and the curtain for the cover. 35. The Ark of the Testimony and its poles, as well as the cover. 36. The table and all its accessories, and the display bread. 37. The pure lampstand, its lights—the lights arranged in rows together with all its accessories, as well as the oil for lighting. 38. The gold altar, and the oil for anointing, and the aromatic incense, as well as the cover for the entrance of the sanctuary. 39. The copper altar and its grating of meshwork, its poles and all its accessories, the laver and its base. 40. The hangings for the courtyard, its posts, its sockets, and the cover for the entrance to the courtyard and its ropes and its pins as well as all the vessels for the service of the Sanctuary, for the Tent of Meeting. 41. The officiating garments for officiating in the Sanctuary, the garments for the Sanctuary for Aaron the priest, as well as his sons' garments for officiating. 42. According to all that the Lord had commanded Moses, so did the Israelites do all the work. 43. When Moses saw that they had done all the work; performing it just as the Lord had commanded them, so had they done, then Moses blessed them.

Notes, Chapter 39

[1]See above Chap. 28, n. 3.

[2]See above *ibid.*, n. 5.

[3]The Targum has the singular for the Hebrew plural. The LXX is here in agreement with the Targum.

[4]Lit. placed.

[5]Lit. place.

CHAPTER 40

1. Then the Lord spoke *with*[a] Moses saying, 2. "On the first day of the first month you should set up the Sanctuary—the Tent of Meeting. 3. Then place there the Ark of the Testimony and *throw the curtain over the ark.*[b] 4. And bring in the table and arrange its *settings,*[c] then bring in the lampstand and kindle its lights. 5. Then place the gold altar for aromatic incense in front of the Ark of the Testimony and place <in position> the cover for the entrance of the sanctuary. 6. And place the altar for burnt offerings in front of the entrance of the *Sanctuary*[d]—the Tent of Meeting. 7. And place the laver between the Tent of Meeting and the altar, and put water therein. 8. Then set up the courtyard round about it, and place the cover over the entrance to the courtyard. 9. And take the oil for consecration and consecrate the sanctuary and everything that is in it, and sanctify it as well as all its vessels, so that it be sacred. 10. Then consecrate the altar of burnt offerings and all its vessels and sanctify the altar, so that the altar should be most sacred. 11. And consecrate the laver with its base, and sanctify it. 12. Then bring Aaron and his sons forward to the entrance of the Tent of Meeting and wash them with water. 13. And dress Aaron with the garments of the Sanctuary and consecrate him and sanctify him, so that he may officiate *before*[1] Me. 14. Then bring his sons forward, and dress them <with> tunics. 15. And consecrate them as you consecrated their father, so that they may officiate *before*[1] Me; now their consecration should be for them an everlasting priesthood for their <future> generations." 16. Now Moses did according to all that the Lord had commanded him; so he did. 17. Then it came about on the first month of the second year, on the *first*[e] of the month, that the Sanctuary was set up. 18. When Moses set up the Sanctuary he put its sockets <in place>, placed its planks <in position>, put its bars <in place> and set up its posts. 19. Then he spread the *cover*[2] over the Sanctuary and placed the covering *of*[f] the tent on top of it, as the Lord had commanded Moses. 20. And he took the Testimony and placed it in the ark and *affixed*[3] the poles to the ark; then placed the cover on top of the ark. 21. Then he brought the ark into the Sanctuary and set up the curtain for the cover, and thew <it> over the Ark of the Testimony, as the Lord had commanded Moses. 22. And he placed the table in the Tent of Meeting on the north side of the Sanctuary outside the curtain. 23. And he arranged upon the *settings*[g] of bread before the Lord, as the Lord had commanded Moses. 24. Then he placed the lampstand in the Tent of Meeting opposite the table, on the south side of the Sanctuary. 25. And he kindled the lights before the Lord, as the Lord had commanded Moses. 26. Then he placed the altar of gold in the Tent of Meeting in front of the curtain. 27. And he offered upon it aromatic incense, as the Lord had commanded Moses. 28. Then he set up the cover for the entrance of the Sanctuary. 29. As for the

Apparatus, Chapter 40

[a] b has; "to," as does the Hebrew.
[b] n has: "cover the ark with a curtain," as does the Hebrew.
[c] A, E, v, and c have the singular, as does the Hebrew.
[d] l adds: "of."
[e] n adds: "day."
[f] l has: "for."
[g] l has the singular, as does the Hebrew.
[h] c and l omit, as does the LXX which also omits it in vs. 2.
[i] n omits.
[j] i adds: "was hanging."

altar for the burnt offerings, he placed <it> at the entrance to *the Sanctuary,*[h] the Tent of Meeting; and he offered upon it the *burnt offerings* [4] and the *meal offerings,*[4] as the Lord had commanded Moses. 30. Then he placed the laver between the Tent of Meeting and (between) the altar, and put water there for *ritual purification.*[5] 31. Now Moses and Aaron *would ritually purify*[5] their hands and their feet from it. 32. When they would enter the Tent of Meeting and when they would approach the altar, *they would undergo ritual purification,*[5] as the Lord had commanded Moses. 33. And he set up the courtyard round about the Sanctuary and the altar, and placed the cover for the entrance to the courtyard in position; whereupon Moses finished the work. 34. Then the cloud covered the Tent of Meeting, and the Glory of the Lord permeated the Sanctuary. 35. Moses, however, was unable to enter the Tent of Meeting for the cloud had settled upon it, and the Glory of the Lord permeated the Sanctuary. 36. Whenever the cloud lifted from above the Sanctuary, the Israelites would set out on all their journeys. 37. Whereas if the cloud did not lift, then they did not set out, until the day it did lift. 38. For the cloud of *the Glory of*[i] the Lord <*was*[j]> over the Sanctuary by day and *a vision of*[i] fire was in it at night, in sight of all the house of Israel throughout their journeys.

Notes, Chapter 40

[1]See Gen. Chap. 4, n. 1.
[2]The Hebrew has "tent," which the LXX renders "curtains" or "hangings."
[3]Lit. "placed."
[4]See Gen. Chap 21, n. 7.
[5]See above Chap. 30, n. 6.

Bibliography

Adler, N. *Netinah La-Ger* in Pentateuch edition *Sefer Torat Elohim*. Wilna, 1886.

Behaq, Y. "Gemara' WeTargum." *Hakarmel* 8 (1870-1): 110-111, 117, 183, 189-190.

Behaq, Y. *Tosefot Millu'im*. Warsaw, 1898.

Berkowitz, B.Z.J. *Leḥem Abirim* in *Leḥem WeSimlah*. Wilna, 1850-5.

Berkowitz, B.Z.J. *Ḥalifot Semalot*. Wilna, 1874.

Berliner, A. *Einleitung Zum Targum Onkelos*. Berlin, 1884.

Cohn, A. "Onkelos und die Halacha." *Magazin* 1 (1874):110.

Díez-Macho, A. "The Recently Discovered Palestinian Targum: Its Antiquity and Relationship with the other Targums." *VT Sup* (1959):222-245.

Díez-Macho, A. *Neophyti* I: Madrid-Barcelona (Consejo Superior De Investigaciones Cientificas), 1970.

Driver, S.R. *The Book of Exodus*. Cambridge Bible for Schools and Colleges. Cambridge, 1918.

Eisenberg, J. *Yanḥenu*. Warsaw, 1900-01.

Friedlander, M., transl. *Maimonides' Guide for the Perplexed*, New York, 1904.

Gesenius, W. *Hebrew Grammar*. Second Edition. Oxford (At the Clarendon Press), 1910.

Goshen-Gottstein, M. *Fragments of Lost Targumim*. (in Hebrew). Part I. Ramat Gan (Bar Ilan University Press), 1983.

Grossfeld, B. "The Relationship between Biblical Hebrew *brḥ* and *nws*, and their Corresponding Equivalents in the Targumim—*'rq, 'pk, 'zl:* A Preliminary Study in Aramaic-Hebrew Lexicography." *ZAW* 91 (1979):107-123.

Heinemann, J. "Targum šemôt 22:4 wĕ-hă-hălākāh ha-qĕdûmāh" *Tarbiz* 38 (1969): 294-296.

Heller, C. *Peshitta in Hebrew Characters with Elucidatory Notes.* Berlin, 1927-9.

Hoffmann, D., ed. *Midrash Tannaim to Deuteronomy.* Berlin, 1909.

Kasher, M.M. *Torah Shelemah* 18 (1958):182-185.

Korah, Y. *Marpe Lashon* in Pentateuch edition *Sepher Keter Torah:* Ha-Ta' ağ Ha-Gadol. Jerusalem, 1960.

Krauss, S. *Griechische und Lateinische Lehnwörter im Talmud, Midrasch und Targum.* Berlin, 1899. Hildesheim (Georg Olms Verlagsbuchhandlun 1964 r.p.)

Kuiper, G.J. *The Pseudo-Jonathan Targum and its Relationship to Targum Onkelos.* Studia Ephemerides "Augustinianum" 9 Rome (Institutum Patristicum "Augustinianum"), 1972.

Lowenstein, M. *Nephesh Ha-Ger: Exodus.* Pietrokov. 1908.

Luzzatto, S.D. *Ohev Ger,* Second Edition. Krakow, 1895.

Rieder, David *Targum Jonathan Ben Uziel of the Pentateuch.* 2 Volumes. Jerusalem, 1984-5.

Rosenbaum, M. & Silbermann, A.M. *Pentateuch with Targum Onkelos, Haphtaroth and Rashi's Commentary:* Exodus. New York (Hebrew Publishing Company), 1934.

Schefftel, B. *Bi'ure Onkelos.* Munich, 1888.

Schelbert, G. "Exodus 22:4 in palastinischen Targum." *VT* 8 (1958):253-263.

Schmerler, B. *Ahavat Yehonatan.* Exodus. Pieterkov. 1908.

Singer, S. *Onkelos und das Verhältniss seines Targums zur Halacha.* Berlin, 1881.

Talmon, S. "The Three Scrolls of the Law that were found in the Temple Court" (in Hebrew) in *Studies in the Bible: Presented to Professor M.H. Segal, ed. J.M. Grintz & J. Liver.* Jerusalem (Kiryath Sepher Ltd.), 1964.

Wertheimer, S. *Or Ha-Targum.* Jerusalem, 1935.

Indexes

BIBLICAL

TARGUMIM

Targum Onkelos

Pseudo-Jonathan

Neofiti I

Neofiti M

Fragment Targum

CTgA

CTgD

CTgF

CTgG

Targum Nebi'im

Targum Ketubim

RABBINIC

I. Tosefta, Mishna Talmud

II. Midrash

POST-BIBLICAL

Ancient Versions

Samaritan Hebrew

LXX

Syriac

Vulgate

Samaritan Targum

Historian

Commentaries

AUTHORS

CPSIA information can be obtained
at www.ICGtesting.com
Printed in the USA
BVHW010205221020
591600BV00003B/7